Washington's Festivals Fairs & Celebrations

Janaya Watne

GladEye Press
SPRINGFIELD, OREGON

Washington's Festivals, Fairs, & Celebrations

Copyright © GladEye Press, April 2016
All Rights Reserved

No part of this book may be reproduced in any form, by photocopying or by any electronic or mechanical means, Including information storage or retrieval systems, without permission in writing from both the copyright owner and the publisher of this book.

Publisher and founder: *Sharleen Nelson*
Publisher and founder: *J.V. Bolkan*
Cover/Book Design and Production: *Sharleen Nelson*
Proofreader: *Julie Bolkan*

Notice: The information in this book is true and complete to the best of our knowledge. It is offered without guarantee by the authors or publisher who disclaim any liability in connection with the use of this book.

First Edition
ISBN: 978-0-9911931-4-1

Printed in United States of America

GladEye Press
Springfield, Oregon
www.gladeyepress.com

About GladEye Press

GladEye Press is an independent publisher of books and other printed (and electronic) materials. Located in the heart of the Pacific Northwest, we specialize in books for and about the people of the Northwest. We are a husband and wife team with more than 50 years combined professional experience as editors and writers. We're also deeply rooted in the region, both of us are native Oregonians and have lived, worked, and played along the coast, in the cities, smaller towns, and many of the places populated by little more than moss, ferns, and trees, or jackrabbits, juniper, and cattle. We love the Northwest. We understand that there are a great many special stories and so much we can all share about this place and we look forward to being a part of the storytelling.

GladEye Press is actively seeking authors and stories. For information about how you can work with us, check out the author submission guideline under the Authors section at our website: www.gladeyepress.com.

About the Author

Janaya Watne has spent most of her adult life in the Pacific Northwest, in Oregon and Washington. As a native-born Montanan, she believes that mountains can only be called "mountains" if they have snow year-round, a hike with less than a 1,500-foot elevation gain is a "walk," and for the best cardio, nothing beats splitting wood.

For many years, she served as a magazine editor for technical trade magazines, and now works in marketing. She currently resides in Vancouver, Washington, which is an hour-and-a-half away from the Pacific Coast to the west, and an hour away from the Cascade Mountains to the east. On weekends, she has trouble deciding between the two.

She and her friends are always up for checking out new places and festivities, and if they can get there via kayak, even better. She shares her house with two cats who find her fascinating, and shares her life with several close friends who find her to be an incorrigible smart ass.

Acknowledgments

I'd like to thank my friends Sharon, Pati, Sherri, Linda, Lisa, Mina, and Kristin for keeping me sane and routinely talking me down off the ledge.

This book is dedicated to the memory of two loves who are no longer around to brighten my day. Philip Helm provided love, support, and home-cooking during the creation of this book, but, sadly, is not around to see its completion. He was both a gentle soul and a dynamo, who had a voice like thunder, an infectious goofy laugh, a soft spot for kittens, and a hug so strong you'd have to tap out to breathe. This big man was both a blessing and an exasperation in my life. He taught me a lot about forgiveness, redemption, patience, unconditional love, and life's unexpected turns. He was taken from his family and I too early, and I grieve his absence every day.

My dog Chloe was the best friend and traveling companion a girl could have. For 14 years, she shared my love for adventure—bounding with me on every hike, guarding the tent on every camping trip, surveying all waterways west of the Mississippi, protecting the yard from evil squirrels and possums, and relishing every ice cream cone and french fry. She had a fantastic sense of humor, and she was my muse. I miss her dearly.

Table of Contents

Introduction..1

Washington Peninsula..5
Regional Map..4
Art Events.. 6
Beer, Wine & Spirits...13
Ethnic & Cultural Celebrations............................15
Family Fun...23
Food & Agricultural Festivals...............................29
Music...40

Southwest Washington.....................................47
Regional Map..46
Art Events...49
Beer, Wine & Spirits...51
Ethnic & Cultural Celebrations............................56
Family Fun...62
Food & Agricultural Festivals...............................70
Music...77

Seattle/South Puget Sound..............................85
Regional Map..84
Art Events...87
Beer, Wine & Spirits...93
Ethnic & Cultural Celebrations..........................102
Family Fun...112
Food & Agricultural Festivals.............................122
Music...128

Northwest Washington...................................135
Regional Map..134
Art Events...136
Beer, Wine & Spirits...143
Ethnic & Cultural Celebrations..........................148

Family Fun...154
Food & Agricultural Festivals...161
Music..169

Central Washington..179
Regional Map..178
Art Events...180
Beer, Wine & Spirits...185
Ethnic & Cultural Celebrations..191
Family Fun...198
Food & Agricultural Festivals...204
Music...211

Eastern Washington...219
Regional Map..218
Art Events...220
Beer, Wine & Spirits...221
Ethnic & Cultural Celebrations..225
Family Fun...233
Food & Agricultural Festivals...242
Music...248

Index..256

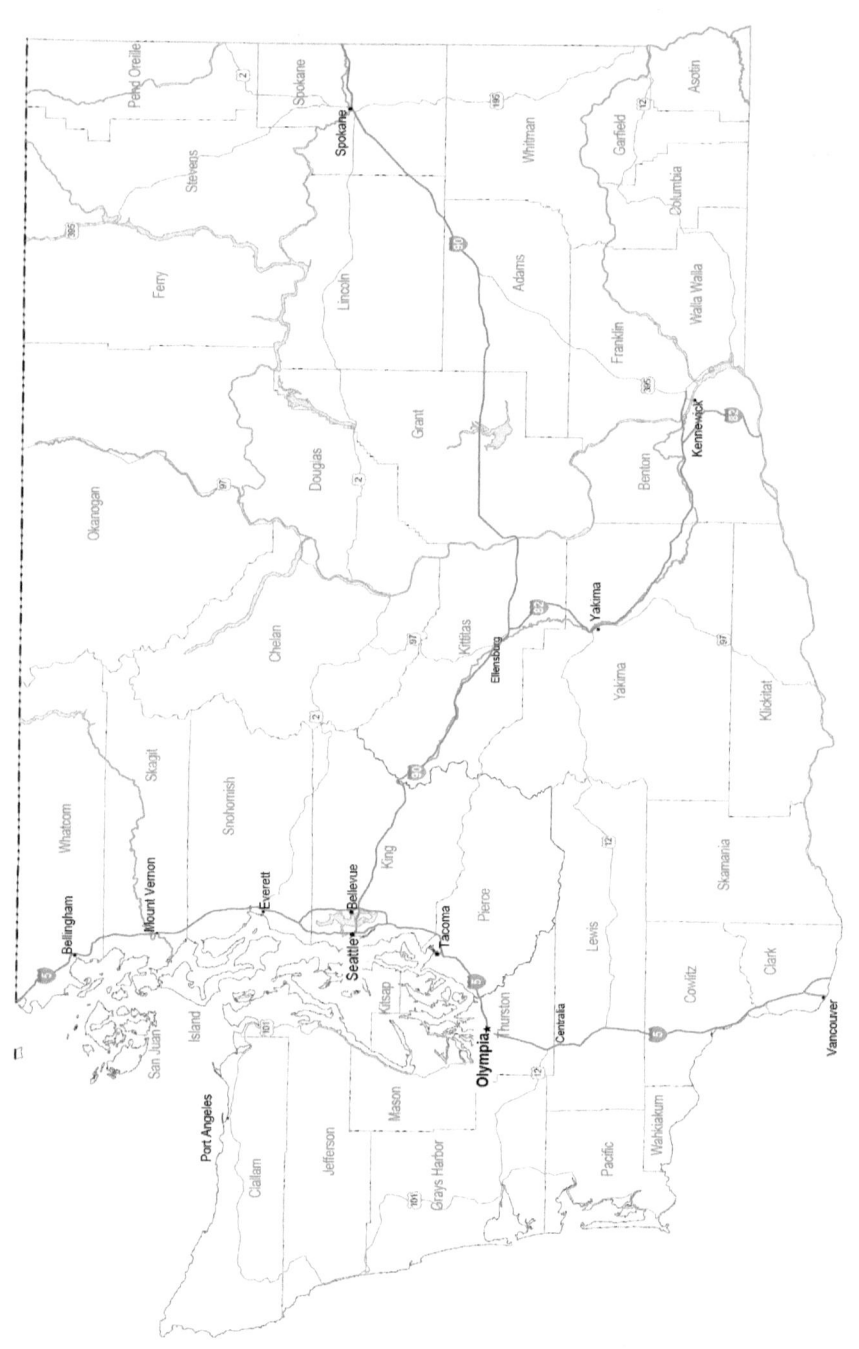

Introduction

Comprised of around 71,000 square miles of terrain, the state of Washington is by no means domestically or geographically uniform. Climate and landscape varies widely from east to west, ranging from sprawling farmlands, to desert plateaus, to high-peaked mountain ranges, to coastal beaches. So, it is not easy to generalize Washington and its residents in one fell swoop. But some consistencies throughout the state help us get a better picture of what makes Washingtonians tick.

Washington State is rainy. Everybody knows that, and it's sort of true. With around 38 inches of rain each year, Washington doesn't even break into the top 10 of rainiest states. But the places that do get rain, get quite a bit of it. Most of the precipitation occurs west of the Cascade Mountain Range, which is where much of the population of Washington resides. Washingtonians are hardy folks, and have learned to adapt to the dampness. It takes a tremendous downpour to keep them from enjoying the outdoors.

Washington is an outdoor enthusiast's paradise. The state is framed on two sides by the Columbia River and the Pacific Ocean, and its nearly 8,000 lakes, and 100+ rivers provide an Eden for water recreation activities. The snow-covered Cascade volcanoes give skiers and snowboarders a chance to chase their bliss. And with forests still covering around 50% of the state (thus the state nickname of The Evergreen State), campers, hikers, hunters, and fishermen have plenty of places to go on the weekends. And now that Mt. St. Helens has calmed down a bit, the chances of getting overtaken by an exploding volcano have lessened a tad.

Washington is a place to go for a good mystery. If you are titillated by conspiracy theories and unexplained phenomenon, you probably watched a lot of *X-Files*, and would feel right at home in Washington. The term "flying saucer" was coined here in 1947 after a mysterious sighting near Mt. Rainier. Yakima County has one of the highest UFO-reporting rates per capita in the U.S. The state has its own Sasquatch refuge that levies stiff fines and penalties for causing the untimely demise of said beast. And the fate of D.B. Cooper—famed hijacker who, in 1971, parachuted out of a plane over Southwest Washington—is still being investigated, as is the whereabouts of the $200,000 ransom money that he had with him.

In general, Washington is a great low-key place to hang, and nobody gets uptight if you wear high-top Converse sneakers to a wedding. Its residents have a unique mix of easy-going and hard-working, and some of the state's accomplishments are remarkable. It is the birthplace of Microsoft, Boeing, Starbucks, Amazon, Nordstrom, Eddie Bauer, Expedia, Cinnabon, Almond Roca, and Costco. It has cultivated home-grown talent like Jimi Hendrix, Kurt Cobain, Bing Crosby, and Kenny G., and it is a leading producer of many crops, including apples, raspberries, hops, mint, pears, grapes, and sweet cherries. With hundreds of wineries, distilleries, and breweries, there's also no shortage of party replenishments.

Not only do Washingtonians work hard, they play hard. The sheer number of festivals and events is staggering. This book is not intended to be a comprehensive list of every festival in Washington State. Such a list would be impossible to maintain, simply because new ones crop up every year, and established events often change, relocate, and sometimes even cease. During the compilation of this book, some events had to be removed at the last minute because organizers decided the festivals were no longer tenable. Instead, this book is intended to offer a representative sample of the fun things to do throughout the state. Although a majority of the events occur during the summer, several off-season events are also included. Because nearly every community in the state holds Fourth of July and holiday/Christmas celebrations, those events are excluded from this book. If you are interested in learning about events during these holidays in a particular location, check out the city's Chamber of Commerce website.

This book is organized into five areas, determined by several inexact factors including geography, climate, and population: Eastern, Central, Northwest, Seattle/South Puget Sound, Southwest, and Peninsula/West Puget Sound.

The Eastern section covers the Rocky Mountain Foothills area of the Okanogan Highlands, the population centers of Spokane and the Tri-Cities, as well as the southeastern Palouse region that is replete with rolling wheat fields and cattle ranches. The festivals in this region are as varied as the geography. Some celebrate the old west and the rich history of the community, some celebrate the crops produced in the region, and some just, well . . . celebrate.

The Central region covers the sunny area that meanders right down the center of the state, in the rain shadow of the Cascade Mountain Range. This area is a vast agricultural and fruit-growing region, and is responsible for producing 75% of the nation's hops. This region also contains

150+ wineries, many within a one-hour drive of each other. You will find a lot of wine- and beer-related festivals here.

The Northwest region contains the area of the Cascades known as the "American Alps," which is traversed by the Skagit River. Salmon and wildlife are the focus of several events. The climate of this area is also perfect for growing crops such as raspberries, strawberries, and tulips. The Skagit Valley Tulip Festival is one of the most popular events in the state, and dazzles nearly one million visitors a year with its 300 acres of blooming tulips. This area also includes the San Juan Islands, whose spring and summer months are packed with art and music festivals, as well as many seafood festivals.

The Peninsula/West Puget Sound area is probably the most secluded area in the state. It includes the Olympic Mountain Range, and its western border ends at the Pacific Ocean. Much of this area is still wild forest, and festivals celebrating wildlife and sea creatures abound. A good portion of this region lies on Reservation land, and several tribes offer festivals that celebrate their rich heritage in the area. Other events focus on the area's maritime beginnings.

Most of the events in the state of Washington occur in the Seattle/South Puget Sound area, which makes sense, because most of the state's population lives here. A multicultural mecca, the metropolis celebrates the best of food, beer, art, food, wine, film, food, music, food, and delightful oddities. The area also has many cultural festivals that celebrate the rich cultural tapestry that is Seattle. And you get to enjoy food at all of them.

Southwest Washington is home to two major population centers: Olympia and Vancouver, each with its own distinct character. As the capitol city of Washington, Olympia nurtures an up-and-coming art scene, while Vancouver and neighboring communities along the Columbia River corridor like to show off and celebrate the scenic landscape that is the Columbia River Gorge. The southwest Washington coast provides some of the most accessible sandy beaches in the country, and beach-centered festivities abound.

Hopefully this book will help you discover new areas in the fabulous state of Washington. And if study of the history and trivia presented here enables you to dazzle other festival-goers as you party with the locals, even better. Cheers!

Peninsula/West Puget Sound Region

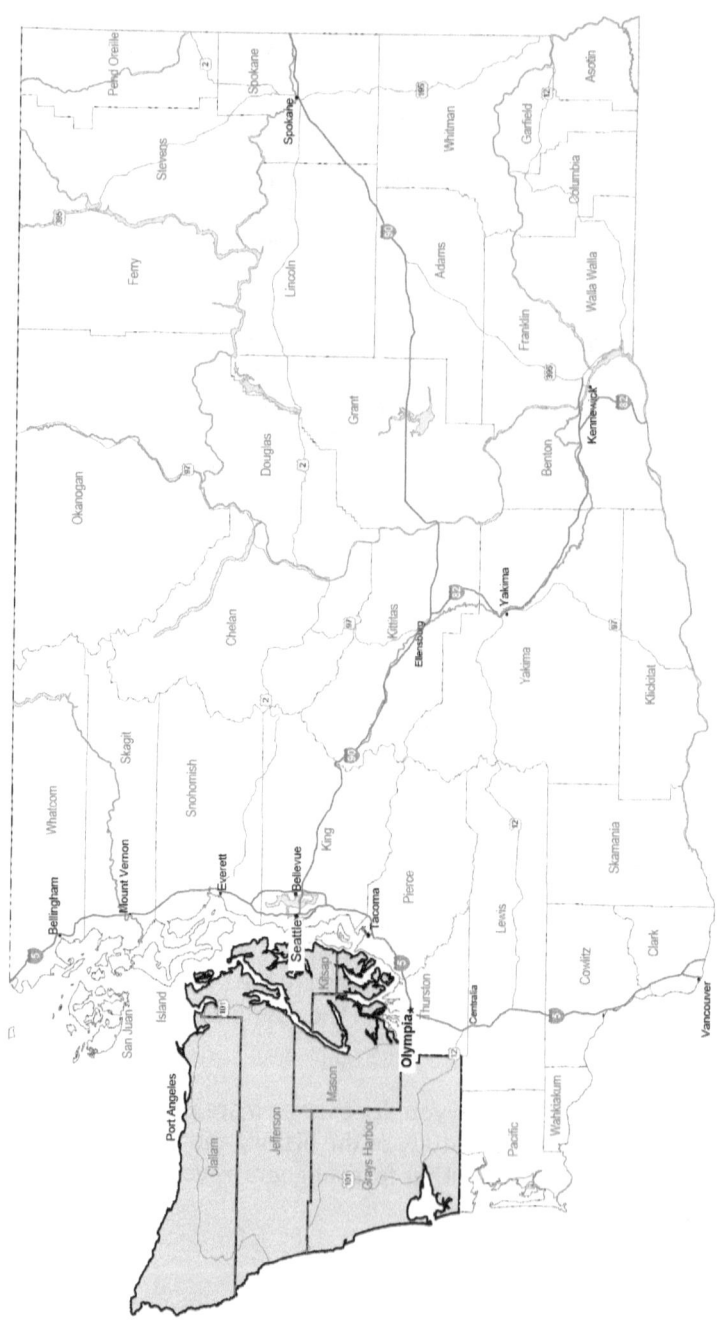

Peninsula/West Puget Sound

Bordered by Puget Sound on the west, the Strait of Juan De Fuca on the North, and the Pacific Ocean on the east, much of the Olympic Peninsula is still wild and secluded, and, in fact, it was one of the last places to be explored in the continental U.S. Olympic National Park comprises nearly one million acres. It features the rugged Olympic Mountains at its backbone, as well as beaches that range from sandy, to rocky, to boulder-strewn. The northern peninsula hosts three temperate rain forests (Hoh, Quinault, and Queets), which receive an average of 140–170 inches of rain per year—that's 12–14 feet, folks. This rainy climate provides the perfect ecosystem for flora and fauna. In fact, the rain forests boast five species of conifer trees that are the largest in the world (Yellow Cedar, Western Red Cedar, Sitka Spruce, Douglas Fir, and Mountain Hemlock). It stands to reason that logging was a main draw for settlers, and their hard work and tenacity is celebrated annually by events such as Shelton's Mason City Forest Festival and Hoquiam's Logger's Playday. Many of the area's denizens are also represented at events like McCleary's Bear Festival, Neah Bay's Eagle Festival, and Silverdale's Whaling Days.

The area's abounding natural resources means that many Native American tribes call the Peninsula home. Several Indian Reservations celebrate their history at events such as Quileute Days in La Push. From the early days, fishing, crabbing, clamming, and oystering have been staple industries. Allyn's Geoduck Festival, Brinnon's ShrimpFest, Shelton's OysterFest, and Port Angeles' Dungeness Crab and Seafood Festival provide the opportunity to sample the abundance of delicious sea bounty. The city of Poulsbo celebrates Viking Fest, which honors the nationality of many of the fisherman that settled in the area.

The east side of the Olympic Mountain Range has a completely different climate. Directly in the rain shadow of the mountains, the relatively sunny town of Sequim and the surrounding area grow lavender, and lots of it. Known as the Lavender Capital of the North America, the area holds its yearly Lavender Festival in July. Not too far away, the city of Port Townsend also celebrates blooms with its Rhododendron Festival in May.

Other fun events in the region include Port Gamble's June Faire, Westport's Rusty Scupper's Pirate Daze, and the tantalizing Chocolate on the Beach Festival, which takes place over a 10-mile, several-town stretch along the coast.

Art Events

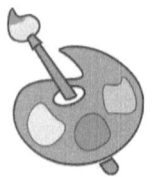

RainFest and River and Ocean Days
Forks/LaPush, Clallam County
April

RainFest is a celebration of the arts sponsored by the West Olympic Council for the Arts. The first week of the festival focuses on arts that are inspired by marine and river environments, and begins with a Quileute drum circle that invites you to bring along a drum and join in. The second week focuses on Westend artists and quilting arts, with a Piecemakers Quilt Show. Other events include jazz music, a swap meet, an umbrella parade (where you bring your own decorated umbrella), and the River and Ocean Film Festival. The event coincides with the annual Washington Coast Beach Cleanup, so time for that is built into the festival schedule.

Address: Various locations
Admission: Free
Parking: Street, parking lot
Accessible: Yes
Pets: No
Lodging: http://forkswa.com/wp-content/uploads/pdf/Lodging%20Guide.pdf
Website: http://forkswa.com/ai1ec_event/rainfest-2014-river-ocean-days/?instance_id=1994
Attractions: Olympic Peninsula Waterfall Trail, Tillicum Park, Forks Timber Museum, First Beach, Second Beach, Third Beach, Sul Doc Salmon Hatchery
Trivia: Forks was the key setting in Stephanie Meyer's vastly popular *Twilight* book series. The average annual number of tourists visiting the town rose from 10,000 before *Twilight* to 19,000 in 2008, the year of the first film, and 73,000 by 2010.
Directions: Forks is located on US Hwy 101, which crosses Washington State's north Olympic Peninsula and follows the Pacific coast south through Oregon and California. The town is about 56 miles from Victoria, BC (via ferry); 132 miles from Seattle (via ferry); 226 miles from Vancouver, BC (via ferry); and 251 miles from Portland, OR.

Juan de Fuca Festival of the Arts
Port Angeles, Clallam County
May/Memorial Day Weekend

The five-day Juan de Fuca Festival of the Arts presents nearly 80 performances on four stages, as well as a lively street fair in a beautiful setting nestled between the Olympic Mountains and the Strait of Juan de Fuca. Head to the Art Shack to get acquainted with many of the fine local artists as they display their paintings, sculptures, and other works of art. Many paintings are actually created during the festival, and all artwork is available for purchase. The colorful street fair includes more than 50 food, artisan, and craft booths. A highlight of the festival is the After Hours in the Clubs program for the 21+ crowd. At 10:30 each night, a few downtown establishments that are within walking distance of the festival feature late-night performances of some of the festival's favorite bands.

Address: Vern Burton Community Center, 308 E 4th Street
Admission: Daily tickets cost $20 for Thursday, Friday, and Monday, and $25 for Saturday and Sunday. All-festival passes cost $55 in advance, $70 at the gate.
Parking: For parking, turn right on to Peabody, then left into the Clallam County Courthouse lot, located just beyond the street fair.
Accessible: Yes
Lodging: http://business.portangeles.org/list/ql/lodging-travel-15. Find B&B information at Olympic Peninsula Bed and Breakfast Association at: www.opbba.com
Website: http://jffa.org/festival-2014-2
Attractions: Olympic National Park and Hurricane Ridge, Port Angeles Fine Arts Center, Arthur D. Feiro Marine Lab, Clallam County Historical Society, Olympic Game Farm
Trivia: Famed Denver Bronco quarterback John Elway and his twin sister Jana were born in Port Angeles, where his father Jack, was the head football coach of Port Angeles High School. John played baseball and football for Stanford from 1979 to 1982 and was ranked #15 on ESPN's "Top 25 Players in College Football History" list. He was selected by the New York Yankees in the second round of the 1981 MLB Draft, and then selected as the first overall pick in the 1983 NFL Draft. He decided to focus on football, which worked out pretty well in the end. His career ended with a record 148 victories and a berth in both the NFL and College Halls of Fame.

Directions: From US-101, enter town on Front St (one way heading west), staying in the left lane until you reach Race St (the second light). A sign for Hurricane Ridge is prominently displayed at this light. Turn left on to Race St. Turn right on to 5th St and head for the first light located at Peabody St. At this light, you will see the festival grounds to the right. Travel time from the Hood Canal Bridge to Port Angeles is a little more than an hour. From the Seattle corridor, take the Bainbridge Island ferry and continue northwest through Poulsbo and cross the Hood Canal Bridge. Merge onto US-101 N and follow signs to Port Angeles.

From North Seattle, take the Edmonds Ferry to Kingston. Follow US Hwy 104 west to the Hood Canal Bridge. Merge on to US-101 N and follow signs to Port Angeles. From Whidbey Island and Port Townsend, Take the Keystone ferry to Port Townsend. From Port Townsend take Hwy 20 to US-101, following the signs to Port Angeles. Travel time from Port Townsend to Port Angeles is about one hour.

From Bellingham or Vancouver, BC, head south on I-5 to exit 230 (Burlington/Anacortes) onto WA-20 W. Turn left on to WA-20 (Oak Harbor/Ferry turn) and proceed to the Coupeville/Port Townsend Ferry. Travel time from Bellingham to the Coupeville ferry dock is about 1.5 hours. Follow the Port Townsend directions above. From Victoria, BC, cross the straits on the MV Coho. Once you disembark, head east on Railroad St for one block, turn right on to Lincoln St, and walk four blocks to the main festival grounds on 4th St. The shuttle to the main festival grounds is located at 1st and Lincoln if you'd rather not walk.

Westport Art Festival
Westport, Grays Harbor County
Third weekend in August

The Westport Art Festival features more than 80 juried art, craft, and food exhibits, plus Discovery Days for the kids, featuring nature-based craft projects at the historic Westport Maritime Museum. The event features invited nautical artists, strolling musicians, and live performances in the band shell on the Maritime Museum grounds. In addition, Corvettes of Grays Harbor hosts Vettes at the Marina during the weekend.

Address: Port of Gray's Harbor, Westport Marina, 326 Lamb Street
Admission: Free
Parking: Street and parking lot parking

Accessible: No info
Lodging: Information about motels, condos, vacation rentals, RV parks, and campgrounds: http://westportgrayland-chamber.org/category.php?Category_id=12
Website: www.westportartfestival.org
Facebook: www.facebook.com/WestportArtFestival
Attractions: Westport Maritime Museum, Westport Light State Park, Westport Observation Tower, Grays Harbor Lighthouse

Trivia: One of the outstanding museum pieces featured at the Westport Maritime Museum is the Destruction Island Lighthouse lens. The Destruction Island Lighthouse, which began operation in 1892 was positioned on Destruction Island, a lonely 30-acre piece of land in the Pacific, 3.5 miles off the Washington Coast. Interestingly, the island did not get its name because any ships were destroyed there, but because a British landing party was massacred by hostile Indians at a nearby mainland river (initially coined Destruction River, now called the Hoh River). In 1995, the lighthouse's Fresnel lens was replaced by a modern beacon, and the lens was soon relocated to the Westport Maritime Museum. The lens is housed in a 70-foot specially constructed building, with an encircling ramp that allows you to view it at various levels. The lens rotates, just like it did when it was in service at the lighthouse, and the skylight above lets in natural light that reflects off the more than 1,100 separate hand-polished prisms. Because of the lens condition and viewer access, the exhibit has been said to be the best first-order Fresnel lens display in the world.

Directions: The festival is approximately 2.5 hours from both Portland and Seattle. From I-5, take exit 104 (Aberdeen, Ocean Beaches) Hwy 101 N. Stay on the main highway; it turns into Hwy 8 W, and then at Elma it changes to Hwy 12 W. Upon reaching Aberdeen, Hwy 12 W becomes Hwy 101 and NE Wishkah St. Get in the left lane and turn left at the third stop light (follow the signs to Westport turn off). Go over the Chehalis River bridge and stay in right lane. You are now on Hwy 105, which you follow for approximately 20 miles. Exit at the first Westport exit and follow signs to the marina (you are on Montesano St). Follow Montesano St to the stop sign at the docks. Turn right at stop sign, the Westport Maritime Museum is on the right.

Port Townsend Film Festival
Port Townsend, Jefferson County
Late September

Since its launch in 2000, the Port Townsend Film Festival has stuck with the motto "A film lover's block party, celebrating great films and filmmakers." The festival screens more than 80 films in seven venues (7,000+ seats), is completely walkable, includes a big outdoor dinner for pass holders, Q & A and panel discussions with filmmakers, and great parties. The event closes off Taylor Street for three evenings, brings in hay-bale seating, and invites everyone to a free outdoor movie. Other free films are presented throughout the festival at the Peter Simpson Theater. The festival attracts film historians, critics, famous screenwriters, producers, directors, and industry specialists. Each year, organizers select a special guest, which in the past has included Elliott Gould, Tony Curtis, Dyan Cannon, Debra Winger, Karen Allen, and Bruce Dern. An award ceremony on Sunday presents awards for best narrative feature, best documentary feature, best narrative short, best documentary short, best adventure film, best animated film (of any length), and an audience choice award in all categories. In addition, a Spirit of PTFF award is bestowed, as well as The Big Cheese Award given by Mount Townsend Creamery. Children younger than six are permitted only at the Taylor Street Outdoor Cinema, but kids still have plenty of opportunity for fun at the Firefly Academy Film Camp. Kids aged 2.5 and older participate in Lego animation, claymation, and arts and crafts.

Address: Various locations, downtown
Admission: All passes include a year-long membership to PTFF, which entitles you to invitations to year-round events, library privileges, and discounts at the Rose Theatre and Pane d'Amore Bakery. A one-film pass is $35. A six-film pass costs $100 and is shareable with others. An unlimited-films festival pass (not shareable) costs $185. A Director Pass costs $650 and includes unlimited films, exclusive party invitations, and concierge service (no waiting in line). A Mogul Pass costs $1,250 and includes unlimited films, exclusive party invites, concierge service (no waiting in line), and an invitation to the filmmakers' reception. When a theater does not fill up for a showing, Rush tickets are sold for $12. Firefly Academy Film Camp costs $10/hr for the first child, $5/hr for the second child, or $100 for an unlimited kids' pass for the entire weekend.
Parking: Parking downtown is limited, but you can easily walk to all

seven venues. A free festival shuttle goes to all of the venues. Park at the Jefferson Transit Park-and-Ride (440 12th Street). Take Jefferson Transit downtown and continue on the free PTFF shuttle bus. Jefferson Transit does not operate Sunday, so your best bet on that day is to park uptown or on the hill and take the shuttle bus downtown.
Accessible: All venues are wheelchair accessible.
Pets: No
Lodging: Accommodations sell out quickly for festival weekend. Screenings begin on Friday at 9 am, so arrive on Thursday to catch the most films.
Website: www.ptfilmfest.com
Facebook: www.facebook.com/PTFF.PTFI
Attractions: Fort Worden State Park, Water Street, Jefferson County Historical Museum and Library, Chetzemoka Park
Trivia: Port Townsend resident Artis the Spoonman is a street performer, known throughout the Pacific Northwest, who uses spoons as a musical instrument. He has performed regularly at Pike's Place Market in Seattle, and has also performed at Seattle's Bumbershoot music festival, and with Frank Zappa, Aerosmith, and Phish. He is best known for his 1994 collaboration with Washington-based hard rock band Soundgarden on the song "Spoonman," which is about, and features, Artis.
Directions: Port Townsend is 60 miles northwest of Seattle via WA-305 N/WA-3 N/WA-104 W/WA-19 N/

Kitsap Arts and Crafts Festival
Kingston, Kitsap County
Last weekend in July

The Kitsap Arts and Crafts Festival has been featuring and promoting talented local artists since it first began in 1960. The weekend includes artisan craft booths, local food vendors, live music, and juried and student art shows featuring photography, painting, sculpture, and mixed media. Proceeds from the festival support art scholarships and art docent programs, as well as awards to winning artists.

Address: Kingston's Village Green, West Kingston Road
Parking: Plenty of free 2-hour parking nearby, or pay to park in the Marina parking lot.
Accessible: No info
Pets: Yes

Lodging: www.visitkitsap.com/lodging/search.asp
Website: www.kitsapartsandcrafts.com
Facebook: www.facebook.com/PTFF.PTFI
Attractions: Kingston Ferry walk-on tour, Stillwaters Environmental Center, Kingston Farmers Market, The Point Casino, Mike Wallace Park, White Horse Golf Club

Trivia: Kitsap County, wherein Kingston resides, was originally named Slaughter County, after Lt. William Alloway Slaughter, who had been killed in 1855 in the Yakima War. The name went into effect in January 1857. In July of that same year, once voters were given a chance for input, the overwhelming majority chose to rename it Kitsap County after Chief Kitsap of the Suquamish tribe. In the wake of the confrontations between the local tribes and settlers, it might be difficult to get homesteaders excited about relocating to a place named Slaughter County.
Directions: Kingston is located about 1.5 hours northwest of Seattle (via ferry). The festival is within walking distance of the Kingston ferry terminal.

Washington designated the Columbian Mammoth as the official state fossil in 1998. Fossilized remains of the Columbian mammoth were found on the Olympic Peninsula.

Beer, Wine & Spirits

Far West Beer Fest
Sequim, Clallam County
July

The Far West Beer Fest is an outdoor event hosted by the 7 Cedars Casino at the base of the Olympic Mountains. Enjoy some of the finest craft brews from 20+ breweries, live music, delicious food, games, and contests. All proceeds benefit the Hurricane Ridge Winter Sports Foundation. Breweries represented in the past have included 10 Barrel, 21st Amendment, Alaskan, American, Brickyard, Deschutes, Elysian, Fremont, Hilliards, Hood Canal, Iron Horse, Laurelwood, Mac & Jack's, Ninkasi, No-Li, Pelican, Pike, Seven Seas, Silver City, and Unibroue.

Address: 7 Cedars Casino, 270756 Hwy 101
Admission: Admission costs $20 in advance, $25 at the door, which gets you five tasting tokens and a 5-oz souvenir tasting glass. Sample pours cost one token and are 4–5 oz. You can purchase additional tokens ($5 for four tokens).
Parking: Free on-site
Accessible: Yes
Pets: No
Lodging: www.olympicpeninsula.org/places-to-stay
Website: www.7cedarsresort.com/far-west-beer-fest.html
Facebook: www.facebook.com/events/688031504583436
Attractions: The Cedars at Dungeness golf course, 7 Cedars Casino, Dungeness National Wildlife Refuge, Olympic National Park
Trivia: 7 Cedars Casino is owned and operated by Jamestown S'Klallam Tribe. The S'Klallam language (called Clallam or Klallam) belongs to the Salisha family of Native American languages. The word S'Klallam means "strong people."
Directions: Sequim is located two hours northwest of Seattle, 17 miles east of Port Angeles on Hwy 101.

Bremerton Summer Brewfest
Bremerton, Kitsap County
Mid-July

In 2014, the Bremerton Summer Brewfest featured more than 75

Washington summer-style beers poured by 30 Washington breweries, including several with intriguing names such as Der Blokken Brewery (Bremerton), Dirty Bucket Brewing (Centralia), Laht Neppur Brewing (Waitsburg), Slaughter County Brewing (Port Orchard), Slippery Pig Brewery (Poulsbo), and Valholl Brewing (Poulsbo). In addition, to highlight the creativity of the Washington brewers, many of them offer beer poured through a Randall. A Randall is double-chamber filter that you fill with flavor-enhancing ingredients, such as hops, spices, herbs, and fruit, and connect to the tap of your favorite beer. At the event, grilled sausages, chili, baked potatoes, soft pretzels, and other treats are available to purchase. Dining at downtown Bremerton establishments is also highly encouraged. Live music is presented throughout the event.

Address: Pacific Ave and 4th Street, downtown
Admission: Tickets cost $20 in advance, $25 at the door (military discount tickets are $15 at the door w/ID). Entry includes a tasting cup and six tokens, each good for a 5-oz taste. Additional tokens may be purchased at $1.50 each or four for $5. Designated Driver admission is available at the gate for $5 (includes free water and soft drinks).
Parking: Free street parking is available in downtown Bremerton for 2–3 hours. The Brewfest encourages public transportation and carpooling.
Accessible: Yes
Pets: No
Lodging: Fairfield Inn and Suites has been the official hotel of the Summer Brewfest, and it offers a discounted rate for attendees: www.marriott.com/hotels/travel/seasb-fairfield-inn-and-suites-seattle-bremerton
Website: http://washingtonbeer.com/bremerton-summer-brewfest
Facebook: www.facebook.com/BremertonSummerBrewFest
Attractions: Puget Sound Navy Museum, Blake Island State Park, USS Hornet, USS Turner Joy (DD-951) Naval Destroyer Museum Ship
Trivia: Puget Sound Naval Shipyard's main job during World War II was to repair the Pacific Fleet's warships that were damaged in battle. These included five of the six battleships that survived Pearl Harbor: USS Tennessee, USS Maryland, USS Nevada, USS California, and USS West Virginia.
Directions: Bremerton Summer Brewfest is just a five-minute walk from the Bremerton Ferry Terminal. If you are coming from Seattle, event organizers encourage you to walk on the ferry and avoid the ferry lines.

Ethnic & Cultural Celebrations

June Faire
Port Gamble, Kitsap County
First weekend in June

June Faire is a public demonstration dedicated to the study and recreation of the Middle Ages and the Renaissance. It is put on by the Barony of Dragon's Laire, of the Society for Creative Anachronism (SCA). The full weekend includes armored combat, weaponry, dancing, bardic performances, arts and crafts, and a bustling marketplace. Woodworkers and metal workers demonstrate their craft, and the Moneyers' Guild demonstrates how to mint coins using medieval technology. Learn about glass bead making, and see historical examples of clothing from a cross-section of cultures, such as Russian, Viking, Tutonic or Germanic, Japanese, and Mongol. Combat and weaponry demonstrations are a highlight of the weekend. Witness archery, full-contact armored combat, rapier duels, and knife, axe, and spear throwing. Other entertainment includes European dancing, gaming and human chess, musicians, singers, jugglers, dancers, and storytellers. The marketplace sells costumes and clothing, hats, footwear, toys, hand-turned wooden goods, fibers for needlework and sewing, fabrics, games, and books. You can also buy armor, swords, battle axes, pikes, and daggers.

Address: State Hwy 104 and Pacific Avenue NE
Admission: $5 per person. Children aged 11 and under are admitted for free.
Parking: Street and parking lot parking
Accessible: No info
Pets: Yes
Lodging: http://portgamble.com/living-working-in-port-gamble/lodging
Website: www.junefaire.com
Facebook: www.facebook.com/Junefaire
Attractions: Port Gamble Historical Museum, St. Paul's Church
Trivia: The Battle of Port Gamble in November of 1856 was an engagement between the U.S. and the Tlingit/Haida tribe of British Columbia. A Haida raiding party landed at Port Gamble and set up camp outside of town. The entire community was evacuated to a local blockhouse. The USS Massachusetts arrived in the port and deployed soldiers ashore in an attempt to get the raiding party to withdraw peaceably. After two

refusals to evacuate, the Massachusetts began shelling the encampment with deck guns, which caused the tribe to retreat to the forest. During the retreat, small arms gunfire killed coxswain Gustave Engelbrecht, who was the only American casualty in the battle and the first U.S. Navy battle death in the Pacific. (Englebrecht is buried in the Port Gamble Historic Cemetery). Two days later, the raiding party surrendered. During the battle, one of the Haida chiefs was killed. According to custom, that meant that a chief of the enemy must also be killed in revenge. Nine months after the battle, the Haida returned to Whidbey Island and began asking settlers if any chiefs were nearby. They determined that island resident Colonel Isaac N. Ebey (who had nothing to do with the Port Gamble skirmish) fit the role of "chief" well enough, and subsequently shot and decapitated him, and left with his head as a trophy. Three years later, Captain Charles Dodd was able to purchase Ebey's scalp back from the tribe, and return it to Ebey's brother to be interred with his long-buried headless body. Rumor has it, however, that the scalp never reached its final resting place, but instead was passed down through the family.

Directions: From Tacoma, take I-5 N or S to Hwy 16 (exit 132). Take Hwy 16 which turns into Hwy 3 N at Gorst. Stay on Hwy 3 N all the way to Hood Canal Bridge. At the bridge Hwy 3 turns into 104 (do not cross bridge). Follow Hwy 104 to Port Gamble and follow SCA signs to site. From the Edmonds/Kingston Ferry, take Hwy 104 out of Kingston and follow to intersection with the Texaco. Turn right and continue on Hwy 104 to the site.

Quileute Days
La Push, Clallam County
Third weekend in July

Stephenie Meyer's *Twilight* series was a mixed bag for the Quileute Nation. In the books, a main character in the human-vampire-wolf love triangle, Jacob Black (who plays the human/wolf), is a member of the Quileute tribe. Although this series brought a lot of attention to the Quileute Nation and fostered public interest in their culture, the fictionalized story has prompted a tourist influx of misguided teenage girls and their mothers, each hoping to catch a glimpse of a hunky Quileute teenager shape-shifting into a wolf, his shirt flying off, yet, mysteriously, his pants remaining completely untattered. Quileute Days is a celebration of the actual culture of the Quileute tribe, which is a nation of fishermen and whalers who are known for their basket artistry and canoe craftsmanship, creating small boats as well as boats that were 200-ft. long that could carry 6,000 pounds. This festival features exciting canoe races, stick games, traditional singing and dancing, and a salmon bake. The grand parade takes place on Saturday afternoon, and Friday and Saturday nights offer a street dance. Other events include horseshoes, a softball tournament, a three-on-three basketball tournament, bingo, live music, and a fun run. None of these events allow participation by werewolves, mostly because they are notoriously sore losers, and most likely fictional.

Address: Downtown
Admission: Free
Parking: Street and parking lot parking
Accessible: Yes
Pets: Yes
Lodging: http://forkswa.com/wp-content/uploads/pdf/Lodging%20Guide.pdf
Website: www.quileutenation.org
Facebook: www.facebook.com/quileute.days
Attractions: First Beach, Second Beach, and Third Beach, Olympic National Park, Rialto Beach, Hole in the Wall hike
Trivia: Third Beach is accessible via a mostly level 1.5-mile trail through natural second-growth forest. The first-growth trees were destroyed in 1921 in a terrible Pacific storm that packed winds of up to 170 mph. The 1921 Olympic Blowdown leveled nearly 8 billion board feet of timber, enough to construct 600,000 three-bedroom homes.
Directions: La Push is on the coast, 150 miles (4 hours) east of Seattle via US-101 W.

Viking Fest
Poulsbo, Kitsap County
Third weekend in May

Because of its similarity to their native countries, Poulsbo was founded and settled by a large number of Norwegian and other Scandinavian immigrants. In fact, Poulsbo retained Norwegian as a primary language until World War II, when a nearby naval shipyard in Bremerton brought in a large influx of English-speaking shipyard workers. Viking Fest is a celebration of this proud Norwegian heritage. The festival features a carnival, art and craft vendors, live music and entertainment, a pancake breakfast, a road race, a stand-up paddleboard race in Liberty Bay, and lots of yummy Scandinavian treats such as lefse and krumkake. Viking Fest is definitely not a place you want to go if you are counting calories. With eating contests for donuts, lutefisk, and oysters, and a cupcake baking and presentation contest called Kupkake Krigen (Cupcake War), you are bound to find many tasty ways to fill your belly. The parade features creative floats, local marching bands, and military entries.

Address: Muriel Iverson Williams Waterfront Park, 18809 Anderson Parkway
Admission: Admission is free. Carnival rides require a fee.
Parking: Places to park in downtown Poulsbo are limited. Vehicles with disability placards can park at the Edward Jones Investment Offices, 19032 Jensen Way NE, or across the street in front of the old city hall. On Saturday, all other attendees may park at the North Kitsap High School and Middle School campuses and ride the shuttle bus to downtown ($2 roundtrip for everyone older than two-years old). During certain times, you may also park in the Gateway Fellowship Church or First Lutheran Church lots for a suggested $5 donation.
Accessible: Yes
Lodging: www.visitkitsap.com/lodging/search.asp
Website: www.vikingfest.org
Facebook: www.facebook.com/PoulsboVikingFest
Attractions: Poulsbo Marine Science Center, Kitsap Memorial State Park, Sawdust Hill Alpaca Farm, Suquamish Clearwater Casino
Trivia: The Marina Market, located in historic downtown Poulsbo, sells a large selection of Scandinavian, European, and Dutch foods. One of the things it is best known for, however, is its Licorice Shrine, where you can choose from more than 350 licorices from around the world, as well as licorice-related items such as licorice pasta, licorice salt, licorice pretzels, licorice tea, licorice shampoo, and licorice toothpaste. Licorice-a-riffic!
Directions: Poulsbo is 1.5 hours west of Seattle (via Bainbridge Island Ferry). For detailed directions to Viking Fest, go to: www.vikingfest.org/docs/directions.pdf.

Hood Canal Highland Celtic Festival
Belfair, Mason County
Last weekend in August

The goal of the Hood Canal Highland Celtic Festival is to promote Highland and Celtic culture, and have a great time doing so. The festival includes many traditional Scottish festival activities, including the gathering of the clans, pipe bands, Celtic dancers, and herding dog demonstrations. The Gathering of the Clans Sanctioned Highland Games events include stone toss, hammer toss, weight for distance, weight for height, and the ever-popular caber toss. Food vendors serve up standard fair favorites, as well as traditional Scottish foods such as meat pies, sausage rolls, haggis, and scones. Because the northwest weather can be kind of iffy, the inclusion of a beer garden that is both indoor and outdoor is pure dead brilliant.

Address: Belfair State Park, 1351 NE SR-300
Admission: Adults $13/day, $18 for two days; military and senior $11/day, $15 for two days; ages 7–12 $8/day; ages 6 and younger are free
Parking: State park entry fee is waived for this event.
Accessible: Yes
Lodging: www.hoodcanalscots.org/accommodations.html
Website: www.hoodcanalscots.org
Facebook: www.facebook.com/pages/Hood-Canal-Highland-Celtic-Festival/122650661123082
Attractions: Coulter Creek Heritage Park, Belfair Farmers Market, Belfair State Park, Kitsap Peninsula breweries, Bloedel Reserve, Fort Ward
Trivia: Scotland has a land-area comparable to the state of Maine. About five million Americans report being of Scottish ancestry. The highest concentration of Americans of Scottish descent lives in New England and in the Northwest.
Directions: Belfair is 45 miles north of Olympia via US-101 N and WA-3 N.

Eagle Festival
Neah Bay, Clallam County
Late April

Celebrate the arrival of the bald eagles when they pair off and build their nests. The Makah tribe hosts guest lecturers and eagle-inspired art during the time that the eagles are concentrated along the water's edge and throughout the area. This is a great opportunity to view the magnificent birds performing courtship and mating rituals at the height of mating season. Many activities take place at the Makah Cultural and Research Center or at the Makah Tribal Marina. Visit the Makah Museum, also located at the research center site, to view their eagle exhibit. Participate in a guided bird walk at Cape Flattery, and then head to Makah Community Hall where vendors sell native art, as well as food. Children can participate in activities at the community hall. The Makah Village Market features eagle nest watching, as well as food. Two meals are served in connection with the event. A traditional lunch of chowder, or chili, and buckskin bread is available for a fee, as well as a fish dinner that features live music.

Address: Makah Marina
Admission: Admission to the festival is free. The museum entrance fee is $5. The Cape Flattery hike, itself, is free, but to participate, you need to purchase a $10 Makah Reservation Recreation Use Permit for each car. Chowder/chili lunch costs $4–$5, and the fish dinner costs $15.
Parking: Street, parking lot
Accessible: Yes
Pets: No
Lodging: www.olympicpeninsula.org/places-to-stay.
Website: www.olympicpeninsula.org/event/eagle-festival
Attractions: Cape Flattery, Makah National Fish Hatchery, Tattoosh Island, Shi shi beach
Trivia: The wingspan of an adult bald eagle generally ranges from 5.5–7.5 feet. They fly at 35–43 MPH when gliding and flapping, and diving speeds can reach 100 mph. Bald eagles are not bald; the name derives either from an old English word "balde," which means "white," or from the word "piebald," which describes something that has irregular patches of two colors, typically black and white.
Directions: From Seattle, WA (approximately 4.5 hours depending on route and weather) via the Bainbridge Ferry: The ferry is located at the Seattle Ferry Terminal (801 Alaskan Way Pier 52, Seattle) Follow 305 N to 3 N to the Olympic Peninsula. Take 104 W over the Hood Canal Bridge. Merge on to 101 and follow signs to Port Angeles. Drive through Port Angeles. Continue on 101 W to 112 Strait of Juan de Fuca Hwy. Turn right and follow signs to Neah Bay. Turn right to stay on 112 and continue through Clallam Bay onto Neah Bay. Via the Edmonds/Kinston Ferry (199 Sunset Ave S, Edmonds, located north of Seattle). Take the WSDOT

ferry from Edmonds to Kingston. From the ferry, continue straight onto SR-104 W/WA-104 W and follow the directions from the Hood Canal Bridge as noted above.

Rusty Scupper's Pirate Daze
Westport, Grays Harbor County
Late June

For one weekend in June, the city of Westport is invaded by marauding pirates. Rusty Scupper's Pirate Daze begins with a pirate horde invasion at the marina, and fun ensues throughout the weekend. The festival features pirate crews roaming the streets, family-friendly music, tall ship tours, sword and cannon demonstrations, a balloon-making crocodile, inflatable amusements for children, mermaids, the Scalawag Alley Game Zone, a pirate train, exotic belly dancers, a parade, and costume contests for both people and pets. Food vendors are open throughout the weekend, and a beer garden and pirate ball top off Saturday night's festivities. In 2014, the event also hosted an actual pirate wedding on Saturday, where Cap'n Sharkbyte LePirate (aka Curtis) and his pirate queen Gemz A'Plenti (aka Gail) walked the matrimonial plank at six bells in the afternoon. Guests were requested to wear their best pirate finery, and Aloysius MacKnucklepeck served as the master of ceremonies and toastmaster.

Address: Westport waterfront
Admission: Free
Parking: Free street and parking lot parking
Accessible: Yes
Pets: Yes, especially parrots
Lodging: http://westportgrayland-chamber.org/category.php?Category_id=12
Website: www.rustyscupperspiratedaze.com
Facebook: www.facebook.com/rustyscupperspiratedaze
Attractions: Grays Harbor Lighthouse, Westport Maritime Museum, Twin Harbors Beach State Park, cranberry bog tours, John's River Wildlife Area, clamming and crabbing
Trivia: At a height of 107 feet, Grays Harbor Lighthouse (located in Westport) is the tallest in Washington state, and the third tallest on the West Coast. The interesting thing about the lighthouse is that it seems to be

migrating. When it was built in 1898, it was 400 feet from the Pacific Ocean. As it stands currently, the lighthouse is 3,000 feet from high tide. Did the lighthouse finally get sick of putting up with the Pacific's relentless harping? Actually, massive amounts of accretion, due in large part to the jetty system at the entrance to Grays Harbor, built up the land around the lighthouse.

Directions: Westport is located 70 miles west of Olympia via SR-8, US-12 W, SR-105 S.

The state of Washington boasts three national parks, 1,462 National Register of Historic Places, 17 national natural landmarks, 24 National Historic Landmarks, and 186 state parks.

Family Fun

Whaling Days
Silverdale, Kitsap County
Last weekend in July

Whaling Days is a three-day, family-oriented festival that has taken place in Old Town Silverdale since 1972. The weekend starts off with carnival rides, musical performances, and fireworks on Friday night. Saturday morning begins with a pancake breakfast put on by the Silverdale Rotary, Whale of a Run fun runs, and the Grand Parade. Sunday includes the popular Tour de Kitsap bike ride, which promises marvelous scenery on various routes, as well as themed rest stops along the way. Throughout the weekend, enjoy carnival rides, craft and information booths, food vendors, live music and entertainment, a beer and wine garden, outrigger canoe races, and the Great Kitsap Duck Race. Whaling Days is a non-profit organization, and monies made from the festival go to various scholarships and community projects.

Address: Silverdale Waterfront Park, 3293 NW Byron Street
Admission: Admission is free. Carnival rides charge a fee. The beer and wine garden charges a $1 cover charge, and drink tickets (good for one beer or one glass of wine) cost $5 each.
Parking: Arrive early, park at a distance, and walk in to the area. Handicapped parking is available along Washington Avenue south of Carlton Street to Lowell Street, as well as along McConnell Avenue, south of Lowell Street. Event organizers recommend Kitsap Transit, which operates throughout the festival. It is $2 for a ride (exact change is needed).
Accessible: Yes
Lodging: www.visitkitsap.com/lodging/search.asp
Website: http://whalingdays.com
Facebook: www.facebook.com/pages/Whaling-Days/112016315485584
Attractions: Kitsap Mall, Clear Creek Trail, Anderson Landing Nature Preserve, Old Mill Park, Pheasant Fields Farm, Kitsap Historical Museum
Trivia: The orcas that are seen in Puget Sound are part of the Southern Resident Killer Whales (SRKW) community. Orcas live, travel, and hunt in matrilineal pods, which means they are led by their oldest females. Calves never leave their mothers, so the pods can be quite large. The J, K, and L pods that are seen near Puget Sound consist of approximately 79 individuals (J pod has 25 members, K pod has 19 members, and L

pod has 35 members). Each of these pods uses a characteristic dialect to communicate, but some calls are common between all three pods. The calls used by Southern Resident community are unique and are unlike the calls used by any other killer whale communities. J pod received an unexpected new baby member at the tail end of 2014, who is now named J-50. Its 43-year-old mother was thought to be too old to bear a calf, and none of the monitoring scientists even knew she was pregnant. J pod also has the world's oldest known killer whale, Granny (or J2). Scientists have estimated that she was born around 1911, which makes her over 100-years old.

Directions: Driving directions from the North: Merge onto WA-3 S toward Bremerton and take the Newberry Hill Rd exit. Turn left onto NW Newberry Hill Rd. NW Newberry Hill Rd becomes Silverdale Way NW. Turn right onto NW Byron St. End at Silverdale Waterfront Park. Driving directions from the South: Merge onto WA-16 W via exit 132 toward Gig Harbor/Bremerton/Sprague Ave. WA-16 W becomes WA-3 N. Take the Newberry Hill Rd exit. NW Newberry Hill Rd becomes Silverdale Way NW. Turn right onto NW Byron St. End at Silverdale Waterfront Park.

Logger's Playday
Hoquiam, Grays Harbor County
Early September

Hoquiam's Logger's Playday pays homage to the long logging history of the town, and to the strong, burly men and women who helped settle the area. Each year, the festival begins with the Rotary Club pancake feed, then the Elks Lodge Grand Parade, followed by the Lions Club's salmon bake. A street fair features food concessions, craft vendors, and other activities. The festival concludes with Hoquiam's renowned Loggers Show at Olympic Stadium, which attracts loggers from all over the country. Competitions include choke setting (where competitors race over logs and through water, while maintaining their balance on a floating log), log chopping, double bucking, speed climbing, tree topping, log rolling, axe throwing, power saw, and obstacle pole, where competitors race to carry a power saw up a log at a 30-degree incline, cut the end off of the log, and then race back down. The show ends with a fireworks display, and hopefully very few ambulance rides.

Address: Downtown Hoquiam and Olympic Stadium, 101 28th Street

Parking: Parking is available at Olympic Stadium
Accessible: Yes
Lodging: http://chamber.graysharbor.org/list/QL/lodging-travel-24.htm
Website: http://cityofhoquiam.com/events/loggers-playday
Facebook: www.facebook.com/pages/Hoquiam-Loggers-Playday/188168771253103
Attractions: Historic Olympic Stadium, Polson Museum, Grays Harbor Public Market, Hoquiam's Castle
Trivia: In 1988, Hoquiam native George Herbert Hitchings was co-winner, along with fellow scientist Gertrude Elion, of the Nobel Prize in Medicine, for their work in chemotherapy, including development of a compound to treat leukemia. Born in 1905, Hitchings' research with Elion at Wellcome Research Laboratories also yielded new drug therapies for malaria, gout, organ transplantation, and bacterial infections. The work by this team also led the way for major antiviral drugs for herpes infections and AIDS.
Directions: Hoquiam is located 55 miles west of Olympia via SR-8 and US-12 W.

McCleary Bear Festival
McCleary, Grays Harbor County
Second weekend in July

McCleary Bear Festival started as a bet between the newspaper editor of the McCleary Stimulator and his friend in Stevenson, WA as to whose local bears were the tastiest. More than 50 years later, the tradition continues, in festival form, and provides a rare opportunity to feast on McCleary's world famous bear stew. It is served immediately following the Grand Parade which always starts at noon on Saturday. The stew includes 100+ pounds of meat (a small portion of that is beef for flavoring), as well as hundreds of pounds of potatoes, carrots, onions, and a large kettle of special spicy sauce and seasonings. The stew is cooked in enormous iron kettles on stoves in the City Park kitchen. It takes about 40 people, working round the clock, to handle the cooking chores. The meal also features a ton (literally) of watermelon, 3,000 rolls, and baked beans by the kettle-full. [Note: this is NOT the single-serving amounts] Although the bear stew is the big attraction, the festival also includes food and craft vendors, a softball tournament, a reptile zoo, Rods and Rides car show, bouncy houses, a kiddie parade, pony rides, music and entertainment, a petting zoo, a trout pond, a fun run, and a soap box derby. Friday evening hosts the annual "Guns and Hoses" softball game between local law enforcement officers and firefighters.

Address: McCleary City Park and various venues around town
Admission: Admission is free. A kick-off dinner and royalty coronation on Thursday evening costs $10.
Parking: Street and parking lot parking
Accessible: Yes
Lodging: Event organizers suggest GuestHouse Inn and Suites Elma, 800 E Main Street, Elma (360.482.6868), or Little Creek Casino and Resort, 91 West SR-108, Shelton (800.667.771)
Website: www.mcclearybearfestival.org
Facebook: www.facebook.com/pages/McCleary-Bear-Festival/77114972357
Attractions: McCleary Hotel, McCleary Museum–Carnell House, Capitol State Forest, Summit Lake
Trivia: When he was a child, Clarence Chesterfield Howerton lived in McCleary with his family. Howerton is famous for being an American circus performer who starred in sideshows from the early 1920s to the late 1940s. Known as Major Mite, he was 2' 4" tall and weighed only 20 pounds at the age of 22. He was billed as the smallest man in the world. In contrast to his public persona as "childlike," it was reported that Howerton enjoyed cigars and beer, and frequently threw around obscenities. In the 1930s, he took a break from the circus to star as a munchkin in *The Wizard of Oz*, and in several *Our Gang* comedy shorts, including one titled "Free Eats." In 1975, he died of pneumonia in McMinnville, Oregon at the age of 62. He is buried in Mountain View Cemetery in nearby Oregon City.
Directions: McCleary is 25 minutes from I-5 at Olympia.

Allyn Days/Geoduck Festival
Allyn, Mason County
Third weekend in July

This combined event provides three days of family fun. Allyn Days events include a youth talent competition, entertainment, a baked goods sale, a beer and wine bar, dozens of food and vendor booths, a salmon dinner with salmon that is grilled over a giant pit barbecue, and a kids' area.

Geoduck Festival includes dragon boat races, dozens of food and vendor booths, entertainment, amateur oyster shucking contests, and a touch tank with live geoducks and other bivalves.

Address: Downtown
Admission: Free
Parking: Free. Shuttle service provided to various parking areas.
Accessible: Yes
Pets: Yes
Lodging: http://explorehoodcanal.com/lodging_2.html
Website: www.allynwashington.com/allyn-days-geoduck-festival
Facebook: www.facebook.com/AllynCommunityAssociation/info
Attractions: Allyn Waterfront Park, Belfair Farmers Market, Mary E. Theler Wetlands Nature Preserve
Trivia: The Geoduck clam is native to the west coast of Canada and the northwest coast of the U.S. It is the largest burrowing clam in the world, weighing 1.5 pounds on average, but some specimens have been recorded at more than 15 pounds and as long as two meters in length—a size at which their appearance can best be described as "icky." They are also one of the longest-living organisms in the world. The oldest recorded specimen was 168 years old.
Directions: Allyn is located 40 miles north of Olympia via US-101 N and WA-3 N.

Mason County Forest Festival
Shelton, Mason County
Starts last Thursday in May

For 70 years, Mason County Forest Festival has been proud to host a party that welcomes friends, families, neighbors, and visitors to celebrate the area's rich forest traditions. Events include a carnival, car show, a fun run, a firefighters pancake breakfast, a family and pets parade, a wood duck race, fireworks, the Paul Bunyan parade, Stihl Timbersports Western Regional Qualifier, a bike tour, music, and entertainment.

Address: Downtown. Timbersports take place at Loop Field, 1020 W Franklin Street
Admission: Free
Parking: Street and parking lot

Accessible: Yes
Pets: allowed at some events
Lodging: www.explorehoodcanal.com/lodging_1.html
Website: http://masoncountyforestfestival.org
Facebook: www.facebook.com/masoncountyforestfestival
Attractions: Hope Island State Park, Jarrell Cove State Park, local area wineries, Olympic National Park
Trivia: The Paul Bunyan parade is so named because of the 20' tall fiberglass statue of Paul Bunyan that has been featured in the parade. The statue was originally created in 1957 to advertise a chain of gas stations in Washington State. He has experienced several rough patches throughout his life. He has been knocked down, beheaded, dismembered into 13 pieces, and had his axe stolen by ne'er do wells from a local rival high school. He also spent a deeply depressing year in seclusion at a wastewater treatment plant. In 1995, local businessman and entrepreneur Lloyd Prouty took pity on Paul, gained custody, and gave him some much-needed body work. Paul began traveling around, acting as a good will ambassador at various events and parades. However, it soon became evident that Paul had another problem. The typical powerline height over many of his parade routes was not enough to accommodate someone of Paul's size. Prouty created a trailer with a hydraulic lift so that when confronted with offending power lines, Paul would slowly recline into a laid back position (making it appear as if he had suddenly become sleepy) so that he could pass, unscathed, underneath. He would then pop up, as if rejuvenated from his cat nap, and continue along the parade route. He is the happiest he's ever been. Paul is also no longer alone—he has a 17-ft long, 8-ft wide companion, Babe the Blue Ox. Check out Paul and Babe's adventures at his Facebook page: www.facebook.com/PaulBunyanAndBabe.
Directions: Shelton is 20 miles northwest of Olympia via US-101 N.

Food & Agricultural Festivals

Blackberry Festival
Bremerton, Kitsap County
September/Labor Day weekend

The annual Blackberry Festival takes place on Bremerton's picturesque waterfront. The three-day event promises unique entertainment and culinary delights, blackberry style, but without all of the pesky thorns. Enjoy free entertainment while you sample the best blackberry jams, jellies, pies, and cobblers, or check out the beer garden and taste blackberry cider and blackberry wine. More than 100 vendors offer a variety of food, drink, and art. Kids' activities include performances by magicians and musicians, games, face painting, and art activities. Other events include a car show, a Berry Fun Run, and the Blackberry Criterium Bike Race.

Address: Bremerton Boardwalk, 100 2nd Street
Admission: Free
Parking: Park and ride costs $2 each way and runs from Olympic College at 16th and Warren Lot S-4. Diamond Parking locations donate $1 of the daily paid fee to the Blackberry Festival. Bremerton has more than 2,000 downtown parking spaces available on the street or in public pay lots. The Bremerton/Port Orchard Foot Ferry runs begin each day of the festival at 10 am and the last run from Bremerton is at 8 pm on Saturday, 7 pm on Sunday, and 6 pm on Monday. The ferry runs every half hour on the whole and half hour from the Port Orchard side, and on the quarter hour from the Bremerton side. The ferry costs $2 each way.
Accessible: Yes
Lodging: www.ci.bremerton.wa.us/BusinessDirectoryII.aspx?lngBusinessCategoryID=26.
Website: www.blackberryfestival.org
Facebook: www.facebook.com/BremertonBlackberryFestival
Attractions: Gold Mountain Golf Course, Kitsap County Historical Museum, USS Turner Joy, aircraft carriers on Charleston Beach Road, Bug Museum, Elandan Gardens
Trivia: Have you ever heard of Bill Gates? Not THAT Bill Gates, but the elder Mr. Gates? Turns out that the dad of Bill Gates, Jr. (founder of Microsoft) is no slouch either. The elder Mr. Gates, who was born in Bremerton, graduated from Washington State University, and practiced

law in the Seattle area from 1950–1998. He has served on the Board of Regents for UW, served as director of Costco Wholesale, was a founding co-chair of the Pacific Health Summit, served on the Board for Judicial Administration of the Washington State Supreme Court, served as president of the Seattle-King County Bar Association as well as the Washington State Bar Association, authored the book Showing Up for Life: Thoughts on the Gifts of a Lifetime, was inducted into the Academy of Arts and Sciences in 2003, was a recipient of the Washington Medal of Merit in 2009, serves as an Honorary Co-Chair for the World Justice Project, and is currently the co-chair of the Bill and Melinda Gates foundation, a philanthropic organization that is one of the largest private foundations in the world.

Directions: From I-5, take the Hwy 16/Bremerton exit near Tacoma. Continue on Hwy 16 across the Tacoma Narrows Bridge. Come to the communities of Gig Harbor, Port Orchard, and Gorst, in that order. After looping through Gorst, meet the interchange where Hwy 16 becomes Hwy 3. Continue straight and follow the signs to downtown.

Sequim Lavender Festival
Sequim, Clallam County
Third weekend in July

Touted as the largest lavender event in North America, the Sequim Lavender Festival includes a street fair, as well as free self-guided tours of seven great lavender farms that normally require an entry fee. The street fair provides a great selection of Olympic Coast cuisine for every appetite, from vegan to hot-dog lover. Enjoy barbecue, at least six flavors of lavender ice cream, crab cakes and salmon, Greek and Thai food, coffee, and freshly made crepes, all while enjoying continuous live music from Northwest bands and ensembles while sitting at tables in tree-shaded lawns. The street fair also includes more than 150 juried art and craft booths. Sequim Lavender Growers Association members offer many lavender products, including hydrating oils, lotions and soaps, culinary ingredients, and pet apparel. And, of course, unique and hard-to-locate lavender plants are available at the street fair and the farms. Kids' activities include a scavenger hunt, music, hula hooping, dancing, a photo booth, and face painting. Bicycling to the lavender farms is encouraged. The Sequim-Dungeness Valley is well known for its gentle rolling roads—you can easily ride your bike to all the Farms on tour. If you buy something that is too big for your bike, the farms happily hold it until you can pick it up later with a car.

Address: Various locations
Admission: Free
Parking: Street, parking lot
Accessible: Yes
Pets: No
Lodging: www.olympicpeninsula.org/places-to-stay
Website: www.lavenderfestival.com
Facebook: www.facebook.com/Sequimlavenderfestival
Attractions: The Cedars at Dungeness golf course, 7 Cedars Casino, Dungeness National Wildlife Refuge, Olympic National Park
Trivia: The city of Sequim and the surrounding area are particularly known for the commercial cultivation of lavender, supported by the unique climate. Sequim is billed as the Lavender Capital of North America, rivaled worldwide only by France.
Directions: Sequim is located two hours northwest of Seattle, 17 miles east of Port Angeles on Hwy 101.

Rhododendron Festival
Port Townsend, Jefferson County
Third week in May

In 1935, a Port Townsend businessman convinced the Hearst Metrotone News organization to come to Jefferson County and film the rhododendrons in bloom for one of Hearst's "short subject" presentations provided to theaters throughout the U.S. Hearst agreed to visit Jefferson County that year to photograph the wild rhododendrons. As a prelude to Hearst's arrival, the business community organized a Queen competition so that Hearst would also have a group of young women to photograph with the rhododendrons. Nominations were made and the community could vote on their favorite by shopping at participating merchants. Dollars spent equaled votes. Myrtle Olsen was voted the first Rhododendron Queen and filmed by Hearst. The townsfolk so enjoyed the festivities, that community organizers decided to make it a yearly event to celebrate Washington's state flower. Events include an art and craft fair, trike races, pet parade, kiddie parade, carnival, fish fry, hair and beard contests, bed races, pancake breakfast, golf tournament, fun run, cake picnic, and the Rhody Festival Grand Parade. The event also provides scholarships to selected royalty.

Address: Downtown
Admission: Free
Parking: Street and parking lot parking
Accessible: Yes
Lodging: http://ptguide.com/accommodations-and-lodging
Website: www.rhodyfestival.org
Facebook: www.facebook.com/rhodyfestival
Attractions: Fort Worden State Park, Northwest Maritime Center, Jefferson County Historical Society, Port Townsend Aero Museum
Trivia: Honey made from the nectar of rhododendrons can cause a rare poisonous reaction called grayanatoxin poisoning, also known as honey intoxication or rhododendron poisoning. Initial physical symptoms of the poisoning include excessive salivation, perspiration, vomiting, dizziness, weakness, and tingling or burning in the extremities and around the mouth, low blood pressure, and decreased heart rate. In higher doses, the toxins can produce loss of coordination, severe and progressive muscular weakness, and electrocardiographic changes. Despite the heart issues, however the condition is rarely fatal and generally lasts less than a day. In the 18th century this "mad honey" was exported to Europe where it gave alcoholic drinks an extra kick. The toxin is used in the 2009 film Sherlock Holmes to induce an "apparently mortal paralysis" in Lord Blackwood, and in Gladstone, Watson's bulldog.
Directions: Port Townsend is located northwest of Seattle (via ferry). Find specific driving directions at: www.ptguide.com/maps-a-directions/driving-directions

Dungeness Crab and Seafood Festival (Crabfest)
Port Angeles, Clallam County
Mid-October

The Dungeness Crab and Seafood Festival, Crabfest, celebrates not only the aquaculture, agriculture, and maritime traditions of the Olympic Peninsula, but brings food, art, music, Native American activities, and children's events into one three-day weekend. Located on the gorgeous Port Angeles waterfront next to Olympic National Park and a short ferry ride from Victoria, Canada, the event celebrates the world-famous

Dungeness crab and the bounty of the sea. Rain or shine, Crabfest features 14 restaurants, cooking demonstrations with celebrity chefs, a chowder cook-off, the Grab-A-Crab Tank Derby (a $5 entry fee lets you crab for 10 minutes), local wine tasting, a 5K run/walk/scuttle, crafts, and music. The hub of the festival is Crab Central Pavilion, also known as the Big Tent, which houses the old-fashioned crab feed complete with large kettles of fresh crab caught in local waters, brought live to the festival, and served with fresh corn and coleslaw. Eight of the finest local restaurants complement the crab feed with more than 25 seafood dishes and great desserts. Enjoy wine tasting, Northwest microbrews, and live music under the big top. Sunday morning, bring the family and enjoy the Crab Revival—gospel music, a sing-along, words of peace, a blessing for the day, and breakfast. And, of course, you can purchase cooked, cleaned, and chilled fresh crab, at market price, to take home for your own crab feast.

Address: 122 N. Lincoln Street (Red Lion Hotel)
Admission: Free. The half-crab dinner is $15.
Parking: More than 2,000 free parking spaces in downtown Port Angeles. You can also park in paid lots.
Accessible: Yes
Pets: Dogs are allowed on the grounds; however, none are allowed in the Crab Central Tent because it is considered a restaurant.
Lodging: The event's official host hotel is the Red Lion Hotel in Port Angeles. Other lodging information: http://business.portangeles.org/list/ql/lodging-travel-15. Bed and breakfast information: www.opbba.com
Website: www.crabfestival.org
Facebook: www.facebook.com/pages/Dungeness-Crab-Seafood-Festival/54517750078?ref=br_tf
Attractions: Olympic National Park, Coho Ferry, Port Angeles Fine arts Center and Webster's Woods Art Park, Olympic Game Farm, Hurricane Ridge, Cape Flattery Trail — the most northwestern point of the continental U.S.
Trivia: The Dungeness crab gets its name from the village of Dungeness, located near Sequim, Washington. The oldest commercial shellfish fishery on the Pacific Coast began in this small village in 1848.
Directions: Port Angeles is located 2.5 hours northwest of Seattle (via ferry), or 120 miles (2.5 hours) north of Olympia via US-101 N.

Chocolate on the Beach Festival
Five miles of chocolate events in Pacific Beach, Aloha, Copalis Beach, Moclips, and Seabrook in Grays Harbor County
Last weekend in February

Spend the weekend tasting your way through 10 miles of chocolate. This fun family festival offers something for every chocolate lover. Enjoy chocolate vendors, artists, and crafters. Attend a cooking class or enter your favorite recipe in the recipe contest. Turn your penchant for mowing your way through a bowl of chocolate pudding into a competitive edge for the pudding eating contest. (Who knew your guilty pleasure could lead to prizes?) Enjoy many types of chocolate, including gluten free, dairy free, vegan, organic, fair trade, and raw. You can also purchase healthy treats for your favorite furry friends.

Address: Vendors and demonstrations are located in the town of Pacific Beach. The vendor building is located at Pacific Beach Elementary, 11 4th Street, and demonstrations are given at North Beach Community Center, 4579 SR-109.
Admission: $5 gets you admission to both Saturday's and Sunday's events. On Sunday, free entry for EMS, police, fire dept., and active/retired military.
Parking: Street and parking lot
Accessible: Yes
Lodging: The festival has several participating accommodation providers, which are listed at the event website at http://chocolateonthebeachfestival.com/accomodations. All guests who choose to stay at one of these places receive a Golden Ticket the weekend of the festival. By entering the Golden Ticket at the Information Booth, guests could win a free stay on the North Beach.
Website: www.chocolateonthebeachfestival.com
Facebook: www.facebook.com/ChocolateontheBeachFestival
Attractions: Grays Harbor National Wildlife Refuge, Olympic National Park, Pacific Beach State Park
Trivia: *The Annie Larsen* was a three-masted schooner that came into the spotlight during World War I when it was seized in June 1915 by U.S. customs officials at Grays Harbor and found to be carrying large quantities of small arms and ammunition in violation of the Neutrality Acts. The arms were on their way to the SS Maverick at a rendezvous off the coast of Mexico, where they would be shipped to India. The An-

nie Larsen affair was one of the major setbacks of the Hindu German Conspiracy, which was an ill-fated Indo-German-Irish plot to aid in the overthrow of the British Raj in the Indian subcontinent.
Directions: Pacific Beach and Moclips are located 18 miles north of Oceans Shores on SR-109, directly on the Pacific Ocean.

OysterFest
Shelton, Mason County
First weekend in October

OysterFest is not only a celebration of all things oyster, but is also Washington State's official seafood festival, and home to the West Coast Oyster Shucking Championships. From a delicate herbed seafood ceviche to corn on the cob, with nearly 100 food vendors to choose from, you'll find something for every palate: Washington wines, a microbrew garden (complete with its own live music stage), and dozens upon dozens of fresh oysters prepared in every way imaginable. The event (which supports nearly 100 local non-profit service clubs and organizations, as well as funds scholarships and community improvement projects) features a popular cook-off, hands-on water quality exhibits, and live music throughout the weekend. It also includes an art and photography show. The Oyster Shucking Championships are a centerpiece of the festival. Speed is the primary factor on Saturday, when each shucker is given 24 oysters to shuck as quickly as possible—with the fastest usually doing so in less than two minutes (2014's winner Alejandro Leon did so in one minute, 16 seconds). At the half-shell trials on Sunday, not only must the shuckers shuck 24 oysters quickly, but they also must place each on its back in the half shell. Shuckers lose points for any cuts to the oyster, or any shell pieces. A prize is awarded for Best Presentation for the tray of oysters on the half-shell that looks the nicest. The shucked oysters from each heat are passed out to audience members after judging, either for them to eat, or to lovingly transport home as an aromatic souvenir.

Address: Port of Shelton
Admission: $5
Parking: Free. Also a free shuttle service is provided from other parking locations throughout Shelton.
Accessible: Yes
Pets: No
Lodging: RV camping $15/day for Thursday and Sunday nights, $35/day

for Friday and Saturday nights
Website: www.oysterfest.org
Facebook: www.facebook.com/oysterfestwa
Attractions: Mason County Historical Museum, local wineries, Oakland Bay Historic Park, Olympic National Forest, Overlook Park
Trivia: According to Guinness World Records, the largest oyster in the world measured in at 13.97" long and 4.21" wide. Not to be taken without his friends, the super-sized mollusk was harvested from the water with five smaller oysters attached. The total cluster weighed more than 3.5 pounds. It was a Pacific oyster found in 2013 on the Danish shores of the Wadden Sea. It is estimated to be 15–20 years old, and is alive and well, and on display at the Wadden Sea Center in Ribe Denmark.
Directions: From Seattle/Tacoma, take I-5 S to Olympia. Take exit 104 to Hwy 101 N. After approximately 6 miles, take the Port Angeles-Shelton exit to continue on Hwy 101. Follow Hwy 101 N approximately 16 miles to Shelton. One-half mile past mile marker 345, take a left at the second Port of Shelton entrance/Industrial Park/Sanderson Way. Take the immediate left onto the access road to W 21 Sanderson Way.

From Bremerton/Gig Harbor, take Hwy 3 into Shelton. Bayshore Golf Course is on the left. Take the next right onto Johns Prairie Rd. Stay on Johns Prairie Rd into Shelton to the Wallace-Kneeland exit. Get on Hwy 101 N/Industrial Park/Sanderson Way. Turn onto the access road to W 21 Sanderson Way.

From Portland, take I-5 N to Olympia. Take exit 104 to Hwy 101 N. After approximately six miles, take the Port Angeles-Shelton exit to continue on Hwy 101. Follow Hwy 101 N approximately 16 miles to Shelton. One-half mile past mile marker 345, take a left at the second Port of Shelton entrance/Industrial Park/Sanderson Way. Take the immediate left onto the access road to W 21 Sanderson Way.

ShrimpFest
Brinnon, Jefferson County
Fourth weekend in May

Brinnon ShrimpFest is a family festival, situated on the banks of Hood Canal, that celebrates the rare, delicious, Hood Canal Spot Shrimp, which is the largest species of shrimp in Puget Sound—they can be as long as nine inches (excluding the antennae). The Spot Shrimp season is extremely short—usually four hours a day for only four days in May. So the folks at Brinnon decided that Memorial Day Weekend was a great time to celebrate the delicious bounty. The festival is one of the very few places that you can buy Hood Canal Spot Shrimp. Although you better come early, because they sell out quickly. The event features craft and food booths (with local fare and typical festival food, in case you're not a shrimp fan), exhibits, live music, and a beer garden. Kids' activities include carnival rides and an air-gun booth. Enjoy the view of Hood Canal as you attend the event, and if you want, you can sit and eat your lunch on the beach. The tides are usually low enough during this weekend for easy harvest of clams and oysters on the public beaches near the festival (license required). The popular belt-sander races invite you to bring your decorated sander and pit its racing prowess against formidable local and Canadian competitors.

Address: ShrimpFest is located between the Yelvik General store and the Cove RV Park and Country Store, 303375 U.S. 101.
Admission: Admission costs $4 a day, or you can get a two-day pass for $6. Kids under age 12 and active military and veterans (with ID) get in free.
Parking: Free
Accessible: Yes
Pets: No
Lodging: http://emeraldtowns.com/things-to-do/camping or http://emeraldtowns.com/things-to-do/lodging.
Website: www.emeraldtowns.org/shrimpfest
Facebook: www.facebook.com/BrinnonShrimpfest
Attractions: Rocky Brook Falls Trail, kayaking in Hood Canal, Olympic National Park, and fishing, clamming, crabbing, shrimping, and oystering
Trivia: Brinnon is the home of Camp Parsons, the oldest Boy Scout camp west of the Mississippi River, and one of the few camps that uses an open-water saltwater base for all scouting aquatic activities. On July 7th, 1919 the first scouts arrived after a boat ride to Brinnon and a five-mile overland hike in to the camp. Camp food was cooked over an open fire on an old 60-inch saw blade. Mountain hikes were a regular program feature, and scouts from Camp Parsons made the second recorded ascent of Mt. Anderson, made the first recorded ascent of Mt. Tom (named after a young scout who was the first in his group to summit that peak), and developed most of the trails from the Dosewallips watershed.

Directions: Three route options from Seattle: 1) Take the ferry from downtown to Bainbridge Island. Travel 13 miles west on SR-305 to SR-3. Travel north 7 miles on SR-3 to the Hood Canal Bridge. Travel west 11 miles on SR-104 to the Port Townsend/Quilcene exit. Exit right and turn right at bottom of ramp onto Center Rd. Travel south on Center Rd 8 miles to Quilcene. Continue on Hwy 101 to Brinnon; 2) Travel north on I-5 to the Edmonds Ferry exit. Take SR-104 to the ferry. Take the ferry to Kingston. Continue west on SR-104 20 miles to the Port Townsend/Quilcene exit. Exit right and turn right at bottom of ramp onto Center Rd. Travel south on Center Rd eight miles to Quilcene. Continue on Hwy 101 to Brinnon or; 3) Travel south on I-5 to Tacoma. Exit on to SR-16. Travel northwest on SR-16 to SR-3. Travel north on SR-3 to the Hood Canal Bridge. Travel west 11 miles on SR-104 to the Port Townsend/Quilcene exit. Exit right and turn right at bottom of ramp onto Center Rd. Travel south on Center Rd 8 miles to Quilcene. Continue on Hwy 101 to Brinnon.

From Olympia, on I-5 take the exit for US-101. Travel north on US-101 approximately 62 miles to Brinnon. From Port Angeles, take US-101 east approximately 45 miles to Quilcene. Continue on Hwy 101 to Brinnon.

Taste of Hood Canal
Belfair, Mason County
Second Saturday in August

Taste of Hood Canal is a day of fun, food, music, and cars. The main draw of the event is, of course, the wonderful food, including oysters, burgers, lumpia, prawns, polish dogs, barbecue garlic shrimp, pulled pork, barbecue brisket and tri-tip, shrimp cocktails, baked potatoes, meatball sliders, nachos, a taco bar, Italian sodas, popcorn, shaved ice, strawberry shortcake, chocolates, peanut brittle, jams and relishes, ice cream, glazed nuts, doughnuts, cookies, fudge, and last, but not least, chocolate dipped bacon. Yum! Enjoy a nice cold beer in the beer garden, or participate in wine tasting. Another major part of the festival is the Customs and Classics Car Show, which features cars from all over the greater Puget Sound area, and attracts nearly 10,000 car show fans. Taste also features informational displays, art and craft booths, fire engines, family entertainment, and live music. The Mason County Fire District hosts its annual pancake breakfast on the morning of the festival.

Address: Clifton Lane
Admission: Free
Parking: Parking is available on old Belfair Hwy, 500 feet from the event, and a free shuttle runs from Sandhill Elementary School. Just follow the signs.
Accessible: Yes
Lodging: www.explorehoodcanal.com/lodging.html
Website: www.tasteofhoodcanal.com
Facebook: www.facebook.com/tasteofhoodcanal
Attractions: Hood Canal, Mary E. Theler Wetlands Nature Preserve, Tahuya State Forest, Belfair State Park, Harstine Island Trail, Belfair Farmers Market
Trivia: Hood Canal was named by Royal Navy Captain George Vancouver on May 13, 1792, in honor of British Admiral Lord Samuel Hood. On October 29 of that same year, a member of Vancouver's party, Lieutenant William Broughton, also named Oregon's Mt. Hood after the same man.
Directions: Belfair is 45 miles north of Olympia via US-101 N and WA-3 N.

Named in honor of President George Washington, Washington is the 42nd state, entering the Union on Nov. 11, 1889.
Capitol: Olympia
State Motto: Al-Ki (Indian word meaning "by and by")
Nickname: Evergreen state
Tree: Western Hemlock
Bird: Willow Goldfinch
Marine Mammal: Orca
State flower: Coast Rhododendron
State Fruit: Apple
State Song: "Washington, My Home"

Music

Galway Bay's Irish Music Festival
Ocean Shores, Grays Harbor County
Last weekend in October

Galway Bay's Irish Music Festival is touted by organizers as the West Coast's largest Irish music festival, featuring six stages, three venues, and 20 great bands. The event has traditionally taken place at Galway Bay Irish Pub and Restaurant, the Ocean Shores Convention Center, and the 8th Street Ale House. Venues serve traditional Irish food, as well as other tasty offerings. The music is an eclectic mix that ranges from more mellow traditional songs to high-energy rock. Galway Bay Irish Pub and the 8th Street Ale House venues are for those 21 and older. The convention center venue is family friendly, and provides kids' activities, including face painting, Irish crafts, and Irish step dancing demonstrations. Saturday workshops for adults include Irish dance, voice lessons, and workshops for various instruments, including accordion, bodhran, Irish guitar, fiddle, and tin whistle.

Address: Galway Bay Irish Restaurant and Pub, 880 Point Brown Avenue NE; Ocean Shores Convention Center, 120 W Chance a La Mer NW; and 8th Street Ale House, 207 8th St, Hoquiam
Admission: Single-day passes range from free to $75 depending on venue and additional ticket options. An all-days pass is $80.
Parking: Street and parking lot parking is available. Also, the festival provides shuttle service between venues and to participating hotels.
Accessible: Yes
Pets: No
Lodging: www.galwaybayirishpub.com/hotels
Website: www.galwaybayirishpub.com/irishmusicfestival
Facebook: www.facebook.com/pages/Galway-Bay-Irish-Restaurant-Pub/229222094556
Attractions: Deep-sea, surf, and freshwater fishing and crabbing; Damon Point State Park; Ocean Shores Golf Course; Weatherwax Trail; Coastal Interpretive Center; Oyhut Wildlife Recreation Area
Trivia: In 1974, the police-drama film *McQ* starring John Wayne and Eddie Albert, was filmed in Ocean Shores and the surrounding area. Wayne's character, trapped in his car after an auto accident, utters the

fabulous line "I'm up to my butt in gas."
Directions: Ocean Shores is located 75 miles (1.5 hours) west of Olympia via SR-8, US-12 W.

Olympic Music Festival
Quilcene, Jefferson County
11 weekends in the summer, late June through early September

When the Olympic Music Festival was founded in 1984, it was originally intended to be a summer home for the Philadelphia String Quartet. It soon became clear, however, that Northwest audiences were great appreciators of chamber music. The Festival has grown from three weekends to 11, and performances take place inside a barn on an idyllic turn-of-the-century dairy farm on 55 acres on the Olympic Peninsula. These "concerts in the barn" feature world-renowned musicians, casually clad, providing outstanding music from the most beloved classical composers. Pack a picnic, bring your friends, and spend a wonderful day roaming the festival grounds before the concert. The farm has plenty of picnic tables and places to explore.

Address: 7360 Center Road
Admission: Barn tickets for adults cost $30 in advance, $33 at the gate; seniors 62 and older cost $28 in advance, $31 at the gate; youth ages 7–17 cost $18 in advance $21 at the gate. Children under age 7 are not permitted at performances in the barn. Lawn tickets cost $20 for adults, $14 for youth, and children under 7 are admitted free. For lawn seating, remember to bring your own blanket or lawn chairs. A Barn Flex Pass costs $300 for 11 performances. A Lawn Flex Pass costs $200 for 11 performances.
Parking: Parking is free on the festival grounds. RVs must park outside the Festival on adjoining roads.
Accessible: Yes. Please call the festival office ahead of time at 360.732.4800 so that appropriate arrangements can be made.
Pets: No
Lodging: www.olympicmusicfestival.org/index.php?page=lodging
Website: www.olympicmusicfestival.org
Facebook: www.facebook.com/home.php#!/theolympicmusicfestival
Attractions: Quilcene Historical Museum, Olympic National Forest, Mt.

Walker, Leland Lake

Trivia: Hood Canal is famous for its Pacific Razor Clams as well as Dabob Oysters and Quilcene Oysters, which were named after nearby Dabob and Quilcene Bays. The world's largest seafood hatchery, owned by Coast Seafoods Company, is located in Quilcene. It is capable of producing over 45 billion oyster eyed-larvae (Diploid and Triploid) each year. Diploid oysters are natural wild oysters. Triploid oysters are generally created at hatcheries and they grow faster and are more disease-resistant than diploids. Triploids are also sterile. This means that they don't have to spend their time primping their comb-overs or desperately trying to flex at the beach. Instead, they use that energy toward growing faster, and maintaining their flavor and texture much longer than the diploids.

Directions: The festival is an enjoyable trip by car and ferry from Seattle or Edmonds. From Seattle and east of Puget Sound, take the Bainbridge Island or Edmonds/Kingston Ferry. Cross the Hood Canal Bridge and travel 10 miles west of the bridge (Route 104). Take the Olympic Music Festival and Quilcene exit and turn right. The festival is 1/2 mile ahead on the right.

From Port Angeles, Sequim, and the west, travel east on Hwy 101 past Discovery Bay. Take Rte 104 (toward Hood Canal Bridge). Travel 8 miles east on 104, then turn left at the Olympic Music Festival and Quilcene exit. Turn right on to Center Rd. The festival is 1/2 mile ahead, on the right.

From Port Townsend and the north, travel south on Hwy 19 and turn right on Center Rd at the Chimacum intersection. Travel south approximately 7 miles. The festival is 1/2 mile past the 104 interchange on the right.

From Tacoma, cross the Tacoma Narrows Bridge and follow Rte 16 and Rte 3 to Hood Canal Bridge. Travel 10 miles west of the bridge (Rte 104) and take the Olympic Music Festival and Quilcene exit. Turn right onto Center Rd. The festival is 1/2 mile ahead, on the right. From Olympia and the south, travel north on Hwy 101 to Quilcene and exit onto Center Rd, toward Chimacum. The Festival is 10 minutes ahead on the left.

Bluegrass from the Forest Festival
Shelton, Mason County
Third weekend in May

The three-day Bluegrass from the Forest festival brings top quality national and regional bands to Shelton for a weekend of music, camping, jamming, contests, workshops, and youth programs. Bring your instrument and join in the Slow Jam, which is a jam session that is novice-player friendly. Band Scramble bandmates are determined by names drawn out of a hat. Ideally, each band ends up with a bass, a banjo, a mandolin, one or two guitars, other instruments, and maybe even a singer. The newly formed bands have 40 minutes to come up with an instrumental and vocal tune that they all happen to know (or can learn quickly). They then take it to the Showcase Stage for a live contest performance. The Mandolin Tasting gathers knowledgeable and talented mandolin players in a room with some very nice mandolins. This differs from a mandolin workshop in that the focus in less about playing technique and more about understanding the features that make a good instrument. Admission gets you in to the Master Workshops where instructors discuss techniques and anecdotes, share their philosophy about performing, and answer questions. The Chick Rose School of Bluegrass is a special program for kids who want to play bluegrass music. Children are divided into small groups according to their musical ability, and are coached by advanced musicians. The program culminates in a special performance of all the kids on Sunday morning on the main stage. The event also includes a banjo contest, vendors, plenty of jamming at the festival and in the campground, and midnight hot dogs on Saturday night.

Address: Shelton High School, 3737 North Shelton Springs Road
Admission: Weekend pass (Fri–Sun) $35. Family weekend pass (for two adults and four kids) $90. Friday evening $15. Saturday afternoon $15 and Saturday evening $15. All day Saturday (two shows plus all events) $25. All-day Sunday $15. Kids ages 12–17 get in for half price, and kids aged 11 and under get in free with an adult. Dry camping is $10 for the day/$20 for the weekend.
Parking: Free
Accessible: Yes
Pets: No
Lodging: www.explorehoodcanal.com/lodging.html
Website: http://bluegrassfromtheforest.com

Facebook: www.facebook.com/bluegrassfromtheforest
Attractions: Jarrell Cove State Park, Little Creek Casino, Taylor Shellfish Farm, Puget Sound, Olympic National Forest, Hood Canal
Trivia: Shelton is the last City in Washington to utilize the Mayor/Commission form of government. The Commissioner in Position One wears the title of Mayor and has the same authority as the other Commissioners.
Directions: From southbound on Hwy 101, take the Wallace Kneeland Blvd exit. Keep going straight past Wal-Mart, then take a left on Shelton Springs Rd. Keep going straight, and Shelton High School is on your left. From northbound on Hwy 101, take Wallace Kneeland Blvd exit. Turn right at the stop sign, and keep going straight past Wal-Mart. Take a left on Shelton Springs Rd. Keep going straight, and Shelton High School is on your left. Coming from Hwy 3, turn right on 1st St (after PROBuild). Keep following 1st St. When the road splits, stay on the right side (you have to merge onto 13th St). Get into the left lane and turn left on Shelton Springs Rd. Keep going straight, and Shelton High School is on your left.

Seattle's Space Needle is an icon for the city. Located in Seattle Center, the futuristic structure was erected in 1962 for the Seattle World's Fair. It features an observation deck at 520 ft. and a gift shop with the rotating SkyCity restaurant at 500 ft.

Peninsula/West Puget Sound County Fairs

Clallam
Port Angeles
www.clallam.net/Fair

Grays Harbor
Elma
www.ghcfairgrounds.com

Jefferson
Port Townsend
www.jeffcofairgrounds.com/JeffCo_Site/Welcome%21.html

Kitsap
Bremerton
www.kitsapgov.com/parks/Fairgrounds/Pages/Fair_Main_Page.htm

Mason
Shelton
www.masoncountyfair.org

Southwest Region

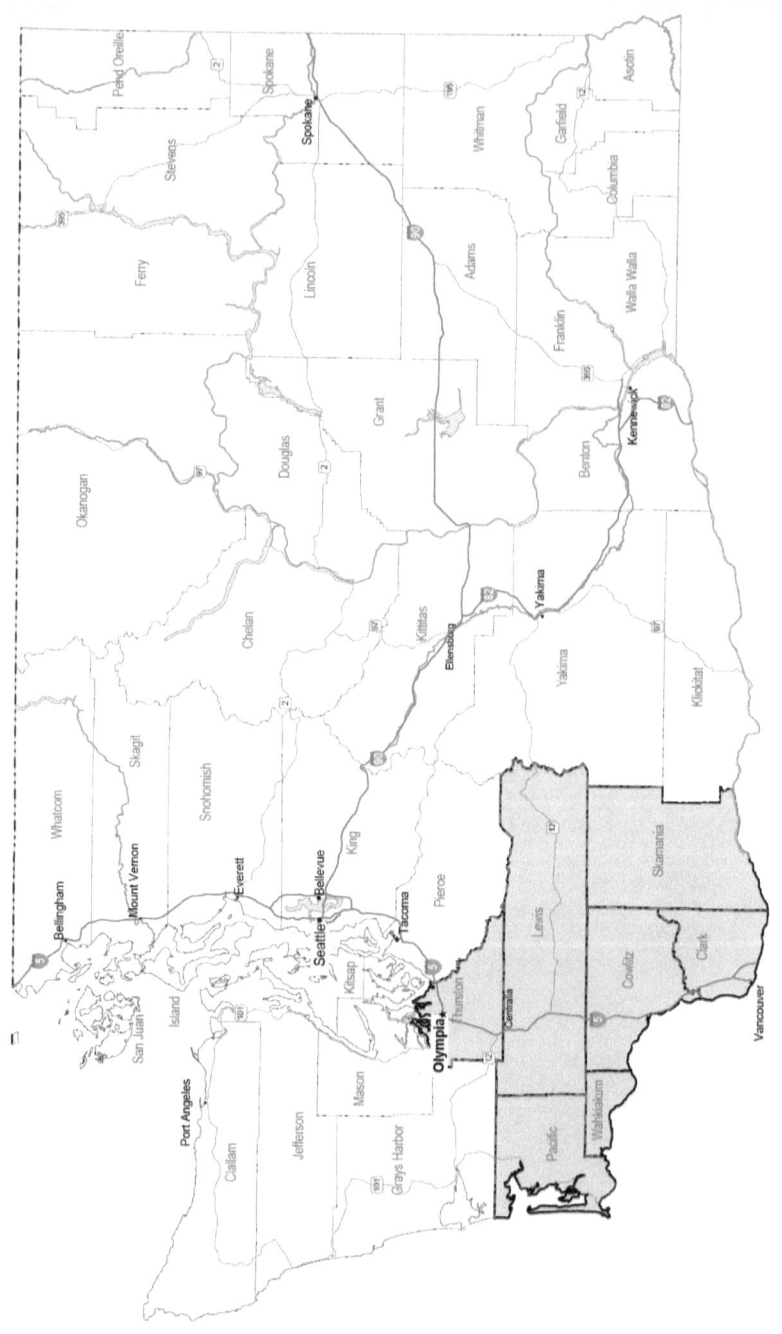

Southwest Washington

Southwest Washington has two main metropolitan areas: The Olympia/Tumwater/Lacey region at the south end of Puget Sound, and Vancouver, which sits on the northern bank of the mighty Columbia River. The area around the capitol city of Olympia has a burgeoning art scene, and hosts annual events such as the Olympia Film Festival and America's Classic Jazz Festival (Lacey). Vancouver, one of the first settlements in the Northwest spurred by the Hudson's Bay Company, often shares its event calendar with Portland, Oregon, which lies just across the Columbia River. However, Vancouver does host a few events that feature its own southern-Washington flair, including a Recycled Arts Festival, and the popular Vancouver Wine and Jazz Festival.

In between Olympia and Vancouver near the I-5 corridor, you can enjoy tasty treats at Chehalis Garlic Fest and at the Mossyrock Blueberry Festival.

East of Vancouver, on the banks of the Columbia, is the gateway to the awe-inspiring scenic Columbia River Gorge. The drive along highway 14, paralleling the north bank of the Columbia, provides some amazing vistas of the river on one side and dense forests and snowy mountain peaks on the other. These forests provide tons of summer and wintertime recreation, and are rumored to be the home of the long-sought-after Sasquatch. The tiny town of Home Valley holds the yearly Bigfoot Bash and Bounty festival for both the serious and the curious.

A majority of Southwest Washington is replete with small-town Americana. Much of it is densely forested, and dotted with small communities, some of which are former logging towns, and some of which are logging towns still. Amboy Territorial Days celebrates the extensive logging history of the area. In addition to fueling the logging industry, these forests provide ground cover for several dramatic volcano-covered peaks that rise from the Cascade Mountain Range, including the notoriously ill-tempered Mt. St. Helens.

Although not as prevalent as in other parts of the state, Southwest Washington does have a growing number of micro-breweries that put out some fantastic beer. Find your new favorite at the Olympia Brew Fest, the Tumwater Artesian Brewfest, the Vancouver Brewfest, or at Centralia's Olympic Club Brewfest.

The Southwest Washington coast is a sand-castle builder's dream. Much unlike the Pacific Coast to the north, the southern beaches are mostly sandy, and as such, invite all sorts of family-friendly beach activities. The Long Beach Peninsula has 28 continuous miles of sand—the longest drivable beach in the world. It hosts the Washington State International Kite Festival every August, as well as the Sandsations festival in July that invites castle-builders of all ability levels.

Other charming small-town festivals in the southwest region include Swede Day Misdsommer Festival in Rochester, as well as the Winlock Egg Day Festival, the Woodland Tulip Festival, the Cranberrian Fair in Ilwaco, and the nutty Longview Squirrel Fest.

In May 1980, Mount St. Helen's erupted, spewing forth one cubic mile of dust, ash, and debris. The mountain lost 1,131 feet of elevation and the blast leveled more than four billion feet of usable timber, enough to build 150,000 homes.

Art Events

Recycled Arts Festival
Vancouver, Clark County
August

The goal of the Recycled Arts Festival is to educate and get the community excited about waste reduction, reuse, and recycling. The festival features more than 130 exceptional artists who create their artwork out of at least 75% recycled or reused materials. Peruse the artists' wares, relax and listen to music, and learn what you can do to improve the environment. Kids enjoy jugglers, a stilt walker, Eartha the Ecological Clown, games, and a chance to make their own art out of recycled materials.

Address: Esther Short Park, 301 W 8th Street
Admission: Free
Parking: Limited on-street parking or in the parking garage across the street, just east of the corner of 6th Street and Columbia
Accessible: Yes
Pets: Yes
Lodging: www.visitvancouverusa.com/visitors/lodging
Website: www.recycledartsfestival.com
Facebook: www.facebook.com/pages/Clark-County-Recycled-Arts-Festival/118234454877432
Attractions: Fort Vancouver, Columbia River Waterfront Trail and Renaissance Park, Hulda Klager Lilac Gardens, Moulton Falls State Park, Officer's Row, Pearson Air Museum, Ridgefield National Wildlife Refuge, Vancouver Farmers Market
Trivia: Esther Short Park, the five-acre park that is the location of the Recycled Arts Festival, is the oldest public square in the state of Washington.
Directions: From I-5 N, immediately after crossing the bridge over the Columbia River, exit right on to City Center/6th St, exit 1-B. Follow the ramp around the loop and back under I-5. As you go under I-5, you are now on C St. Go one block to 8th St and turn left. Go 3 blocks to Columbia St. Esther Short park is on Columbia and 8th St. From I-5 S, take the Mill Plain exit. Turn right at the bottom of the exit onto Mill Plain. Go west four blocks to Columbia St. Turn left on Columbia and go south to 8th St. Esther Short Park is on Columbia and 8th St.

Olympia Film Festival

Olympia, Thurston County
10 days in November

This 10-day 'round-the-clock festival features films, filmmakers, film-related guests, special performances (including an opening-night concert), discussion panels, and educational workshops, all in the historic Capitol Theater, built in 1924. The festival has something for everyone, including animated kids' films, foreign language films, local Northwest films, award-winning experimental films, comedies, and dramas. Don't miss the Q & A sessions at which filmmakers, actors, and screen writers discuss their works. The festival attracts between 5,000 and 7,000 attendees each year.

Address: Capitol Theater, 206 5th Avenue SE
Admission: $85 general admission, which gets you in to most events. A student pass is $30 with ID, A partial pass is available, which gets you in to five titles, and costs $40. Single tickets are $10 general admission, $4 for kids 12 and younger. All Freakin' Night gets you in to all movies on opening night for $15. Opening night includes a reception, a movie, and a concert.
Parking: Street and paid lot parking
Accessible: Yes
Pets: No
Lodging: www.visitolympia.com/lodging
Website: http://olympiafilmsociety.org/olympia-film-festival
Facebook: www.facebook.com/home.php#!/OlympiaFilmFestival
Attractions: Priest Point Park, Washington State Capitol, Olympic Flight Museum, Red Wind Casino, WET Science Center, Mima Mounds Natural Area Preserve
Trivia: One of the first documentary films was *South* (1919), created by Frank Hurley, official photographer for the Imperial Trans-Antarctic Expedition led by Ernest Shackleton in 1914. The film chronicles the failed Antarctic expedition. You can rent and watch this movie on the British Film Institute website: www.bfi.org.uk.
Directions: From I-5 N, take the exit toward State Capitol/City Center. Merge on to 14th Ave SE. At the traffic circle, take the first exit on to Jefferson St SE. Jefferson St SE turns slightly right and becomes Adams St SE. Turn left on to 5th Ave SE. The theater is on the right.

Beer, Wine & Spirits

Vancouver Brewfest
Vancouver, Clark County
Early August

Vancouver Brewfest is the biggest outdoor beer event in the city. It features more than 70 beers, ciders, mead, spirits, and wine in the heart of downtown Vancouver. This event also includes gluten free and organic beers, art/craft vendors and merchants, outstanding food from the best restaurants in Vancouver, and live music. Brewfest is a charity fundraiser and has supported Disabled American Veterans, NW Battle Buddies (service dogs for wounded Vets), and Second Chance Companions.

Address: Esther Short Park, 301 W 8th Street
Admission: General Admission is $15 in advance, $20 at the door. General Admission ticket includes entrance all days, a glass, and $5 in Brewfest tokens. VIP admission is $30. VIP ticket includes entrance all days, a glass, a $10 food voucher, $10 in Brewfest tokens, and one entry to the Frisbee Golf hole-in-one competition held each day.
Parking: Street or paid lot parking
Accessible: Yes
Pets: Yes
Lodging: www.visitvancouverusa.com/visitors/lodging/
Website: http://vancouverbrewfest.com
Facebook: www.facebook.com/VancouverBrewfest
Attractions: Fort Vancouver, Columbia River Waterfront Trail and Renaissance Park, Hulda Klager Lilac Gardens, Moulton Falls State Park, Officer's Row, Pearson Air Museum, Ridgefield National Wildlife Refuge, Vancouver Farmers Market
Trivia: Vancouver's Old Apple Tree Park is home to what is thought be Washington's oldest apple tree, planted in 1826. The Urban Forestry Commission gives away tree cuttings from this matriarch every year during the Old Apple Tree Festival in October.
Directions: From I-5 N, immediately after crossing the bridge over the Columbia River, exit right on to City Center/6th St, exit 1-B. Follow the ramp around the loop and back under I-5. As you go under I-5, you are now on C St. Go one block to 8th St and turn left. Go 3 blocks to Columbia St. Esther Short park is on Columbia and 8th St. From I-5 S, take the Mill Plain exit. Turn right at the bottom of the exit onto Mill Plain. Go

west four blocks to Columbia St. Turn left on Columbia and go south to 8th St. Esther Short Park is on Columbia and 8th St.

Olympic Club Brewfest
Centralia, Lewis County
April

The Olympic Club Brewery in Centralia opened in 1997 as part of a renovation project taken on by McMenamins Pubs and Breweries to restore the notorious and storied gentlemen's resort. The hotel, which is now on the U.S. National Register of Historic Places, has a history of railway bootlegging, captured train robbers, secret call buttons, subterranean tunnels, and rumored hauntings. The Olympic Club Brewfest, which takes place at this location, gathers Washington brewers, as well as guest brewers and importers to pour their finest creations. Beer enthusiasts can tour the brewery, relax in the outdoor seating area, play a round or two of pool, and enjoy specials from the open-pit barbecue, including bratwurst, tri-tip steak, burgers, and "the world's best baked beans." Past guest participants have included Eliot Bay Brewing Company (Seattle), Loowit Brewing Company (Vancouver), Mt. Tabor Brewing Company (Vancouver), Fishtail Brewing Company (Olympia), Double Mountain (Hood River, OR), Burnside Brewing (Portland), Dick's Brewing (Centralia), Snoqualmie Falls Brewing Company (Snoqualmie Falls), Iron Horse Brewery (Ellensburg), Merchant Du Vin Importer (Tukwila), and Diamond Knot Brewery (Mukilteo).

Address: Olympic Club and Hotel Theater, 112 N Tower Avenue
Admission: $12 for a 10-sample punch card
Parking: Street and parking lot parking
Accessible: Yes
Pets: No
Lodging: You can rent a room in the Olympic Club Hotel (360.736.5164) although rooms sell out early. The nearby Holiday Inn at 730 NW Liberty Place (360.740.1800), offers a hotel package and shuttle service. Other lodging accommodations in the Centralia area: www.cityofcentralia.com/Page.asp?NavID=648
Website: www.mcmenamins.com/1482-mcmenamins-brewfests-oly-club
Attractions: Centralia Train Depot, Centralia Factory Outlet stores, Fort

Borst Park, Lewis County Farmers Market, historic downtown murals, Great Wolf Lodge

Trivia: NBA player Detlef Schrempf attended Centralia High School as an exchange student from the former West Germany (1980–81). He played college basketball with the University of Washington Huskies, and was a first round draft pick by the Dallas Mavericks in 1985. He then played for the West German, and later German, national team in the 1984 and 1992 Summer Olympics.

Directions: Centralia is located 30 miles south of Olympia on I-5.

Olympia Brew Fest
Olympia, Thurston County
August

Every year, the Olympia Brew Fest invites a hand-picked selection of the best craft brewers in the Northwest to one place, allowing beer lovers to experience a variety of delicious Pacific Northwest brews. Not just every brewer who wants to participate gets an invitation. Breweries must impress the palates of a panel of event organizers. Because the Northwest is home to so many great brews, more than 30 breweries wind up with an invitation, and they serve up more than 60 beers. Breweries have included Olympia's own Fish Brewing Co., Three Magnets Brewing Co., and Whitewood Cider Co. Enjoy great food as well, including salmon cooked in the traditional style by the Chehalis tribe and provided by the Lucky Eagle Casino. And as a special bonus, if you happen to get crapped on by a seagull during the event, you get a free crab hat. If only that were always true in life. Proceeds from the event going to support the Thurston County Chamber Small Business Development Program.

Address: Port Plaza Park, Downtown
Admission: $25 in advance, $30 at the gate. Admission includes a commemorative mug and six 5.5-oz. tastes. Additional tastes can be purchased inside the event. Designated drivers receive root beer and water with a $5 admission.
Parking: Street and parking lot parking available
Accessible: Yes
Pets: No
Lodging: www.visitolympia.com/lodging
Website: www.olybrewfest.com

Facebook: www.facebook.com/pages/Olympia-Brew-Fest/363721636993000
Attractions: Monarch Sculpture Park, Washington State Capitol, Yashiro Japanese Garden, Local wineries, Northwest Trek Wildlife Park
Trivia: The Washington State Capitol building has, at 287 feet high, the fifth-tallest masonry dome in the world and the tallest in North America.
Directions: From I-5, take the State Capitol/City Center exit. Merge on to 14th Ave SE and at the traffic circle, take the second exit and stay on 14th Ave SE. Turn right onto Capitol Way S. At the traffic circle, take the second exit and turn left. Port Plaza Park is on the left.

Tumwater Artesian Brewfest
Tumwater, Thurston County
Late August/Early September

The city of Tumwater has had a long history associated with beer brewing. The Olympia Brewing Company was based in Tumwater, brewing its beer with water that came from local artesian wells. The Tumwater Artesian Brewfest celebrates and preserves this history. Enjoy live music while tasting beer from more than 30 Pacific Northwest breweries, including Tumwater's original Olympia Beer. And if beer's not your fancy, you also have several regional wines to taste. Brewfest events include a beer stein holding contest (where contestants see how long they can hold a one-liter beer stein at arm's length that is filled with Olympia beer), a field goal challenge, giant Jenga, a hole in one contest, super-sized beer pong, cornhole, and volleyball.

Address: Tumwater Valley Driving Range, 4611 Tumwater Valley Drive SE
Admission: Beer taster admission: $20 pre-sale, $25 at the gate. Military admission: $15 pre-sale, $20 at the gate. Designated driver admission: $10 pre-sale, $10 at the gate. Beer Taster tickets include a tasting glass while supplies last. Beer and hard cider tastings are 5.5 oz. Additional tastes are available for $1. Wine tastings are 2 oz, and cost 1 token each.
Parking: Parking available on site
Accessible: No info
Pets: No
Lodging: www.visitolympia.com/lodging
Website: www.tumwaterartesianbrewfest.com

Facebook: www.facebook.com/home.php#!/TumwaterArtesianBrewfest
Attractions: Tumwater Falls, Schmidt House, Tumwater Farmers Market, Wolf Haven International, Olympic Flight Museum
Trivia: Originally established as the Capital Brewing Company, in 1902 the brewery changed its name to the Olympia Brewing Company. The company chose the slogan "It's the Water" for its flagship product, Olympia Beer, to explain that Olympia lagers were exceptional because of the excellent quality of the artesian springs at the site of the brewery. Olympia Brewing Company ran from 1896 to 1983, at which time, it was acquired by what would become the Pabst Brewing Company. Today, a plant in Irwindale, California still manufactures beer under the Olympia label.
Directions: Tumwater is located immediately south of Olympia on I-5.

Washington produces 70% of the nation's hops for brewing beer. The majority of the nation's mint is also grown in the state.

Ethnic & Cultural Celebrations

Three Days of Aloha in the Pacific Northwest/ Ho'Ike and Hawaiian Festival

Vancouver, Clark County
July

Three Days of Aloha in the Pacific Northwest is a celebration of Polynesian culture that comprises the Ho'Ike and Hawaiian Festival in Vancouver, and the Hula and Craft Workshop in Portland, Oregon (just across the Columbia River from Vancouver). Together, these events provide a weekend filled with island-style entertainment. The weekend starts with a two-day workshop, where preeminent master instructors from Hawai`i offer instruction on dance, language, oli/chant, mele, history, current Hawaiian issues, and cultural crafts. Saturday starts with the 5K Aloha fun run/walk and then the Ho'Ike and Hawaiian Festival in Esther Short Park in the heart of downtown Vancouver. Sway to the rhythm as hula dancers and Polynesian singers fill the park with the heartbeat of their cultures. The outdoor festival includes raffles, keiki (kids') activities, arts and crafts, a fun run/walk, business and delicious food vendors, and a hula competition. Bring a low-backed chair or blanket and enjoy the tropical festivities.

Address: Esther Short Park, 301 W 8th Street
Admission: Free (workshops have various fees)
Parking: Street or paid lot parking
Accessible: Yes
Pets: Yes
Lodging: Vancouver's Red Lion Inn at the Quay, which is within walking distance of the event, offers discounted room rates for festival-goers. Call 360.694.8341 to reserve a room. Portland's Red Lion on the River also offers a discounted room rate. Call 503.283.4466 to reserve a room. Other accommodations can be found at: www.visitvancouverusa.com/visitors/lodging
Website: http://hawaiianfestivalpnw.com
Attractions: Fort Vancouver, Columbia River Waterfront Trail and Renaissance Park, Hulda Klager Lilac Gardens, Moulton Falls State Park, Officer's Row, Pearson Air Museum, Ridgefield National Wildlife Refuge,

Vancouver Farmers Market
Trivia: Established in 1849 by the U.S. Army, the Vancouver Barracks was the first American military post in the Pacific Northwest. Notable soldiers who served in these barracks include future President Ulysses S. Grant, General O.O. Howard, and General George C. Marshall.
Directions: From I-5 N, immediately after crossing the bridge over the Columbia River, exit right on to City Center/6th St, exit 1-B. Follow the ramp around the loop and back under I-5. As you go under I-5, you are now on C St. Go one block to 8th St and turn left. Go 3 blocks to Columbia St. Esther Short park is on Columbia and 8th St. From I-5 S, take the Mill Plain exit. Turn right at the bottom of the exit onto Mill Plain. Go west four blocks to Columbia St. Turn left on Columbia and go south to 8th St. Esther Short Park is on Columbia and 8th St.

Lacey Ethnic Celebration
Lacey, Thurston County
Late Winter, early March

The Lacey Ethnic Celebration lets you experience traditions from other lands through demonstrations and displays. Listen to music and watch dancing from around the world on three performance stages. Past musical performances have included African and Japanese drums, Scottish pipes, Welsh harps, orchestras, and Brazilian jazz. Enjoy exotic foods and artwork from food and craft vendors. Talk with associations that represent local ethnic groups. The event includes hands-on craft activities for kids as well.

Address: St. Martin's University, Worthington Center and Marcus Pavilion
Admission: Free
Parking: Parking available on site at the university
Accessible: Yes
Pets: No
Lodging: www.visitolympia.com/lodging.
Website: www.ci.lacey.wa.us/living-in-lacey/the-community/arts-and-events/ethnic-celebration
Attractions: Local wineries, Lacey Museum, Nisqually National Wildlife Refuge, Tolmie State Park
Trivia: Lacey boasts the remnants of Donation Land Claims of some of

the earliest settlers to cross the country on the Oregon Trail, including that of the Chambers family, who arrived in the late 1840s. They settled on adjoining claims that would become known as Chambers Prairie.
Directions: From I-5 S, take exit 109 Martin Way. Turn right off the exit onto Martin Way. At the first traffic light, turn left onto College St. Turn left onto Abbey Way/6th Ave SE, then follow the signs to the desired campus location. From I-5 N, take exit 108 Sleater Kinney Rd/College St. After exiting, stay to the left toward College St. Continue on 3rd Ave SE. Turn right on College St. Turn left at the next traffic light onto Abbey Way, then follow the signs to the desired campus location.

Swede Day Midsommer Festival
Rochester, Thurston County
Third Saturday in June

Each year in Sweden, Midsommer is celebrated in late June, coinciding with the Summer Solstice. The town of Rochester captures the same spirit in their yearly Swede Day Midsommer Festival, where everybody gets to be a Swede for the day. The event features a pancake breakfast, a Swedish meatball lunch, a midsummer pole dance, Scandinavian dancing, games, vendors, and a parade. And don't be surprised (or concerned) if one of the other celebrants greets you with "Jag alskar dig," meaning "I love you." They are just being neighborly.

Address: Swede Hall, 18543 Albany Street NW
Admission: Free admission. Pancake breakfast prices are $5 for children (aged 10 and younger), $7 for adults, or $20 for a family. Swedish meatball lunch prices are Adults (aged 12 an up) $7, children (aged 6–11) $4, and children under 6 eat free.
Parking: Street, parking lot
Accessible: Yes
Pets: No
Lodging: www.tourlewiscounty.com/lodgingdining
Website: http://rochester-wa.com/swede_day_events.htm
Attractions: Centralia Outlet Mall, Rochester Farmers Market, Fort Henness, Great Wolf Lodge, Lucky Eagle Casino, Millersylvania State Park, and Mima Mounds Natural Area Preserve, Fort Henness
Trivia: The small village of Jukkasjärvi in Northern Sweden (200 km north of the Arctic Circle) houses the very first ice hotel ever built. ICEHOTEL

covers 5,500 square meters and is constructed from 1,000 tons of Torne River ice and 30,000 tons of "snice," a mixture of snow and ice that strengthens the structure. Between March and April, ice is harvested from the Torne River and kept in cold storage during spring and summer. Construction takes place in November and December and the ICEHOTEL is then open to visitors between December and mid-April.
Directions: Rochester is mid-way between Seattle and Portland, OR, four miles west of I-5 on WA-12.

Oshogatsu in Olympia
Olympia, Thurston County
January

Oshogatsu celebrates the Japanese New Year and provides a unique opportunity to learn about Japanese culture. Live entertainment on the main stage showcases traditional Japanese dance and music, taiko drumming, and vocal performances. The family focused event includes a variety of cultural activities, make and take crafts, Aikido and Kendo/Taido demonstrations, and an art exhibition where visitors can view and purchase Japanese calligraphy, sumi paintings, paper cuttings, and traditional crafts. Japanese foods are prepared and served on site. Sample a taste of fresh Japanese mochi, which is a chewy rice cake served during the Japanese New Year. In addition, experience "Mochitsuki," which is the ceremonial making of mochi. A professional Mochitsuki troupe elevates mochi-pounding to art with traditional implements, chanting, and rhythmic movements. They use large wooden mallets to pound steaming batches of cooked rice into a smooth, stretchy dough. As the pace increases, so does the dexterity, reflexes, and expert timing of the troupe.

Address: Olympia Center, 222 Columbia Street SE
Admission: Event admission is free with a suggested donation of $2/person or $5/family.
Parking: Parking available on site
Accessible: Yes
Pets: No
Lodging: www.visitolympia.com/lodging
Website: http://celebratejapan.org
Attractions: Hands On Children's Museum, Washington State Capitol,

Yashiro Japanese Garden, Daniel R. Bigelow House, Tumwater Falls
Trivia: With an overall life expectancy of 84.6 years, Japan's citizens generally live longer than citizens of any other country on the planet, followed closely by Andorra, Singapore, and Hong Kong. The United States is 34th on the list (compiled by the World Health Organization), with an average life expectancy of 79.8 years.
Directions: From I-5, take the exit toward State Capitol/City Center and merge on to 14th Ave SE. At the traffic circle, take the second and stay on 14th Ave SE. Turn right onto Capitol Way S, then turn left on to State Ave NW. Take the first right on to Columbia St NW. Olympic Center is on the right.

Highlander Festival
Kelso, Cowlitz County
Second weekend in September

Kelso was founded in 1847 by Peter W. Crawford, a Scottish surveyor who named the town site after his home town of Kelso, Scotland. Celebrating these Scottish roots, the city hosts the annual Highlander Festival every year in September. Festival events include traditional Scottish music, Highland dancing, Celtic entertainment, shinty (a team game), food vendors, a parade of clans, pipe bands, historical reenactments and costumes, clan tents, a Scottish baking competition, a golf tournament, and plenty of Celtic and Scottish vendors. The heavy athletics competitions, which start on Saturday morning, are always a crowd pleaser.

Address: Tam O'Shanter Park, downtown
Admission: Free
Parking: Free
Accessible: No info
Pets: No info
Lodging: www.kelso.gov/Visitors/Accommodations. Camping is also available at Tam O'Shanter Park. It costs $8 per night, per space, or $15 for the weekend.
Website: www.kelso.gov/visitors/highlander-festival
Facebook: www.facebook.com/pages/Kelso-Highlander-Festival-and-Scottish-Games/368109010422
Attractions: Mt. St. Helens National Volcanic Monument, Cowlitz County

Historical Museum
Trivia: Actor Connor Trinneer was raised in Kelso and graduated from Kelso High School in the late 1980s. He is best known for his role as Commander Charles "Trip" Tucker III in the *Star Trek: Enterprise* television series, and as Michael Kenmore on the *Stargate Atlantis* television series.
Directions: Take I-5 Exit 39 onto Allen St. Go east to Kelso Dr (at the first light to the east of the freeway). Turn right onto Kelso Dr, going south just past the Red Lion Inn. Turn left at the sign directing to the park, going east approximately 1.5 blocks.

Vancouver, Washington requires all motor vehicles to carry anchors as an emergency brake.

Family Fun

Sandsations
Long Beach, Pacific County
Weekend in July chosen by volunteers based on tides

Sandsations is a sand castle competition for all ability levels. The event starts on Wednesday, with professional artists creating beautiful sand sculptures in the middle of downtown, with sand that is hauled from the beach, in an environment where they don't have to worry about tide and time. This part of the festival, called "City Sandsations," takes place over three days. During this time, the sculptors demonstrate their skill, answer questions, and offer tips and tricks that you can use for your own creation on Saturday. With categories ranging from child to professional, the Saturday competition allows you six hours to work your sand magic. Cash prizes and gift baskets are awarded to category winners at an award presentation on Saturday afternoon. The event closes with a beach fireworks display, a bonfire, live music, and free s'mores.

Address: Long Beach
Admission: Free to attend. Sculpting fees are as follows: masters $65, intermediate $45, novice $35, family $15, kids $1
Parking: Street parking
Accessible: No special accommodations made on beach terrain
Pets: Yes. The Humane Society puts on a Sand Flea Pet Parade.
Lodging: http://funbeach.com/stay/hotels-motels-and-cottages
Website: http://sandsationslongbeach.com
Facebook: www.facebook.com/SANDSATIONS
Attractions: World Kite Museum, Cape Disappointment State Park, North Head Lighthouse, Willapa Bay Interpretive Center, Centennial Murals Tour
Trivia: On October 29, 2013, Ed Jarrett broke the Guinness World Record for the tallest sandcastle for the fourth time. His Sandy Castle stood 38', 2" tall on Jenkinson's Beach in Point Pleasant, New Jersey.
Directions: Long Beach is 107 miles (2 hours) northwest of Vancouver, WA via I-5 N and US-30 W.

Washington State International Kite Festival
Long Beach, Pacific County
Third full week in August

With 28 miles of uninterrupted beach, the Long Beach Peninsula is the ideal spot to host the Washington State International Kite Festival (WSIKF), which is one of the largest kite festivals in North America. This week-long celebration draws famous kite fliers from all around the world, as well as tens of thousands of spectators. At the very first kite festival in 1981, a team from Edmonds Community College (near Seattle) flew a kite for 180 hours straight, setting a Guinness world record. But you don't need to be a world-record setter to enjoy the festivities. Kite enthusiasts of all ages and abilities find something to enjoy. Taking place just a couple of blocks from downtown Long Beach, the event includes kite-making workshops, camera workshops, kids' camps, a handcrafted kite competition, various themed kite demos, and a kite trick demonstration. It also features food booths, as well as merchandise and kite vendors. If you're more of a photog than a kite wrangler, the skies are filled with colorful photo opportunities the entire week.

Address: Beach access at Bolstad Road
Admission: Free to public. Competitions charge an entry fee
Parking: Street parking
Accessible: Beach events take place on sand, so may not be easily accessible
Pets: Yes
Lodging: http://funbeach.com/stay/hotels-motels-and-cottages
Website: http://kitefestival.com/kite-festival
Facebook: www.facebook.com/kitefest/info
Attractions: Columbia Pacific Heritage Museum, Lewis and Clark National Historic Park, World Kite Museum
Trivia: The highest altitude achieved by a single kite is 13,609 ft. above ground level, established by Richard Synergy near Ontario, Canada in August 2000.
Directions: Long Beach is 107 miles (2 hours) northwest of Vancouver, WA via I-5 N and US-30 W.

Bald Eagle Days
Cathlamet, Wahkiakum County
Third weekend in July

In 1940, Congress passed the Bald Eagle Protection Act to give legal protection to the regal national symbol of the United States. The Cathlamet Women's Club decided to show their support for the Bald Eagle by hosting a parade through town and encouraging the continued protection of the bird. Even though the Bald Eagle is no longer endangered, the town still holds its annual celebration. Located directly on the Columbia River, the area is a great place to view the majestic birds. The event includes a sidewalk art contest, a pancake breakfast, a farmers market, trolley rides, a Bald Eagle Run, a parade, train rides, food and craft vendors, kids' games, live music, a beer garden, and a fireworks show.

Address: Main Street
Admission: Free
Parking: Free street parking
Accessible: Yes
Pets: No info
Lodging: www.cathlametchamber.com/accommodations.php
Website: www.cathlametchamber.com/bald_eagle_days.php
Attractions: Willapa National Wildlife Refuge, Grays River covered bridge, Wahkiakum Historical Museum, bicycling on Puget Island
Trivia: Cathlamet began as an Indian village that was home to the Kathlamet people. The village contained nearly 300 residents (which was quite large for the time) when visited by Lewis and Clark in 1805–06.
Directions: Cathlamet is 65 miles northwest of Vancouver, WA via I-5 N and WA-4 W.

Amboy Territorial Days
Amboy, Clark County
Second weekend in July

Originally held in 1961 as a celebration of the 75th anniversary of the Amboy Post Office, Amboy Territorial Days continues in its celebration of the city of Amboy and its history. The three-day festival features a carnival, live music, a beer garden, numerous food booths, a parade, family entertainment, lawnmower races, and the most popular event of all—

the logging show. Over the years, thousands of spectators have come from all over the Northwest in their flannel to watch the finest compete in events that began in the forests of America. Logging events include double bucking, a stock chain saw race, an obstacle pole over water, axe throwing, birling/log rolling, high climbing (75'), precision tree dropping, and speed chopping.

Address: Amboy Territorial Days Park, 21400 NE 399th Street
Admission: Free
Parking: Street, parking lot
Accessible: Yes
Pets: No
Lodging: www.amboywa.com/hotels.htm
Website: http://tdays.org/amboy-territorial-days-2014
Facebook: www.facebook.com/events/519487551501340
Attractions: Ridgefield National Wildlife Refuge, North Clark Historical Museum, Mt. St. Helens National Volcanic Monument, Windy Ridge Viewpoint, Birth of a Lake trail
Trivia: The tiny town of Ariel sits 16 miles outside of Amboy. Ariel's claim to fame is that, in the early 1970s, it served as the headquarters for the team of agents searching for D.B. Cooper. In 1971, Cooper hijacked a Boeing 747 over the Cascade Mountains and parachuted out over Washington with $200,000 in ransom money. Despite an extensive search, he was never seen again, resulting in the country's only unsolved hijacking. Since 1974, every year, the Ariel Store and Tavern hosts the D.B. Cooper Party on the Saturday after Thanksgiving. The event includes a Cooper look-alike contest, food, beer, author discussions, and much story telling about what could have happened to Cooper.
Directions: Amboy is located about 20 miles east of I-5, on WA-503.

Longview Squirrel Fest
Longview, Cowlitz County
Mid-August

Washington State loves to celebrate its critters, from the edible varieties such as shrimp, oysters, and Dungeness crab, to slugs and bald eagles, which are edible only under the direst of circumstances. The Longview Squirrel Fest provides the opportunity to celebrate the furry little excavator. In a nutshell, the day's events include lots of live entertainment, food, art and craft vendors, a parade, and a beer garden. Plenty of kids' activities are on tap, including a flying squirrel zip line, games, circus workshops, and the Great Acorn Scramble, in which kids aged 13–17 search through hay that is loaded with 10,000 acorns, and try to grab as many as they can. The day ends with a fireworks show. Longview is home to the Nutty Narrows Bridge, a bridge built in 1963 specifically for squirrels so that they could cross the street safely, and avoid becoming casualties on the street below. As part of each Squirrel Fest since its inception in 2011, a new squirrel bridge has been unveiled each year. The Squirrel Fest website even has a link to a live squirrel cam sitting atop one of the bridges, so that you can check out squirrel activity any time of the day.

Address: Civic Circle, 17th Avenue, downtown
Admission: Free
Parking: Free street and parking lot parking
Accessible: Yes
Pets: No info
Lodging: http://kelsolongviewchamber.chambermaster.com/members/QL/lodging-travel-15.htm
Website: http://lvsquirrelfest.com
Facebook: www.facebook.com/LVSquirrelfest
Attractions: Lake Sacagawea State Park, Mt. Saint Helens, Columbia River, Hulda Klager Lilac Gardens, Cowlitz County Historical Museum, Historic Monticello Hotel
Trivia: For more than two decades, Longview's Stuffy's II restaurant has served up what they call the "world's largest cinnamon rolls" baked from scratch. Each roll contains almost seven cups of flour and weighs 5–6 pounds. The rolls, which cost less than $10, have been featured on the Food Network's "Outrageous Food" show.
Directions: From I-5 N, take exit 39 and travel west. From I-5 S, take exit 40 and travel west.

Winlock Egg Day Festival
Winlock, Lewis County
Fourth weekend in June

How did the world's largest egg wind up at the top of a pedestal in downtown Winlock? It scrambled up, of course. Okay, it was probably hoisted by a crane to its lofty perch, but either way, it stands out as a monument to Winlock's tremendous pride in its egg-based heritage. The egg, which was originally created in 1923 out of canvas, is now made of fiberglass, is 12 feet long, weighs 1,200 pounds, and was officially declared World's Largest Egg by Ripley's Believe it or Not in 1989. The townsfolk not only celebrate their heritage in statuary, but also with the yearly Egg Day Celebration. The festival starts on Friday evening with the crowning of the festival queen. Saturday begins with an all-you-can-eat breakfast (which is probably no place for an anti-ovotarian), followed by the parade and free egg-salad sandwiches. The event also includes vendors, a car show, a carnival, live music, a library book sale, a street dance, and an annual dog-and-owner fashion show.

Address: Downtown
Admission: Free
Parking: Free street and parking lot parking
Accessible: Yes
Pets: Yes
Lodging: www.tourlewiscounty.com/lodgingdining
Website: http://winlockeggdays.weebly.com
Facebook: www.facebook.com/home.php#!/winlock.day?fref=ts
Attractions: Mt. St. Helens National Park, Renegade Rooster Historical Collection, Winlock Historical Museum, Lewis and Clark State Park
Trivia: In 1931, the town of Long Beach, WA helped Winlock celebrate the egg festival by transporting over its "World's Largest Frying Pan," measuring 9.6-ft across, to help fry up omelets for the crowd. Although its original cast-iron form has since been replaced with a fiberglass replica, and the claim of "world's largest" can no longer be made, the pan is still on display in Long Beach.
Directions: From Portland, take I-5 N to exit 63/WA-505 toward Winlock/Toledo left at WA-505 and travel 3 miles to Winlock. From Seattle, take I-5 S to exit 63/WA-505 toward Winlock/Toledo. Turn right at WA-505 and travel 4 miles to Winlock.

Capital Lakefair
Olympia, Thurston County
Third weekend in July, Wednesday through Sunday

Lakefair is a five-day festival that attracts thousands of spectators to enjoy a wide array of events. The festival includes art and craft booths, a battle of the bands, a car show, a downtown sidewalk sale, live music and dancing, plenty of food booths, a singing competition, kids' activities, 3K and 5K fun runs, an art show, and a volleyball tournament. The highlight of the event is the Grand Twilight Parade, which includes more than 1,200 marchers and participants and approximately 35 floats. The weekend goes out with a bang on Sunday night with a spectacular firework display on the southeastern shore of Capital Lake.

Address: Various locations near Capital Lake
Admission: Admission is free. Carnival rides cost around $35 for a wristband for unlimited rides.
Parking: There are no dedicated parking areas or areas with shuttle service to Lakefair. Parking around Heritage Park is limited unless you get away from the park and park on city streets. You will then need to pay parking meters. Intercity Transit has normal bus service that serves downtown during Lakefair. There are a limited numbered of disabled-parking designated spaces located on Legion Way between Columbia Street and Water Street.
Accessible: Yes
Pets: No, except for service animals
Lodging: www.visitolympia.com/lodging
Website: www.lakefair.org
Facebook: www.facebook.com/CapitalLakefair
Attractions: Washington State Capitol Building and Museum, Nisqually Red Wind Casino, Crosby House Museum, Priest Point Park
Trivia: As the area around Olympia grew in the 1850s, it became apparent that they needed a more efficient way to move people, mail, and freight around. The land was heavily forested, down to the water's edge, which made inland transportation difficult. Myriad ferries were soon making regular runs in the area. The ferry fleet became known as the Mosquito Fleet because, as the story goes, someone commented that the activity on the waterfront looked like a swarm of mosquitos.
Directions: Lakefair is held around the banks of Capitol Lake in Heritage Park, along 5th Avenue and on Water Street. Various other events are held in Marathon Park on Deschutes Parkway, in Sylvester Park on Capitol Way and on 5th Avenue and the Capitol Campus grounds along Capitol Way.

Bigfoot Bash and Bounty
Home Valley, Skamania County
Late August

Are you a believer or not quite sure? This festival is for the serious and the curious investigators of the mysterious Bigfoot. The day opens with a Bigfoot Berry pancake breakfast, then the Sasquatch scavenger hunt begins, in which you win prizes as you locate the elusive creatures that are hidden amongst businesses in Home Valley and nearby Carson. Afterward, enjoy live music and entertainment, a carnival, vendors, and the Yeti Yard beer garden. The event also presents a lineup of Sasquatch speakers who, just to be clear, are speakers and authors who talk about Sasquatch issues, not speakers who are actually Sasquatches (Sasqui?). Discussions in the past have covered topics such as Bigfoot habitat, the legend of Sasquatch, relationships with tribal people, and Pacific Northwest experiences.

Address: Home Valley Park, Just off Hwy 14
Admission: Admission is free, but there is a fee for carnival activities. The pancake breakfast costs $8 for adults and $5 for children.
Parking: Free parking at the event
Accessible: No info
Pets: Yes, on leash
Lodging: Camping is available at the Home Valley Campground for $20 per night. Other lodging information: www.skamania.org/places-to-stay.cfm
Website: www.bigfootbashandbounty.com
Facebook: www.facebook.com/pages/Bigfoot-Bash-and-Bounty/54590278425?sk=info
Attractions: Beacon Rock State Park, Cape Horn Viewpoint, Columbia Gorge Interpretive Center, Dougan Falls
Trivia: So many Bigfoot sightings have occurred in Skamania County that, in 1984, officials passed an ordinance that set up Skamania County as a Sasquatch Refuge, and, thus the slaying of any such beast results in a fine of up to $1,000 and a maximum of one year in jail.
Directions: From Vancouver travel east on SR-14 for 52 miles (seven miles past the town of Stevenson). Look for a brown sign on the right (south) side of the highway that says Home Valley Park. The park is just east of a plywood mill.

Food & Agricultural Festivals

Mossyrock Blueberry Festival
Mossyrock, Lewis County
First weekend in August

It's hard to decide which is the best part of the Mossyrock Blueberry Festival—the blueberry pancake breakfast, the blueberry pie eating contest, or the wiener dog races. The only thing that could possibly make it better is if the wiener dogs raced to their own blueberry pie eating contest stationed at the finish line. At any rate, if you love blueberries, this weekend has a lot to offer. In addition to all things blueberry, the festival includes a collectable car show, a quilt show, and live stage entertainment. Enter your dog in the Family Fun Dog Show, show off your talents at the talent show and taco feed, and relax in the beer garden. The festival also has lots of blueberries to eat and purchase.

Address: Downtown
Admission: Donations requested
Parking: General parking is available off of Isbell Road. Follow the signs. At the stop light on US-12 turn South onto William Street, right on Main Street, left on Isbell Road, and then left into the parking area. Handicapped parking is available in the Klickitat Prairie Park parking lot at 125 W State Street. Follow the signs.
Accessible: Yes
Pets: Yes
Lodging: http://mossyrockfestivals.org/stay.html
Website: http://mossyrockfestivals.org
Facebook: www.facebook.com/pages/Mossyrock-Blueberry-Festival/272983476237601
Attractions: Mayfield Lake, Riffe Lake, Mt. Rainier National Forest, Mt. Saint Helens, Lewis County Historical Museum
Trivia: Mossyrock Dam, on the Cowlitz River near the town of Mossyrock, is the tallest dam in Washington State at 606 feet. Although Grand Coulee Dam in central Washington is one of the largest concrete structures in the world, it's height is registered at 550 feet.
Directions: To reach Mossyrock, take I-5 to the US-12 exit (exit 68) south of Chehalis. Take US-12 E toward Yakima for 21 miles. There is a stop light at the Mossyrock exit. At the stop light, turn right onto Williams St. If you are coming from east of Mossyrock, take US-12 west about 11

miles beyond Morton. At the stop light turn left onto Williams St.

Woodland Tulip Festival
Woodland, Cowlitz County
April

The Woodland Tulip Festival invites you to take a tiptoe through their rows of 140 tulip varieties, and enjoy a weekend full of fun, festivities, and flowers. Every year during the month of April, Holland America Bulb Farms puts together the Woodland Tulip Festival with the support of its retail outlet Holland America Flower Gardens to share the family's love of bulbs and flowers with the rest of the community and visitors from all over the world. The actual festival takes place during two of these April weekends. Events include a 5K Tulip Trot; a food, art, and craft vendor market; a cutest baby contest (chosen from photos submitted of babies with the tulips); a youth photography contest; and a chance to pick your own tulips in a you-pick field. Purchase bulbs, potted flowers, or pre-cut tulips on site.

Address: Holland America Bulb Farms, 1066 S Pekin Road
Parking: Parking available on site
Accessible: No info
Pets: No
Lodging: www.woodlandwachamber.com/lodging
Website: www.habf.net/Woodland-Tulip-Festival.html
Facebook: www.facebook.com/pages/Woodland-Tulip-Festival/106034602750811
Attractions: Hulda Klager Lilac Gardens National Historic Site, Mt. St. Helens National Volcanic Monument, Lewis River
Trivia: The tulip is the national flower of Turkey. Although generally associated with the Dutch, tulips are actually native to central Asia. The name "tulip" is derived from the Turkish word "tulbend" or "turban," which the flower resembles.
Directions: From I-5 N, take Woodland exit 21. At the exit stop light, turn left and drive underneath the overpass. Go straight through the light on Goerig St and continue into Woodland until Goerig St turns in to Davidson St. Take a left onto 5th St and follow until the street turns into S Pekin Rd. At the first Y, veer to the left, and at the second Y veer to the right. Continue for about a mile. Holland America Bulb Farms is on the

left side of the road. From I-5 S, take Woodland exit 21. After the exit, follow the frontage road for about 0.5 mile. Just before the stop light, veer to the right and go to the stop sign. Go straight onto Goerig St and follow the directions above.

Chehalis Garlic Fest and Craft Show
Chehalis, Lewis County
Fourth weekend in August

This is definitely the place to go if you love garlic. The Chehalis Garlic Festival and Craft show offers food, food, and more delicious, stinky food. Sample items such as deep fried garlic, garlic-butter dipped corn on the cob, garlic butter-drizzled fries, garlic sausage on a bun, garlic and stir-fry veggies, garlic pasta, and even garlic ice cream. Scores of talented artisans feature pottery, jewelry, garden art, wooden hand crafts, jams and jellies, soaps and bath goodies, metal art, art prints and paintings, and pet products. Take the opportunity to browse through Antique Alley. The three-day event also includes cooking demonstrations, kids' activities, live music, a beer garden, and wine tasting from local area wineries. Purchase garlic for cooking and planting from northwest farmers who bring more than 60 varieties of fresh garlic to the event.

Address: Southwest Washington Fairgrounds, 2555 North National Avenue
Admission: General Admission is $5. Those aged 65 and older, or military members with an ID, can get in for $4. Children ages 7 and under get in free.
Parking: Parking available on-site
Accessible: Yes
Pets: No info
Lodging: http://chehalisgarlicfest.com/lodging.html. Fairground camping is available for $23 per night with or without hookups. Call the SWWF for more info (360.736.6072).
Website: http://chehalisgarlicfest.com
Facebook: www.facebook.com/pages/Garlic-Fest-Chehalis/196989940333262
Attractions: Vintage Motorcycle Museum, Claquato Church, Lewis County Historical Museum, Chehalis-Centralia Railroad and Museum, Willapa Hills Trail

Trivia: The fear of garlic is known by the psychological term alliumphobia.
Directions: From I-5 S, take the Centralia exit #81 Mellen St. Go left under the overpass, drive approximately six blocks and take a right on Pearl St (one-way street going south) over the viaduct. Pearl turns into Gold St. Go south on Gold St, which turns into National Ave. Southwest Washington Fairgrounds is on the right. The north parking lot is the first entrance on the right side. From I-5 N, take the Chehalis exit #79 Chamber Way and turn right off the exit onto Chamber Way. Turn left on to National Ave (one-way heading north). National turns into Kresky Ave N. To reach the parking lot, continue north on Kresky Ave, turn left on Fair St, then left on Gold St. The north parking lot is the first entrance on the right side.

Cranberrian Fair
Ilwaco, Pacific County
October

The Cranberrian Fair began on the Long Beach Peninsula at the turn of the 20th century and was revived by the Columbia Pacific Heritage Museum in the early 1980s. It celebrates the history and harvest of America's native fruit and all of the rich food resources of the Long Beach Peninsula. Although cranberries are the main focus for this event oysters, fish, and garden harvests are also presented. The event hosts a variety of vendors offering homemade goodies, such as peach/cranberry pie, as well as handmade items such as pottery, jewelry, hand-turned wooden bowls, paintings, and cranberry vine baskets. Fair entrance includes full admission to the museum's exhibits. Hop on the Cranberry Trolley in Ilwaco, which whisks you to the Pacific Coast Cranberry Research Foundation and Cranberry Museum. The trolley runs on the hour from Columbia Pacific Heritage Museum from 11 am until 2 pm Saturday and Sunday.

Address: Columbia Pacific Heritage Museum, 115 Lake Street
Admission: Admission is $5, which gets you a collectible button and admission to all events at the Columbia Pacific Heritage Museum. The Cranberry Museum is free.
Parking: Free
Accessible: Yes
Pets: No

Lodging: https://funbeach.com/stay/hotels-motels-and-cottages
Website: http://columbiapacificheritagemuseum.com/news-events-2/cranberrian-fair
Facebook: www.facebook.com/events/256225441077853/
Attractions: Funland Family Entertainment Center, Columbia River Maritime Museum, Cape Disappointment State Park, NW Carriage Museum
Trivia: There are currently about 235 cranberry growers on the West Coast from Canada to Oregon. Ninety-nine percent of these growers are part of an Ocean Spray cooperative.
Directions: The Columbia Pacific Heritage Museum is located one block off of US-101 at 115 SE Lake St in Ilwaco.

South Sound BBQ Festival
Lacey, Thurston County
First Saturday after July 4th

Do you love slow-smoked traditional barbecue? The South Sound BBQ Festival gives you the chance to satisfy your taste for all things barbecued, including beef, pork, chicken, and seafood. If you REALLY love barbecue, enter the chicken-wing eating contest, and see how many wings you can eat in four minutes. Several professional barbecue vendors sell food, and amateur barbecuers, aka "Back Yard Joes" can enter their own recipes for a chance to win cash and prizes. The day also features live music and entertainment, as well as a beer garden.

Address: Huntamer Park, 629 Woodland Square Loop
Admission: Free admission. Food available for purchase, some items priced as low as $2.
Parking: Parking is free at several parking lots around the Huntamer Park area.
Accessible: Yes
Lodging: www.visitolympia.com/lodging
Website: http://southsoundbbqfestival.com
Facebook: www.facebook.com/SSBBQFest
Attractions: Tumwater Falls, Lacey Farmers Market, Yashiro Japanese Garden, Percival Landing Boardwalk, Red Wing Casino
Trivia: The first U.S. president to host a barbecue at the White House was Lyndon B. Johnson. As a native Texan, Johnson made sure it featured Texas-style barbecued ribs.

Directions: From I-5 N, take exit 108 and take the ramp right for Sleater-Kinney Rd N toward College St. Turn right on to College St SE, then turn right on to Woodland Square Loop SE. The last intersection is College St SE. If you reach 7th Ave SE, you've gone too far. From I-5 S, take exit 109 and take the ramp right for Martin Way toward College St/Sleater-Kinney Rd N. Turn right onto Martin Way E, then turn left onto College St SE. Turn right onto Woodland Square Loop. The last intersection is College St SE. If you reach 7th Ave SE, you've gone too far.

Pacific Northwest Mushroom Festival
Lacey, Thurston County
Late July

This family-friendly festival features speakers, chefs, cooking demonstrations, a mushroom farm tour, children's activities, entertainment, vendors, and a 5K Grow in the Dark fun run, a night-time run where everybody wears their best glow-in-the-dark gear, complete with plenty of glow-in-the-dark necklaces and bracelets. Shroomfeast is a mushroom-tasting area that serves culinary delights such as bacon-wrapped mushroom bites, stuffed portabella sliders, portabella mushroom ice cream, mushroom bacon brittle, and artichoke stuffed mushrooms. The event hosts the Mushroom and Wine Event on Saturday evening which pairs local Washington wine and beer with delicious mushroom hors d'oeuvres, live music, dancing, and a silent charity auction.

Address: Regional Athletic Complex, 8345 Steilacoom Road SE
Admission: General Admission is $5. Kids age 12 and under get in free.
Parking: Free parking and shuttle service at Washington Land Yacht Harbor, 9101 Steilacoom Road SE
Accessible: Yes
Lodging: www.visitolympia.com/lodging
Website: www.pnwmushroomfest.com
Facebook: www.facebook.com/pnwmushroomfest
Attractions: Washington State Capitol Building and Museum, Fort Lewis Military Museum, Olympic Flight Museum, Tolmie State Park, Nisqually Reach Nature Center
Trivia: The most common mushroom in the western United States is the Armillaria solidipes. This type of fungus grows underground and blooms once a year in the fall, showing its above-ground "honey mushrooms."

The underground organism can grow to be quite large. In fact, in the Blue Mountains of Oregon, scientists have discovered a fungal colony of this species that is believed to be one of the largest living organisms in the world. It has been growing for around 2,400 years and covers 3.4 square miles (around 2,200 acres). It is colloquially known as the Humongous Fungus.

Directions: From I-5 S, take the WA-510 E exit (#111). Turn left onto Marvin Rd NE/WA-510. Turn left onto Steilacoom Rd SE. 8345 Steilacoom Rd SE is on the right. From I-5 N, take the WA-510 E/Marvin Rd S exit (#111) toward Yelm. At the roundabout, turn right on to Quinault Dr NE. Take the first right on to Marvin Rd NE/WA-510. Turn left on to Steilacoom Rd SE.

A Sampling of Famous Washingtonians:

Musicians Jimi Hendrix, Kurt Cobain of Nirvana, Kenny G, Ray Charles, The Wailers, Pat Boone, Bing Crosby, Quincy Jones, Kenny Loggins, Macklemore, Steve Miller and Sir-Mix-a-Lot; golf pro Fred Couples; actors Chris Pratt, Kyle MacLachlan, Dyan Cannon. and Adam West; game show host Bob Barker; cartoonist Gary Larson; authors Ann Rule, Tom Robbins, Chuck Palahniuk; and serial killer Ted Bundy.

Music

XFest NW
Stevenson, Skamania County
September/Labor Day weekend

XFEST is a Christian rock festival that takes place annually on Labor Day weekend, and provides three days of camping, community, and music. Xfest is a venue for artistic expression, and showcases mostly regional bands, but also some national bands.

Address: Skamania County Fairgrounds, 710 Rock Creek Drive
Admission: A 1-day pass costs $12 in advance/$15 at the door. A 3-day pass costs $35 in advance/$40 at the door. A 3-day pass for a group of 10 or more is $25 per person in advance/$30 per person at the door. A 3-day family pass is $80 in advance/$90 at the door. Children aged 12 and under get in free.
Parking: Parking available on site at the fairgrounds.
Accessible: Yes
Lodging: Camping at XFEST is included in the price of admission. Skamania County Fairground offers awesome, scenic views of the Columbia Gorge, as well as plenty of room for parking and setting up tents. The fairground has power hook-ups for your RV or camper, and it offers excellent restroom facilities on site, including hot showers.
Website: www.xfestnw.org
Facebook: www.facebook.com/pages/Xfestnw/194141263968967
Attractions: Columbia River Gorge, Beacon Rock State Park, Bridge of the Gods, Punch Bowl Falls, Columbia Gorge Interpretive Center
Trivia: The Bridge of the Gods is a steel truss cantilever bridge that spans the Columbia River from Cascade Locks, OR to Skamania County, Washington, upriver from Bonneville Dam. The current bridge is named after the Bridge of the Gods of Native American lore, which was a natural dam in the same location, created by a landslide that dammed up the Columbia. The steel bridge was completed in 1926 (updated in 1940), and happens to be where the Pacific Crest Trail crosses the Columbia. In 1927, a few months after his trans-Atlantic flight, Charles Lindbergh flew the Spirit of St. Louis up the Columbia River Gorge, made a low pass over the bridge, banked the plane, flew under the bridge, and headed on his way.
Directions: From downtown Portland, OR or Vancouver, WA drive 45

miles east on I-84 in Oregon or scenic SR-14 in Washington. From I-84, take exit #44 and cross The Bridge of the Gods to SR-14. Take a right onto SR-14, toward Stevenson. From SR-14, take a left at the Skamania Lodge sign—that's Rock Creek Dr. Follow Rock Creek Dr around Rock Cove. The address is 720 SW Rock Creek Dr, which is on the right side of the road, across from the church. From downtown Stevenson, Rock Creek Dr is located at the west end of town past the Main Street Convenience Store.

Columbia Gorge Bluegrass Festival
Stevenson, Skamania County
Fourth weekend in July

Located only 45 minutes from Portland, the Columbia Gorge Bluegrass Festival, in scenic Stevenson, is a unique blend of amazing talent, workshops, and instrument contests for both kids and adults. The Columbia Gorge Fiddle Contest also takes place during the festival. The four-day event features fine craft and food vendors, a beer garden, and nightly dances.

Address: Skamania County Fairgrounds, 720 SW Rock Creek Drive
Admission: Children 12 and under get in free. Thursday and Sunday day passes cost $15. Friday and Saturday day passes cost $35. A full weekend pass (Thurs – Sun) costs $55.
Parking: Parking available on site
Accessible: Handicapped parking is located throughout the fairgrounds. Limited courtesy wheelchairs are available for loan at the festival and can be checked out through the Festival Event Office.
Pets: Dogs allowed in camping area only, not in the festival venue
Lodging: Camping is available with hot showers and an unforgettable vista. Non-electrical campsites cost $88 (includes 1 weekend pass). Electric hook-up campsites cost $105 (includes 1 weekend pass). Premier RV camp sites cost $149 (includes 1 weekend pass). Call 509.427.3980 to make camping reservations. Other lodging information: www.cityofstevenson.com/lodging.html
Website: www.columbiagorgebluegrass.net
Facebook: www.facebook.com/ColumbiaGorgeBluegrass
Attractions: 27 Columbia River Gorge area wineries, Columbia River

Gorge National Scenic Area, Beacon Rock State Park

Trivia: Beacon Rock, in Skamania County, is the name of the 848' tall granite monolith on the north bank of the Columbia River. In 1805, Lewis and Clark named the rock, although they initially called it Beaten Rock, and noted that it marked the eastern extent of the tidal influence on the Columbia. In 1915, Henry Biddle purchased the rock for $1 and set to constructing a trail to the top with more than 50 switchbacks, as well as helpful handrails, and bridges. Most of this mile-long trail is still used today by hikers, and the face of the rock itself is a favorite of rock climbers. The payoff at the top is a fantastic, uninterrupted view of the Columbia River Gorge. That is, unless it's raining . . .

Directions: The Skamania County Fairgrounds is located in the heart of the Columbia River Gorge National Scenic Area in the historic river city of Stevenson. From downtown Portland, OR or Vancouver, WA, drive 45 miles east on I-84 in Oregon or scenic SR-14 in Washington. From I-84, take exit #44 and cross The Bridge of the Gods to SR-14. Take a right onto SR-14, toward Stevenson. From SR-14, take a left at the Skamania Lodge sign — that's Rock Creek Dr. Follow Rock Creek Dr around Rock Cove. The address is 720 SW Rock Creek Dr, which is on the right side of the road, across from the church. From downtown Stevenson, Rock Creek Dr is located at the west end of town past the Main Street Convenience Store.

Vancouver Wine and Jazz Festival
Vancouver, Clark County
Third weekend in August

The Vancouver Wine and Jazz Festival promises hot jazz, great wine, fine art, and delicious Pacific Northwest cuisine. It delights jazz music lovers with internationally and locally acclaimed jazz, blues, and pop musicians. Sample and taste more than 200 wines, many of them Pacific Northwest wines, and get your fill of regional gastronomic specialties. The festival presents a select number of fine artists and crafters from Washington, Oregon, Idaho, and California who feature all forms of artistic genres/media. Also peruse the booths of commercial exhibitors of all types.

Address: Esther Short Park, 301 W 8th Street
Admission: A three-day pass is $60 and is available only in advance. Individual-day ticket prices are Friday - $18 in advance, $20 at the gate; Saturday - $23 in advance, $25 at the gate; and Sunday - $23 in advance, $25 at the gate. Kids under 12 get in free, but must remain with an adult at all times.
Parking: Street or paid lot parking
Accessible: Yes
Pets: No
Lodging: www.visitvancouverusa.com/visitors/lodging
Website: www.vancouverwinejazz.com
Facebook: www.facebook.com/vancouverwinejazz
Attractions: Fort Vancouver, Columbia River Waterfront Trail and Renaissance Park, Hulda Klager Lilac Gardens, Moulton Falls State Park, Officer's Row, Pearson Air Museum, Ridgefield National Wildlife Refuge, Vancouver Farmers Market
Trivia: Pearson Field, located at Fort Vancouver, is the oldest continually operating airfield in the U.S., receiving its first landing of a dirigible in 1905. It was also the landing site of the first transpolar flight from Moscow in 1937.
Directions: From I-5 N, immediately after crossing the bridge over the Columbia River, exit right onto City Center/6th St, exit 1-B. Follow the ramp around the loop and back under I-5. As you go under I-5, you are now on C St. Go one block to 8th St and turn left. Go 3 blocks to Columbia St. Esther Short park is on Columbia and 8th St. From I-5 S, take the Mill Plain exit. Turn right at the bottom of the exit onto Mill Plain. Go

west four blocks to Columbia St. Turn left on Columbia and go south to 8th St. Esther Short Park is on Columbia and 8th St.

America's Classic Jazz Festival
Lacey, Thurston County
Late June

This annual music festival was started in 1991 as a way for fans to get together and share their love of Dixieland music. The festival hosts world-class bands in four venues—one for listening, and three with large dance floors for dancing. Before you head to the dance floor, however, you can take dance lessons to learn the Balboa, the Foxtrot, and the Charleston. The event also includes a parasol parade and an after-glow party. You can purchase food and beverages at the event.

Address: Saint Martin's University Campus, 5300 Pacific Avenue SE
Admission: An all-event pass costs $90 ($15 for students aged 14–22). Prefestival on Thursday costs $15. Friday-only costs $40, Friday-night-only after 7 pm costs $25. Saturday-only costs $50, Saturday-night-only after 7 pm costs $25. Sunday-only costs $25.
Parking: Parking available on the university campus.
Accessible: Yes
Pets: No
Lodging: www.olyjazz.com/festival-lodging
Website: www.olyjazz.com
Facebook: www.facebook.com/pages/Great-Olympia-Dixieland-Jazz-Festival-WWWOLYJAZZCOM/352984478049554?hc_location=timeline
Attractions: Washington State Capitol Building and Museum, Hands On Children's Museum, Priest Point Park, Nisqually National Wildlife Refuge
Trivia: Originally called Woodland, the growing community petitioned for their very own post office in 1891. The federal government denied the request because there was already a town and post office named Woodland in southwest Washington. The townsfolk had to come up with a new name. "Lacey" was chosen, probably after local Justice of the Peace O.C. "Chester" Lacey, but no one's really sure of its origin.
Directions: From I-5 N, take exit 108 to College St, turn right. Go south on College St to one-way Pacific Ave, to one-way Lacey Blvd, and maneuver to the left lane. Turn left at Lacey Blvd. Stay in the left lane, turn

left on Franz, and proceed to Saint Martin's University. From I-5 S, take exit 109 to Martin Way/Sleater Kinney, turn right on Martin Way, and maneuver to the left lane. Go left at the stop light to College St, south on College St to one-way Pacific Ave, to one-way Lacey Blvd, maneuvering to left lane. Turn left at Lacey Blvd. Stay in the left lane, turn left on Franz, and proceed to Saint Martin's University. From Downtown Olympia, take 4th Ave to Pacific Ave where it becomes a one-way on to Lacey Blvd. At the traffic circle, follow to Franz, turn left to Saint Martin's University.

In the 1920s, Clark County was considered the prune capital of the world, which was then the nation's most popular breakfast fruit.

Southwest Washington County Fairs

Clark
Ridgefield
www.clarkcofair.com

Cowlitz
Longview
www.cowlitzcountyfair.com

Lewis/Southwest Washington
Chehalis
http://southwestwashingtonfair.net

Pacific
Menlo
www.co.pacific.wa.us/pcfair/

Skamania
Stevenson
www.skamaniacounty.org/facilities-rec/homepage/skamania-county-fair-timber-carnival-2

Thurston
Olympia
www.co.thurston.wa.us/fair/

Wahkiakum
Skamokawa
www.co.wahkiakum.wa.us/depts/fair/

Seattle/South Puget Sound Region

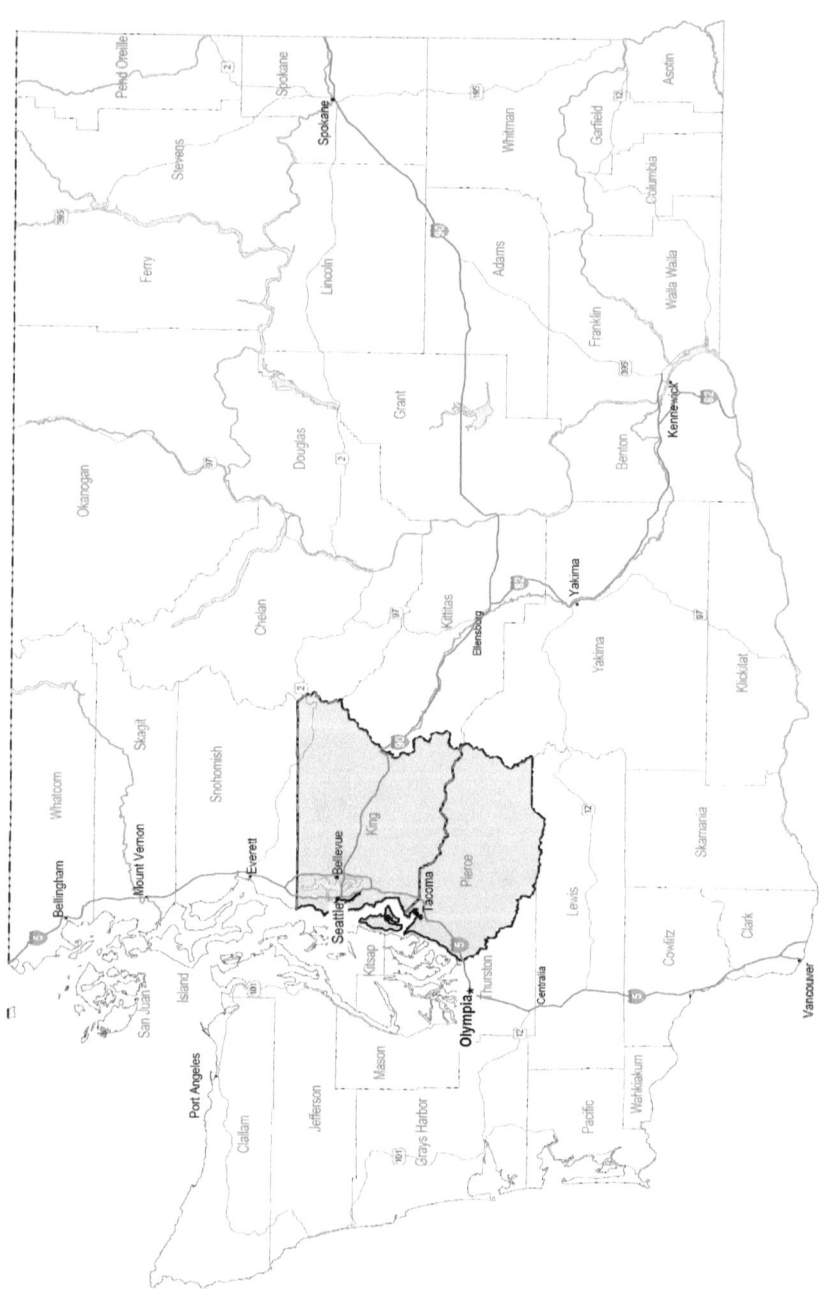

Seattle/South Puget Sound

The Seattle metropolitan area is the embodiment of the Pacific Northwest. It is unapologetically the best of all of its stereotypes: a rainy, caffeine-riddled, microbrew-thronged, bike-obsessed, laid-back cosmopolitan area where you're just as likely to find employees clad in flannel and jeans as business suits and ties. On the east lies the Cascade Mountain Range, and on the west lies the Olympic Mountain Range and the Pacific Ocean, providing a breathtaking backdrop, and an endless natural playground for hardy folk who aren't afraid to venture out under skies that produce an average rainfall of 39 inches per year. And venture outside, they do. It is a particular badge of honor that the rain doesn't prevent the inhabitants of Puget Sound from doing anything, except perhaps sunbathing. And when the sun does come out, festivals and celebrations abound, as do lily-white legs framed by cargo shorts and sandals.

As a multi-cultural area, many nationalities are honored at events around the Sound. Bellevue's Aki Matsuri Fall Festival, Kenmore's Mid-sommarfest, Des Moines' Native American Flute Festival, and Seattle's Northwest Folklife Festival, Polish Festival, and CroatiaFest provide a chance to experience the traditions and epicurean specialties of the people who have settled the area.

Speaking of epicurean specialties, one of the many things that Seattle does well is food. Local food festivals offer the best of culturally diverse cuisine, farm-fresh produce and seafood, and local wild mushrooms and wild salmon. Enjoy such mouthwatering treats at events like Seattle's Taste Washington, Issaquah's Salmon Days, and Ballard's Seafood Fest.

Beer is big in this region, followed closely by wine. Ashford's Mt. Rainier Fall Wine and Brew Festival, Redmond's Washington Brewer's Festival, Seattle's International Beerfest, and Kirkland's Uncorked festival serve up some of the country's best microbrews and vintages.

Though this industrious area birthed corporate giants such as Microsoft, Boeing, Starbucks, Amazon, Nordstrom, and Eddie Bauer (to name a few), it has never lost touch with its artistic side. The region's residents are strong supporters of the arts, which is evident by the sheer number of arts-related revelries, such as Bellevue's Festival of the Arts, Kirkland's Summerfest Art and Music Festival, and Seattle's International Film Festival. The music scene is also preeminent, with Seattle's Bumbershoot music and arts festival reigning as king. It is one of the largest festivals of its kind in North America, and routinely attracts major headliners as well as up-and-comers, and indie-music performers.

Outside of the metropolitan area, the foothills of the Cascade Range are decidedly more agrarian, and events such as Puyallup's Daffodil Festival and Sumner's Rhubarb Days are evidence of this.

No event listing for the Puget Sound region would be complete without a shout-out to off-beat offerings, such as Snoqualmie's Gigantic Bike Festival, and Seattle's burlesque Moisture Festival, as well as its much-razzed Hempfest.

> At low tide, there can be as many as 786 islands in the Puget Sound.

Art Events

Bellevue Festival of the Arts
Bellevue, King County
Last full weekend in July

Bellevue Festival of the Arts is a juried art and craft fair located just across Lake Washington from Seattle. The festival began in the 1980s because of disenchantment within the local artist community about the way normal arts festivals were being run, charging the artists for-profit commissions to display their art. The group wanted to create a fair in which participation would excite fellow artists. They did away with the for-profit commissions and gave the flat-fee proceeds back to the community that supported them. And this is what the Bellevue Festival of the Arts still does today. The three-day event provides a venue for more than 200 talented artists, local food vendors, and musicians from the Northwest and beyond to share their most recent works with the public. This event coincides with the Bellevue Art Museum's ARTSfair and Bellevue's 6th Street Fair.

Address: Cost Plus World Market Parking Lot, 10300 NE 8th Street, just north of Bellevue Square
Admission: Free
Parking: information http://en.parkopedia.com/parking/neighborhood/Downtown-Bellevue-WA
Accessible: Yes
Lodging: The festival recommends several hotels, some of which may give special Arts Festival rates: Courtyard Seattle Bellevue/Downtown (425.454.5888); Le Residence Hotel (425.455.1475); Hyatt Regency Bellevue (800.591.1234); Residence Inn Marriott (425.882.1222); The Sheraton Bellevue (425.455.3330) or (866.837.4275); Embassy Suites Hotel–Bellevue (425.644.2500); Coast Bellevue Hotel (425.455.9444) or (800.716.6199). Other lodging information: www.visitbellevuewashington.com/hotels
Website: www.bellevuefest.org
Facebook: www.facebook.com/BellevueFest
Attractions: Marymoor Park, Burke-Gilman Trail, Lake Sammamish, Bellevue Arts Museum, Eastside Heritage Center, Bellevue Farmers Market
Trivia: In 2010, Bellevue City Council member John Chelminiak was at-

tacked by a black bear while walking his dogs near his family's vacation home at Lake Wenatchee. During the attack, he received wounds to his abdomen and lower body, and the wounds were so severe to his face, he lost an eye. Remarkably, despite these injuries, he not only survived, but was in good spirits afterward and had no qualms about returning to the vacation house in the woods. As of 2014, Chelminiak was still serving on the Bellevue City Council.

Directions: The Bellevue Festival of the Arts is located four miles east of Seattle in downtown Bellevue, north of I-90 and south of 520. It is outdoors along NE 8th at Bellevue Way just north of Bellevue Square at the Cost Plus World Market.

Kirkland Summerfest Art and Music Festival
Kirkland, King County
Early August

Kirkland Summerfest—the city's largest festival—is a celebration of art, outdoor entertainment, and community spirit on the beautiful Kirkland waterfront. The three-day gathering offers dozens of performances, activities, exhibitions, and screenings representing the best in music, dance, comedy, circus and street arts, and family entertainment. When it began in 2011, Summerfest emphasized Shakespeare in the park, music, and children's activities. It has since become more popular and diverse, offering a progressive mix of local, regional, and international artists of all disciplines. The event offers admission-free concerts, open-air spectacles, and unique family attractions. In addition to performances, the event includes robot demonstrations, combat robot battles, a dog costume contest, a remote-controlled sailboat regatta, a duck dash, a U.S. Coast Guard search and rescue demo. Take the opportunity to race on a dragon boat team after a brief 20-minute lesson. And don't miss the Moss Bay Cardboard Boat Regatta. Kids' activities include a bouncy house, a giant slide, sand castles, tattoos, waterfront yoga, and Touch a Truck, where kids of all ages can see the ins and outs of big rigs, fire trucks, police cruisers, buses, and work vehicles. The festival also includes lots of food vendors and food carts, as well as a beer and wine garden.

Address: Marina Park, 25 Lakeshore Plaza
Admission: Free
Parking: Street and parking lot

Accessible: Yes
Pets: Leashed dogs allowed
Lodging: www.explorekirkland.com/Stay.htm
Website: www.kirklandsummerfest.com/#save-the-dates
Facebook: www.facebook.com/The.Real.Summerfest
Attractions: Outdoor sculpture walking tour, Juanita Beach Park, Howard Mandville Gallery, farmers markets
Trivia: From 1987 to 1996, Costco's headquarters was based in Kirkland. The company's house brand products are named "Kirkland Signature" after the city.
Directions: From I-405 N, take exit 18 (NE 85th St exit). At the end of the off-ramp, turn left on to NE 85th St. Proceed approximately 0.3 miles and NE 85th St becomes Central Ave. Proceed approximately 0.5 miles and turn left on to Lake St (Market St). Proceed one block and turn right onto Kirkland Ave. From I-405 S, take exit 18 (NE 85th St exit). At the end of the off-ramp, turn right on to NE 85th St. Proceed approximately 0.3 miles and NE 85th St becomes Central Ave. Proceed approximately 0.5 miles and turn left onto Lake St. Proceed one block and turn right onto Kirkland Ave.

Seattle International Film Festival

Seattle, King County
Several weeks in May/June

Touted as the largest and most highly attended film festival in the U.S., the Seattle International Film Festival (SIFF) presents more than 250 features/documentary films and 150 short films to an audience of more than 155,000 every year. The festival brings the world's greatest films to Seattle, showcases every genre imaginable, and provides experiences that foster an informed, aware, and vibrant community of film lovers. Because the festival features so many films, it may be hard to pick out which ones you'd like to see. To make it easier, event organizers have not only placed the movies into traditional categories, but have also categorized the movies into 10 different mood groupings: Love, Make Me Laugh, Open My Eyes, Thrill Me, Provoke Me, Show Me the World, Sci-Fi and Fact, To the Extreme, Creative Streak, and Face the Music. SIFF is recognized by the Academy of Motion Picture Arts and Sciences as a Qualifying Festival in all short film categories. Every year, the festival gives out the Golden Space Needle Audience Awards for Best Narrative

Film, Best Documentary Film, Best Director, Best Actor, Best Actress, Best Short Film, and the Women in Cinema Lena Sharpe Award (an audience award given to the film by a woman director that receives the most votes in the Golden Space Needle balloting). The festival also sponsors seven internationally juried awards in the following categories: Documentary Film, New Directors Showcase, Shorts, and FutureWave Youth Film Shorts (open to filmmakers 18 and younger).

Address: Various locations
Admission: Ticket prices range from $7 for matinee family films, to $9 for regular matinee screenings, to $12 for regular screenings. Multi-screening passes range from $60 for a six-movie pass, to $180 for a 20-movie pass, to $3,000 for an all-access platinum pass that includes many amenities such as concierge service, access to galas and parties (including open bars), and reserved seating. Tickets are also available for the opening and closing night galas ($50 each), and for the red carpet experience ($250).
Parking: Depends on location
Accessible: Yes
Pets: No
Lodging: http://visitseattle.org/Visitors/Stay.aspx
Website: www.siff.net
Facebook: www.facebook.com/SIFFNews
Attractions: Fremont neighborhood, Queen Anne Hill's Kerry Park, Gasworks Park, Seattle Underground Tour
Trivia: In 2014, the festival presented 32,361 minutes of film (539 hours).
Directions: Varies by venue

Seattle Outdoor Theater Festival
Seattle, King County
Second weekend in July

GreenStage is Seattle's longest-running Shakespeare Company. Its mission is to inspire audiences to engage in live theatre as part of their recreation, and to instill and foster an appreciation for live theater, with a strong belief that it can be enjoyed in the same spirit as a picnic or a ballgame. To accomplish this mission, in the early 2000s, the company created the Seattle Outdoor Theater Festival. The family-oriented weekend packs in eight theater companies and 14 performances, and admission is free. The performances take place mainly on the grass, and very few of the venues have any seating at all. So, bring your blanket, your family (kids welcome), and a picnic lunch, dinner, or snack and sit down and enjoy the show. For the best spots on the grass, arrive at least 20 minutes early.

Address: Volunteer Park, 1247 15th Avenue E
Admission: Free
Parking: Parking near the event is limited, so public transportation is strongly advised.
Accessible: Yes
Pets: Leashed dogs allowed
Lodging: http://visitseattle.org/Visitors/Stay.aspx
Website: www.greenstage.org/sotf
Attractions: Museum of Flight, Seattle Art Museum, Lake Union, Ye Olde Curiosity Shop, Magnuson Park
Trivia: For several years in the mid '90s, the Klingon Shakespeare Restoration Project worked dutifully to translate Shakespeare's Hamlet into Klingon. The book (The Tragedy of Khamlet, Son of the Emperor of Qo'noS) was published in 1996 by the Klingon Language Institute. It features the English version of the play alongside the Klingon translation. The impetus for the project came from a line from *Star Trek VI: The Undiscovered Country* in which the Klingon Chancellor Gorkon states "You have not experienced Shakespeare until you have read him in the original Klingon." *Star Trek* publisher Pocket Books republished the paperback version in 2000.
Directions: From I-5 N, take the East Olive Way exit (exit #166) and bear right on East Olive Way. East Olive Way merges into East John St. East John comes to a T at 15th Ave E. Turn left on 15th Ave E. In about 3/4 of a mile, the entrance to Volunteer Park is on your left. From I-5 S: Exit at Bolston Ave/Roanoke St (exit #168A) and turn left on E Roanoke St. Cross I-5, then merge into the right lane. Turn right at 10th Ave E. Turn left onto E Boston St. E Boston becomes 15th Ave E. The entrance to Volunteer Park is on your left (approximately 1/2 mile from 10th Ave E.)

Eatonville Arts Festival
Eatonville, Pierce County
First full weekend in August

The thing that makes the Eatonville Arts Festival unique is that is features all original artwork—no imports allowed. Wares from more than 100 artisans from across the country include ceramics, pottery, jewelry, sculpture, paintings, beadwork, walking sticks, and wind chimes, as well as many other items. The three-day festival includes a live and silent auction, continuous live musical entertainment, specialty cars, tasty food, and a beer garden with Karaoke. An artist's quick draw competition is a crowd favorite. All festival proceeds go to benefit the Lions Club of Eatonville.

Address: Glacier Park, 213 Fir Street
Admission: Free
Parking: Free parking is available on any street around the festival.
Accessible: Yes
Lodging: www.eatonvillechamber.com/business.php
Website: www.eatonvilleartsfestival.com
Attractions: Northwest Trek Wildlife Park, Mt. Rainier National Park, Pioneer Farm Museum, Recycled Spirits of Iron sculptures
Trivia: Former Los Angeles Police Detective Mark Fuhrman, a major player in the O.J. Simpson murder trial, was born and raised in Eatonville.
Directions: From I-5, go east on WA-512. Take the Meridian/161 South/Mt. Rainier exit and follow 161 for 22 miles to Eatonville. Turn right onto Carter St, then turn right onto Fir St. Glacier Park is at the end of Fir St.

Beer, Wine & Spirits

Kirkland Uncorked
Kirkland, King County
Third weekend in July

Kirkland Uncorked is a showcase of art, food, and wine on the picturesque shores of Lake Washington. The three-day event features wines from 20+ world-class Washington wineries, bite-sized feasts from notable Eastside restaurants, and appearances from the Northwest's most prestigious celebrity chefs and culinary personalities. The festival is split into two parts: a 21+ Tasting Garden and an all ages street fair. The Tasting Garden features wine tasting, grilling demonstrations, live music, and a Saturday grill-off. The street fair features a boat show, the Uncorked Market (selling jewelry, canvas art, handmade clothing, and imported goods), the CityDog Magazine's dog modeling contest, and a Sunday Food Truck Feast featuring the area's best mobile kitchens. Other activities at past events have included canvas painting and stand-up paddle board yoga. Kirkland Uncorked is a benefit for Homeward Pet Adoption Center, a non-profit, no-kill animal shelter.

Address: Marina Park, 25 Lakeshore Plaza
Admission: Free to the public. Tasting Garden General Admission is $25 in advance and $35 at the door. Tickets include entrance to the Tasting Garden, a commemorative tasting glass and 10 wine-tasting tokens. Wine tastes (1-oz) cost 1–2 tasting tokens, depending on each wine's value. The Ultimate Wine Admission is $60 in advance and $70 at the door. Ultimate tickets include entrance to the Tasting Garden, a commemorative tasting glass, and all-you-can-sample tastes of wine.
Parking: Plenty of free and paid parking options are available. Find out more information at the festival's website: www.kirklanduncorked.com/festival-info.html#parking.
Accessible: Yes
Pets: Yes
Lodging: Several lodging options are featured at the event website, including The Heathman Hotel (888.264.5494); The Woodmark Hotel, Yacht Club and Spa (888.963.5308); Courtyard by Marriott (425.602.3200; Baymont Inn and Suites Kirkland (425.822.2300); and Loomis House Bed and Breakfast (425.827.7194). Other lodging informa-

tion: www.kirklanduncorked.com/staytheweekend.html
Website: www.kirklanduncorked.com
Facebook: www.facebook.com/KirklndUncorked?ref=br_tf
Attractions: Juanita Bay Park, Arthur Foss tugboat, Kirkland Arts Center, Bridle Trails State Park
Trivia: The 1982 Kirkland National Little League team won the Little League World Series, which is featured in ESPN's 30 for 30 documentary *Little Big Men*.
Directions: From I-405 N, take exit 18 (NE 85th St). At the end of the off-ramp, turn left on to NE 85th St. Proceed approximately 0.3 miles and NE 85th St becomes Central Ave. Proceed approximately 0.5 miles and turn left on to Lake St (Market St). Proceed one block and turn right on to Kirkland Ave. From I-405 S, take exit 18 (NE 85th St). At the end of the off-ramp, turn right on to NE 85th St. Proceed approximately 0.3 miles and NE 85th St becomes Central Ave. Proceed approximately 0.5 miles and turn left onto Lake St. Proceed one block and turn right onto Kirkland Ave.

Washington Brewer's Festival
Redmond, King County
June/Father's Day weekend

The Washington Brewer's festival is a unique all-age beer festival where thousands of beer aficionados and families gather to celebrate Father's Day weekend. Featuring more than 300 beers from 88 different Washington breweries, the festival also offers great food, live music, a brewer's keg toss contest, and wine and cider tasting. The three-day event features plenty of entertainment for kids including a root beer garden, inflatable toys, and a kids' craft tent where they can make Father's Day gifts to surprise dad.
Address: Marymoor Park, 6046 W Lake Sammamish Parkway NE
Admission: Tickets are $20 per day in advance, $25 per day at the door. Admission includes a tasting cup and six tasting tokens. Additional tastes are $1.50 each. Designated driver admission is $5 and available at the door only. On Saturday and Sunday, persons under 21 are admitted free of charge.
Parking: On-site parking is available for $5 cash. A courtesy van is available Saturday and Sunday, that shuttles the .75 miles to and from the West Lake Sammamish Parkway NE and Leary Way bus stop and the

event entrance.
Accessible: Yes
Pets: No
Lodging: The festival's hotel sponsor has been Marriott Redmond Town Center (425.498.4000), which offers a discounted rate for festival attendees: www.marriott.com/hotels/travel/seamc-redmond-marriott-town-center
Website: http://washingtonbeer.com/wa-brewers-fest
Attractions: Idylwood Beach Park, Puget Power Trail, Microsoft Visitor Center, Willows Run Golf Course, K1 Speed indoor go kart racing
Trivia: Marymoor Park is home to the state's only velodrome, a 400-meter, steeply banked, outdoor track dedicated to bicycle racing. The surface is concrete and was completely resurfaced in 2005 to a smoother finish. Over the years, Marymoor has been a regular stop for the Sundance Grand Prix, the 7-Eleven/*Bicycling Magazine* Grand Prix, the regional Olympic Trials, and several Olympic and Pan-Am development meets, as well as the Goodwill Games in 1990. The Friday Night Racing series, which runs all summer long, thrills spectators while they gather with their families and friends to picnic on the lawn or enjoy the view from the stands.
Directions: Marymoor Park is 15 miles east of downtown Seattle and 5 miles east of Bellevue. From I-405 at SR-520 in Bellevue, take SR-520 eastbound to West Lake Sammamish Pkwy NE in Redmond and travel five miles. Take the W Lake Sammamish Pkwy Exit ("exit only" right lane – exit for Redmond Towne Center). At the bottom of the off-ramp, turn right. Go one block to the traffic light at Marymoor Way. This is the Marymoor Park west entrance. Turn left into the park. From Seattle, take SR-520 east from I-5 across the Evergreen Point floating bridge. At I-405, follow the previous directions, or take I-90 east across the floating bridge and across Mercer Island to I-405. Head north on I-405. At SR-520 eastbound, follow the directions listed previously.

Seattle International Beerfest
Seattle, King County
July or August

Seattle International Beerfest is a high-end, three-day beer festival that specializes in rare exotic beers, and invites you to "taste the greatest beers you've never heard of." The event features more than 200 world-class beers, many from the Pacific Northwest, but many hailing from all over the planet (16+ countries). Stroll around the beautiful grounds with a cold one as you listen to great bands play all weekend. In addition to lighter summer beers, Beerfest unapologetically rolls out a selection of top-rated beers that are normally reserved for the colder months, including barley wines, imperial stouts, double IPAs, barrel-aged strong ales, funky farmhouse saisons, and sour ales. The event's indoor/outdoor park space has seating for 600–700, in both shaded and unshaded areas. In addition, the huge lush grass lawn invites you to bring a blanket from home and kick back. Enjoy free darts, chess, checkers, and backgammon throughout the weekend.

Address: Fisher Pavilion and Lawn, 305 Harrison Street (about 200 yards from the Space Needle)
Admission: Tickets cost $25 in advance, $30 at the gate. Admission includes 10 beer tickets and an official SIB glass. Additional tickets can be purchased for $1 each. Each serving is 4-oz and beers cost 1–7 tickets. Non-drinkers pay a $5 cover charge. An online exclusive deal costs $45, and includes 40 beer tickets, an official SIB glass, express entry, and all benefits of regular paid entry.
Parking: Free parking is available north of Mercer Street. Otherwise you can pay to park on the street or in local parking garages.
Accessible: Yes
Pets: Yes
Lodging: http://visitseattle.org/Visitors/Stay.aspx
Website: www.seattlebeerfest.com
Facebook: www.facebook.com/pages/SEATTLE-INTERNATIONAL-BEERFEST/125784954105763?sk=info
Attractions: Seattle Mariners at Safeco Field, Mercer Island, Pike's Place Market, Space Needle
Trivia: Seattle was the first American city to put police on bicycles.
Directions: To get to Seattle Center from I-5 N, take exit 165 on the left for Seneca St. Take a slight right onto 6th Ave, travel for nearly a mile, then turn left on to Denny Way. Seattle Center is on your right. To reach Seattle Center from I-5 S, take exit 167 for Mercer St toward Seattle Center. Continue on Mercer St for approximately 0.7 miles. Seattle Center is on your left.

Wine Rocks

Seattle, King County
Usually July, sometimes June

Wine Rocks is a gathering of local winemakers, craft brewers, and musicians showcasing exceptional wine, unique distillates, outstanding beer, groovy tunes, savory fare, and one helluva of a backdrop. In the late 2000s, Gibson Guitars wanted an event to promote the opening of its new showroom. Local event guru Jen Doak knew that Seattleites love their craft beverages, yummy eats, and rockin' out. So, why not put it all under one roof? Thus, Wine Rocks was born. The event is a sensory feast celebrating Washington State's local abundance. Libations are served up by plenty of winemakers, distilleries, and brew masters who also happen to know a thing or two about music. A diverse playlist features winemakers channeling their inner rock star, as well as several favorite local bands. In addition to complimentary hors d'oeuvres, some of Seattle's best food trucks are parked at the pier, selling their mouthwatering creations. All of this takes place on the waterfront, which offers spectacular views of Puget Sound and the Olympic Mountains. Proceeds from this event benefit local non-profit organizations.

Address: Bell Harbor Waterfront, 2211 Alaskan Way
Admission: Advance tickets are $40 (usually through the end of May), $45 until event. Admission at the door is $50 (cash only). The event typically sells out, so get your tickets early.
Parking: The Bell Street Pier garage (9 Wall Street) is conveniently located directly across from the terminal and offers covered and secure parking. Enter at the corner of Alaskan Way and Wall Street. Twenty-five handicap parking stalls are available. Maximum height is 6'6". You can also find more downtown parking information at: www.seattle.gov/transportation/epark
Accessible: Yes
Pets: No
Lodging: The Inn at El Gaucho (866.354.2824) provides a 20% discount for Wine Rocks guests. Other lodging options: http://visitseattle.org/Visitors/Stay.aspx
Website: http://winerocksseattle.com
Facebook: www.facebook.com/winerocksseattle
Attractions: Lake Union, Maritime Heritage Center, Pike's Place Market, Pacific Science Center

Trivia: Seattle is ranked the most literate city in the country. It has the most book stores and libraries per capita. The Seattle Public Library system has the highest percentage of library card-holders per capita in the country.

Directions: From I-5 S, take exit 165B toward Union St. Turn right onto 4th Ave, then turn left on to Wall St. Turn left onto Elliott Ave. The Bell Street Pier/World Trade Center Garage, located at 2323 Elliott Ave N, is on your right next to the Art Institute of Seattle. From I-5 N, take left exit 165 for Seneca St. Turn right onto 4th Ave, then turn left on to Wall St. Turn left onto Elliott Ave. The Bell Street Pier/World Trade Center Garage, located at 2323 Elliott Ave N, is on your right next to the Art Institute of Seattle.

Seattle Wine and Food Experience
Seattle, King County
Last Sunday in February

Seattle Wine and Food Experience is a premier showcase of gourmet wine and food that features more than 100 wineries from the Northwest and beyond, 25+ Seattle restaurants, 50+ specialty food purveyors, and 28 breweries, cideries, and distilleries. Experience a world tour of wine with a special focus on wines from featured regions as you enjoy the culinary delights prepared by Northwest chefs. Learn about food and wine products through "experiences" and event features. Exhibitors offer a variety of samples ranging from magazines, to cheese, to chocolate. A small sampling of past vendors includes Stella Artois, Washington State Potato Commission, Top Pot Doughnuts, Bill the Butcher, Seattle magazine, Sip Northwest magazine, Allrecipes.com, Honest Tea, J.W. Desserts, Mallow Artisan Marshmallows, Snoqualmie Ice Cream, Tim's Cascade Snacks, Mt. Townsend Creamery, Lynnae's Gourmet Pickles, America Lamb Board, Jonboy Caramels, and Washington Beef Commission. This event, for those 21 and older, is a fundraising event.

Address: Seattle Center Exhibition Hall, 300 Mercer Street
Admission: General Admission is $55. VIP admission (which includes an extra hour to taste and a swag bag) is $70. Make sure to get your tickets early—the event sells out every year.
Parking: Some street parking is available and there are many lots near the Exhibition Hall. Also consider other driving options (such as a cab, a

limo service, or public transportation) to ensure safety after consuming alcohol.
Accessible: Yes
Pets: No
Lodging: http://seattlewineandfoodexperience.com/info#section-hotels
Website: http://seattlewineandfoodexperience.com
Facebook: www.facebook.com/seattlewineandfoodexperience/timeline
Attractions: Pacific Place, Henry Art Gallery, Golden Gardens Park, Space Needle and revolving Sky City restaurant
Trivia: Seattle is the birthplace of Starbucks. The oldest surviving Starbucks location is thriving in historic Pike's Place Market. The first Starbucks was opened in 1971 in a different location in the market, but moved to 102 Pike Street in 1975. It has been serving coffee to caffeine-seeking masses ever since then. Interesting to note that during the construction of the store, owners tried to use as much recycled material as possible. The leather on the bar's outer facing was scrap obtained from shoe and automobile factories. The signage on the bar uses recycled slate from a local high school. The restroom partitions are made from recycled laundry detergent bottles, and the wall tapestry is made of repurposed burlap coffee bags from the coffee chain's local roasting plant.
Directions: To get to Seattle Center from I-5 N, take exit 165 on the left for Seneca St. Take a slight right onto 6th Ave, travel for nearly a mile, then turn left on to Denny Way. Seattle Center is on your right. To reach Seattle Center from I-5 S, take exit 167 for Mercer St toward Seattle Center. Continue on Mercer St for approximately 0.7 miles. Seattle Center is on your left.

On the Road to Paradise, Mount Rainier Fall Wine & Brew Festival
Ashford, Pierce County
Early to mid-November

The Mount Rainier Fall Wine and Brew Festival is your chance to sip, savor, and enjoy a variety of hard-to-find artisanal wines and microbrews from small Washington producers. Local musicians play as you sample and learn about the wines and brews from the winemakers, vintners, and brewers. Past featured participants have included Bateaux Cellars (Toledo), Convergence Zone Cellars (Woodinville), HarMony Wines (Castle Rock), Hoodsport Winery (Hoodsport), Madsen Family Cellars (Silverlake), NW Mountain Winery (Olympia), Piccola Cellars (Woodinville), Redmond Ridge Winery (Walla Walla), Scatter Creek Winery

(Tenino), Stottle Winery (Lacey), Finnriver Farm and Cidery (Chimacum), Narrows Brewing Company (Tacoma), and 7 Seas Brewing (Gig Harbor). Wine is available by the taste, glass, bottle, and case. The festival has no age restrictions—children are welcome.

Address: Mt. Rainier Lions Club, Grand Tasting Hall, 27726 Hwy 706 E
Admission: Admission is $25 with advance purchase (before mid-November). Regular admission is $30. Event entry fee includes wine glass, 10 tasting tickets, and chocolate.
Parking: On site event parking
Accessible: Yes
Pets: No
Lodging: www.mt-rainier.com/lodging_search.php
Website: www.road-to-paradise.com
Facebook: www.facebook.com/pages/On-The-Road-to-Paradise-Wine-Tasting/156953084357508
Attractions: Recycled Spirits of Iron (Ex Nihilo) Sculpture Park, Mt. Rainier National Park, Mineral Lake, Alder Lake
Trivia: The Cedar Creek Treehouse is a privately owned treehouse bed and breakfast in Ashford. The lodging cabin is 50' off the ground, nestled in a 200-year-old Western Red Cedar tree. The facility also offers a guided tour to its Treehouse Observatory, which is 100 feet off the ground. To reach the observatory, you ascend an 82' high spiral staircase (built around a tree trunk) and cross over a suspended bridge that is 43' long and 82' off the ground—probably not for those with a fear of heights. But if you're brave, the payoff is an outstanding view of Mt. Rainier's Muir snowfield and Mt. Wow.
Directions: Ashford is 60 miles southeast of Olympia via WA-7 S.

Gig Harbor Beer Festival
Gig Harbor, Pierce County
May/Mother's Day weekend

The Gig Harbor Beer Festival features a wide variety of Northwest craft brewers offering event-goers a splendid mix of familiar favorites and new brews to taste. Area restaurants also offer patrons a variety of delicious food. The show features Gig Harbor's own 7 Seas Brewing (whose brews include such tantalizing names as Rude Parrot IPA, Ballz Deep Double IPA, Life Jacket Session IPA, Hot Prophet 100% Wet Hop Ale, and Cascadian Dark Ale). Other award-winning participating breweries in the past have included 192 Brewing (Kenmore), American Brewing (Edmonds), Bainbridge Island Brewing (Bainbridge Island), Big Al Brewing (Seattle), Der Blokken (Bremerton), Dicks Brewing Co. (Centralia), Everybody's Brewing (White Salmon), Fremont Brewing (Seattle), Georgetown Brewing Co. (Seattle), Harmon Brewing Co. (Tacoma), Hood Canal Brewer (Kingston), Loowit Brewing Co. (Vancouver), Narrows Brewing (Tacoma), Northwest Brewing (Pacific), Rainy Daze Brewing Co. (Silverdale), RAM Big Horn Brewery (Tacoma), Silver City Brewery (Bremerton), Slippery Pig Brewing (Poulsbo), Sound Brewery (Poulsbo), and Wingman Brewery (Tacoma). The event, which also includes live music, is a fundraiser for Gig Harbor Kiwanis.

Address: Uptown Gig Harbor Pavilion, 4701 Pt. Fosdick Drive
Admission: Admission is $20 in advance/$25 at the door. Tickets sell out quickly. Admission fee includes a 5-oz tasting cup, 8 tasting tokens, and a program
Accessible: Yes
Pets: No
Lodging: www.gigharborguide.com/page.php?id=837
Website: www.gigharborbeerfestival.com
Facebook: www.facebook.com/GigHarborBeerFestival
Attractions: Harbor History Museum, Blue Willow Lavender Farm, Kopachuck State Park, Discovery Village, Harborview Drive, Jerisich Park
Trivia: Until 1940, the only method of transportation between Gig Harbor (on the Kitsap Peninsula) and Tacoma was via steamship. In 1940, the first Tacoma Narrows Bridge was constructed between Tacoma and the peninsula. It was quickly nicknamed "Galloping Gertie" because of its propensity to pitch and sway in high winds. The bridge survived only four months before a gusty November storm caused it to collapse into the sound. No lives were lost in the collapse (with the exception of a cocker spaniel abandoned in a car by a driver who fled the scene). Old 16-mm footage of the collapse has been preserved by the Library of Congress. Part of the film can be viewed on YouTube (www.youtube.com/watch?v=j-zczJXSxnw). The current Tacoma Narrows was built in 1950 (another parallel bridge was completed in 2007 to handle eastbound traffic). In all of that time, the replacement bridge has never once bucked anybody off.
Directions: Gig Harbor is 12 miles northwest of Tacoma via WA-16 W.

Ethnic & Cultural Celebrations

Aki Matsuri Fall Festival
Bellevue, King County
Second weekend in September

The Aki Matsuri (Fall Festival) is a celebration of Japan's rich cultural heritage. The festival features two full days of on-stage performing arts; martial art demonstrations by local dojo members; tea ceremony and Ikebana demonstrations; films; more than 75 exhibit booths (artists, craft persons, businesses, and organizations); Taiko, Japanese gardening, shakuhachi (traditional Japanese bamboo flute), and bonsai workshops; puppet shows; and Nomi-no-ichi, which is a Japanese style flea market. Plenty of Japanese cuisine is also available for purchase, including bento, sushi, gyoza, yakisoba, and yakitori.

Address: Bellevue College Main Campus, 3000 Landerholm Circle SE
Admission: Free. Some workshops and seminars require registration and a fee.
Parking: Free
Accessible: Yes
Pets: No
Lodging: www.visitbellevuewashington.com/hotels
Website: http://enma.org/2014/overview.html
Attractions: Bellevue Arts Museum, KidsQuest Children's Museum, Bellevue Botanical Garden, Lake Sammamish
Trivia: Ann and Nancy Wilson, sisters and front women for the rock band Heart, lived in Bellevue during their teenage years and graduated from local high schools.
Directions: Bellevue is located 12 miles east of Seattle via I-90 E.

Flute Quest, Native American Flute Festival
Des Moines, King County
Third weekend in August

Flute Quest is the largest Native American Flute Festival in the Northwest. It welcomes adults and children interested in the history and culture surrounding the Native American flute, or who want to learn how to play the flute. Beginner workshops are free and world-renowned instructors lead workshops for accomplished musicians. Musicians are invited to play with fellow musicians in circle sessions dedicated to drums, flutes, didgeridoos, and other world instruments. The three-day festival features flute and drum vendors and live music on the festival stage from a great line up of recording artists. Also, check out the array of beautiful rattles, fans, drums, and leather goods for sale.

Address: Saltwater State Park, 25205 8th Place S
Admission: Free. Advanced workshops and main concerts charge a fee.
Parking: Saltwater State Park requires the Discover Pass or one-day pass for parking. However, if you are camping at Saltwater State Park you are exempted from the parking permit. Discover Pass exemptions are given for handicapped folks and disabled veterans.
Accessible: No info
Lodging: To reserve a campsite, call 888.CAMPOUT or 888.226.7688. Make reservations online at: www.parks.wa.gov/reservations
Website: www.waflutecircle.org/flutequest.htm
Attractions: Marine Science and Technology (MaST) Center of Highline College, Saltwater State Park, Art on Poverty Bay
Trivia: From the early 1920s to mid-1940s, Des Moines housed the Big Tree Inn. Originally constructed for the 1915 Panama Pacific International Exposition in San Francisco, the inn was made from two hollowed-out sections of a 2,000-year-old, 300-ft-tall redwood tree that was 20 feet in diameter. Relocated to Des Moines in 1921, the oddity served as a popular chicken shack for several years. In 1938, the business was relocated to a more heavily trafficked road. Eventually, it was destroyed by fire.
Directions: Des Moines is located 12 miles north of Tacoma via I-5 N.

Midsommarfest
Kenmore, King County
Last Sunday in June

Midsommarfest is a traditional Swedish celebration of the summer solstice. The Kenmore event re-creates this festival as authentically as possible, and includes contributions from many Nordic and Baltic countries. Throughout the event, watch performances of folk music and folk dancing on two stages. The grand parade and raising of the majstång (garlanded midsommar pole) happens early in the afternoon. Spectators are invited to help hoist the 45' pole with their muscles or cheers, and then join in the rousing långdans (serpentine running dance) around the pole, accompanied by the music of massed musicians. The Allspel takes place immediately following the pole ceremony, where the musicians play for participatory dancing. Wander through craft and vendor booths in the Hemslöjdsmarknad (craft market), where you can enjoy folk crafts, Nordic sagas, music, snacks, demonstrations, and participatory activities. Traditional midsommar food and other Scandinavian delicacies are offered. To get into the festival spirit, you can purchase a flower crown (the classic midsommarkrans), either ready-made, or ready to decorate to your own taste. Children's activities include crafts, Nordic stories, raising the children's pole, and learning game dances.

Address: St. Edward State Park, 14445 Juanita Drive NE
Admission: Free. Midsommarfest buttons are available for a $2 donation.
Parking: Parking is free. State Parks allow guests' vehicles to be parked on the grass, so no shuttles are needed. However, be sure to park in the Midsommar area, as directed by parking attendants. Please carpool if possible to make the best use of available parking spaces. The regular parking lots still require Discover Passes for visitors to other areas in the park.
Accessible: Yes
Lodging: www.explorebothell.com/business_listings/places-to-stay
Website: www.skandia-folkdance.org/midsommarfest.html
Attractions: Saint Edward State Park, Burke-Gilman Trail, scenic seaplane air tours with Kenmore Air, Inglewood Golf Club
Trivia: The Donald Duck Party is a farcical Swedish political party whose platform boasts "free liquor and wider sidewalks." Although the party has never actually existed (no such party has ever been registered with the Swedish Election Authority), it has received enough write-in votes since 2002 to be the ninth most popular political party.
Directions: From Seattle (I-5), take exit 173, and bear left (north) onto 1st Ave NE. Turn right (east) onto NE Northgate Way, travel 1.3 miles, then bear left (north) onto SR-522 (Lake City Way NE). Travel 4.7 miles, turn right (south) onto 68th Ave NE. Continue south on Juanita Dr NE (68th Ave NE) for about two miles. St. Edwards State Park is on the right. From the east side of Lake Washington (I-405), take exit 23, turn off on to the ramp, and merge onto SR-522 (west). Travel 3.6 miles, then turn left (south) onto 68th Ave NE. Continue south on Juanita Dr NE (68th Ave NE) for about two miles. St. Edwards State Park is on the right.

Northwest Folklife Festival
Seattle, King County
May/Memorial Day Weekend

Every year since 1972, the Northwest Folklife Festival has brought a celebration of diversity and tradition to the heart of the city. The festival showcases all forms of cultural expression practiced in the Northwest, including ethnic, folk, and traditional arts, crafts, and music. There are no headliners and all of the performers play for free. Featuring hip hop MCs, Irish cloggers, Middle Eastern dancers, bluegrass fiddlers, West African drummers, and ska bands, the festival has built a thriving artistic outlet. Buskers, including musicians, jugglers, circus performers, and magicians, perform on walkways throughout the event. Approximately 250,000 attendees visit the event during its four-day run. Each year, the festival spotlights a particular ethnic community or folk tradition. In recent years, this focus has included India and its people, maritime culture, Bulgarian culture, and Arab American life. In addition to live music and dance, enjoy craft vendors, ethnic products from around the world, dance and music workshops, dozens of food vendors, and storytelling.

Address: Seattle Center, 305 Harrison Street
Admission: Admission is free. However, to keep the Festival free, event personnel accept donations of any amount. When asked, they suggest a donation of $10 per person per day (or $20 for family/groups).
Parking: Seattle Center has several paid lots within a three-block radius. However, these lots fill up by midday and can be pricey. Event organizers recommend taking the bus, biking, or walking to the festival. All lots around Seattle Center have designated disabled parking spots. Check with a parking attendant if all the available spaces are full and you are in need of a disabled parking spot. You will also find designated disabled parking spots on 2nd Avenue N just south of Thomas Street and on Warren Avenue just south of Mercer Street.
Accessible: Yes
Pets: No
Lodging: www.nwfolklife.org/festival/experience/where-to-stay
Website: www.nwfolklife.org/festival
Facebook: www.facebook.com/nwfolklife?rf=336995949707342
Attractions: Pike Place Market, Waterfront Park, Washington Park Arboretum, Space Needle
Trivia: January 2015 saw the 6th annual No Pants Light Rail Ride, an

offshoot of the No Pants Subway ride that the New York group Improv Everywhere started in 2002. Seattle-based Emerald City Improv invites you to take off your pants, ride the light rail, and pretend that everything is normal. Participants ride all the way to SeaTac Airport. You do have to follow a few rules, though. First of all, you must be willing to take your pants off. You have to stay in character and don't say what's going on (try to keep a straight face). It's fun to try and create a character and reason you don't have pants (for example, you just arrived on a flight at SeaTac and the airlines lost your pants). Don't wear offensive or overly-skimpy underwear. (If you wear anything too revealing, you will be asked to put your pants back on.) Keep in mind, the general pants-wearing public is also on the ride with you, and most have cell phone cameras.

Directions: To get to Seattle Center from I-5 N, take exit 165 on the left for Seneca St. Take a slight right onto 6th Ave, travel for nearly a mile, then turn left on to Denny Way. Seattle Center is on your right. To reach Seattle Center from I-5 S, take exit 167 for Mercer St toward Seattle Center. Continue on Mercer St for approximately 0.7 miles. Seattle Center is on your left.

Polish Festival Seattle
Seattle, King County
July

Seattle's Polish Festival invites you to explore and experience Polish culture and traditions through live music and dance performances, workshops related to Polish culture, traditional folk costumes, exhibits, a film festival, and children's activities. The vendor marketplace showcases Polish glass art, hand-crafted pottery, amber jewelry, crystal, and cut-out paper art, as well as information about local Polish-American community organizations. The beer garden is well stocked with a variety of imported Polish beer as well as Northwest wines, and food vendors serve plenty of authentic delicious Polish food. If you love Polish sausage, enjoy sampling different varieties at a kielbasa tasting.

Address: Seattle Center, 305 Harrison Street
Admission: Free
Parking: Information for Seattle Center: www.seattlecenter.com/transportation/parking
Accessible: Yes

Lodging: http://visitseattle.org/Visitors/Stay.aspx.
Website: www.polishfestivalseattle.org
Facebook: www.facebook.com/pages/Polish-Festival-Seattle/148276978641970
Attractions: Frye Art Museum, Ye Olde Curiosity Shop, Kubota Garden, Center for Wooden Boats
Trivia: Poland has one of the highest concentrations of lakes in the world, with almost 10,000 closed bodies of water. In Europe, only Finland has a greater density of lakes.
Directions: To get to Seattle Center from I-5 N, take exit 165 on the left for Seneca St. Take a slight right onto 6th Ave, travel for nearly a mile, then turn left on to Denny Way. Seattle Center is on your right. To reach Seattle Center from I-5 S, take exit 167 for Mercer St toward Seattle Center. Continue on Mercer St for approximately 0.7 miles. Seattle Center is on your left.

CroatiaFest
Seattle, King County
First weekend in October

CroatiaFest is a celebration of music, dance, and food that makes the Croatian culture so unique. The festival begins on Saturday evening with Croatian Mass at St. Joseph Catholic Church. Mass is followed by a Croatian dance party, which invites you to the Russian Community Center across the street from the church to dance and sing along, sample delicious Croatian food, and enjoy a no-host bar featuring a variety of wines. Sunday is packed with events, including music, exquisite costumes, and traditional dances performed all day on the main stage by various Croatian musicians, dance ensembles, and singing groups. Also enjoy Croatian cooking demonstrations, films, and lectures. Learn about the history of Croatian communities throughout the Pacific Northwest, trace your Croatian lineage, and plan your next trip to Croatia. Food vendors serve many different items, including traditional grilled ćivapčići, which is meat sausage served on a pita bread with ajvar, which is a red pepper relish. The event also features a beer garden, vendors selling Croatian merchandise and souvenirs, and activities and crafts for children.

Address: Seattle Center Armory, 305 Harrison Street
Admission: Admission to the Saturday night dance party is $10. Admis-

sion to CroatiaFest on Sunday is free.
Parking: www.seattlecenter.com/transportation/parking
Accessible: Yes
Pets: No
Lodging: www.croatiafest.org/hotels.html
Website: www.croatiafest.org
Facebook: www.facebook.com/CroatiaFest
Attractions: Chihuly Garden and Glass, International Fountain, Seattle Center Totem, Space Needle
Trivia: Renowned electrical engineer, mechanical engineer, and inventor Nikola Tesla was born in 1856 in the village of Smiljan in Croatia. Tesla is best known for his inventions of alternating current, lasers, electric motors, and remote controls, as well as his work in robotics and radio. The Tesla Coil is a machine that he invented that generates extremely high voltages, in an attempt by Tesla to transmit electrical power without wires. The results are quite shocking.
Directions: To get to Seattle Center from I-5 N, take exit 165 on the left for Seneca St. Take a slight right onto 6th Ave, travel for nearly a mile, then turn left on to Denny Way. Seattle Center is on your right. To reach Seattle Center from I-5 S, take exit 167 for Mercer St toward Seattle Center. Continue on Mercer St for approximately 0.7 miles. Seattle Center is on your left.

Pacific Northwest Scottish Highland Games and Clan Gathering
Enumclaw, King County
Last weekend in July

The Pacific Northwest Scottish Highland Games and Clan Gathering offers you the chance to enjoy a wee bit of Scotland right here in the Northwest. The three-day festival features the North American Scottish Athletics Championship, U.S. West Coast Drum Corps Championship, NW Regional Harp Finals, individual piping and drumming, pipe bands, and highland and national dancing. During your visit, sample a wide variety of delicious and traditional Scottish foods, as well as Scottish-style ales. Take a stroll through the Avenue of the Clans and the Glen of the Clans and delve into your Scottish ancestry and heritage. The Hall of Celtic Vendors lets you peruse the fine workmanship of Scottish artisans. The Scottish Farm showcases shaggy Scotch Highland cattle, Scottish sheep, and Shetland ponies. The Celtic Kennel features Celtic dog breeds at work and play. Top off Saturday evening with the Ceilidh—a traditional Scottish party with music, sing-alongs, stories, and Scottish country dancing.

Address: Enumclaw Expo Center, 45224 284th Avenue SE
Admission: Admission for adults is $17 for one day, $25 for two days; for seniors 60 and older, as well as active or retired military and veterans get in for $12 for one day, $18 for two days. Admission for children ages 5–12 is $12 for one day, $18 for two days, and children under age 5 are free. Day of Games tickets after 4 pm are available at half price. Admission to the Ceilidh only is $5 for adults, $2 for seniors, military, and children ages 5–12. Children under age 5 get in to the Ceilidh free.
Parking: Lot parking for $5 a day.
Accessible: Yes
Pets: No
Lodging: Camping is available both on and off site. On-site tent and RV camping fees range from $25–$35 per night, depending on hookups. Other lodging: www.sshga.org/games/generalInfo/lodging.htm
Website: www.sshga.org
Attractions: Nolte State Park, Mud Mountain Dam, Mt. Rainier National Park, Anderson Rhododendron Gardens
Trivia: Enumclaw resident Swen Nater is a former NBA and ABA rebounding champion, a two-time ABA All-Star, and the 1974 ABA Rookie of the Year (while with the San Antonio Spurs). He was born in the Netherlands, and was three years old when his parents divorced. His mother remarried, then moved to America with her new husband, and Swen's younger brother, leaving Swen and his sister in an orphanage in the Netherlands because the family could not afford to bring all of the children with them. The understanding was that, once the parents had money, they would retrieve Swen and his sister. After three years in the orphanage, hope for reuniting with the family looked grim, until the television show *It Could Be You* (a predecessor to *You Bet Your Life*) heard of the situation and brought the two siblings to America to be reunited with their family on television. Nater played college basketball at UCLA (1971–1973), backing up Bill Walton. Nater helped the Bruins win two NCAA titles.
Directions: From the north, take I-405 S to the Maple Valley Hwy (SR-169) and south to Enumclaw. From I-5, take SR-18 east to Auburn and SR-164 east to Enumclaw. From Tacoma, take SR-167 and go east on SR-410 to 284th Ave SE. From the south, take SR-512 east and SR-410 east

to 284th Ave SE. From the east on I-5, take SR-18 to Maple Valley and SR-164 south to Enumclaw. Once in Enumclaw, follow signs to the Expo Center. The Center is at the southeast edge of Enumclaw, just off SR-410 at 284th Ave SE.

Oktoberfest Northwest
Puyallup, Pierce County
Early October

Oktoberfest Northwest promises lots of beer and brats, as well as plenty of activities to entertain the whole family. The food and beverage offerings focus on authentic choices one might find at the Oktoberfest in Munich: bratwurst, soft pretzels, schnitzel, crepes, and other German entrees and snacks are featured in the food booths. The Munich-inspired Festhalle Biergarten pours Trumer Pils, Warsteiner Dunkel, Warsteiner Oktoberfest, Hacker-Pschorr Weiss, Hoff Brau Oktoberfest, and Snoqualmie Harvest Moon. Wine is also available. Activities for children include pumpkin decorating, arts and crafts, face painting, and a scavenger hunt. At the Root Bier Garden, kids can also get a glass of keg-poured Crater Lake root beer and floats, treats, and snacks. The 5K Stein Dash (costumes encouraged!) is an all-ages event that takes place on Sunday. All participants receive a limited-edition stein to carry during the run, which can then be filled with the participant's choice of a free drink (alcoholic or not) at the end of the race. You can also participate in a free game of Hammerschlagen, where players attempt to hammer individual nails into the cross section of a stump one stroke at a time. The first player to level the nail with the stump, wins. Don't forget to bring your wiener (dog, that is) to the exciting and hilarious Running of the Wieners, which includes races, awards for longest weiner, a costume contest, and stupid wiener tricks (which could be won, hands down, by my ex-husband).

Address: Washington State Fairgrounds, 110 9th Avenue SW
Admission: Free on Friday from 12–3 pm. Regular price after 3 pm on Friday and all day Saturday is $10. Sunday admission is half price all day ($5). Children 12 and younger are free all weekend.
Parking: Parking is free. Enter the fairgrounds through the Blue Gate.
Accessible: Yes
Pets: Only service animals and wiener dogs signed up for the Sunday

races are allowed.
Lodging: RV camping is available for $23 in advance ($30 at the lot entrance). RV camping spots provide full hook-ups. No tent camping allowed. Call 253.841.5057.
Website: www.oktoberfestnw.com
Facebook: www.facebook.com/oktoberfestNW
Attractions: Foothills Trail, Bradley Lake Park, Meeker Mansion, Mt. Rainier National Park, Historic Walking Tours
Trivia: In 1942, after Pearl Harbor and President Roosevelt's subsequent executive order that authorized the eviction of Japanese Americans from the west coast, the Puyallup fairgrounds was selected by Army officials as a Japanese detention facility. "Camp Harmony" (officially known as Puyallup Assembly Center) served as temporary shelter for more than 7,000 Japanese Americans. The facility was short-lived, however. The Japanese were soon sent to other locations, and Camp Harmony was disassembled in early 1943. As a memorial to those incarcerated, 40 years later, in 1983, Washington State Governor John Spellman and other state representatives helped dedicate on site a 10-foot cylindrical silicon-bronze sculpture by the famed artist, George Tsutakawa.
Directions: Puyallup is located 10 miles east of Tacoma via WA-167 and River Road E.

Family Fun

Moisture Festival
Seattle, King County
Four weeks every spring, Mid-March through Mid-April

The Moisture Festival presents comedy/variété and burlesque performances in numerous venues around Seattle. Featuring more than 200 performers in more than 50 shows, the event delights audiences with the weird and wonderful talents of aerialists, acrobats, clowns, comedians, puppeteers, jugglers, dancers, and musicians. The festival features a rapid succession of acts showcasing comedy alongside awe-inspiring physical and mental dexterity, with poignant moments of strength and delicate beauty to make audiences laugh, wonder, shake their heads in disbelief, and truly appreciate how exhilarating live entertainment can be. The Moisture Festival encourages the contemporary creativity that is constantly emerging in variété, and strives to educate people about the rich history of this genre. A live show band propels each performance. Shows are approximately two hours long. All 3:00 and 7:30 pm variété shows are for all ages. The 10:30 pm variété shows and all burlesque shows are for those 18 and older. Food and beverages are available at each venue.

Address: Hales Palladium, 4301 NW Leary Way; Broadway Performance Hall, Capitol Hill, 1625 Broadway; Teatro ZinZanni, Seattle Center, 222 Mercer Street
Admission: Most events are $10–$25
Parking: Street parking at all venues, or pay-parking also available.
Accessible: Yes
Pets: No
Lodging: http://visitseattle.org/Visitors/Stay.aspx
Website: www.moisturefestival.org
Facebook: www.facebook.com/moisturefestival
Attractions: Olympic Sculpture Park, Seattle Great Wheel, Seattle Asian Art Museum, Washington Park Arboretum
Trivia: The Burlesque Hall of Fame is located on Fremont Street in (where else?) Las Vegas. It features posters, photographs, publicity stills, newspaper clippings, and playbills related to famous burlesque performers including Gypsy Rose Lee, Blaze Starr, Lili St. Cyr, Chesty Morgan,

Candy Barr, and Tempest Storm. The museum includes costume elements and props such as feather boas, fans, gloves, garter belts, gowns, shoes, pasties, g-strings, and jewelry.
Directions: Varies

Gigantic Bike Festival
Snoqualmie, King County
Mid-August

Don't tell Oregon, but in 2014, for the seventh consecutive year, Washington was named the #1 bicycle friendly state by the League of American Bicyclists. The Gigantic Bicycle Festival is the Pacific Northwest's summer celebration of bicycle culture. The festival features a diverse, multi-faceted, and regionally representative mix of live music, hand-built bicycles, visual and performance art, film, comedy, guest speakers, sculpture, interactive installation pieces, and plenty of food. Washington and Oregon are at the heart of an inspired community of bike builders, creating some of the most elegant, functional, imaginative, and well-devised bicycles on the planet. The festival showcases bike, frame, and wheel builders from the greater Cascades region, drawing from British Columbia, Washington, Oregon, Idaho, and Northern California. The Inky Spokes series (part of the festival) is co-produced with Northwest gallery spaces and artists, and features anything from fine art, bicycle poster art, bicycle inspired craft, installation and sculpture, to recycled bicycle creations. The Gigantic Bicycle Film Series features bicycle-inspired independent and short films from the Pacific Northwest. If you want to join your bicycling comrades, many festival goers arrive at the grounds via bicycle along supported Century and 77-Mile road rides leaving Seattle's Magnuson Park on early Saturday morning.

Address: Centennial Fields Park, 39903 SE Park Street
Admission: A weekend pass with a campsite is $40. A weekend pass without a campsite is $30. A one-day pass for Saturday or Sunday is $15. A Friday evening pass is $10. Admission is free for children under age 12. Parking: Parking and overnight parking is free for festival goers at Mt. Si High School and Snoqualmie Elementary. The festival grounds is a short walk from all parking lots. Locked and staffed bike parking is freely available at the festival grounds all weekend. A U-Haul makes $10 trips back to Seattle with bicycles during the day Sunday if you'd like help getting

your bike back to town.
Accessible: Yes
Lodging: Overnight field camping (with a nice view of Mt. Si) is available to registered riders and festival goers for Saturday night. The campground is a short 200-meter walk from the festival grounds, following the paved trail east from the east festival grounds gate. Campers can set up starting at 11 am Saturday, and have to be packed out by 8 pm Sunday. Camping is a $10 add-on option when you buy festival passes or register for the Saturday Century or 77 Mile rides. For more information on hotels and the local RV resort: http://business.snovalley.org/list/QL/lodging-travel-15
Website: www.giganticbicyclefestival.org
Facebook: www.facebook.com/bicyclefestival
Attractions: Snoqualmie Falls, Northwest Railway Museum, Mt. Si
Trivia: After observing Pacific Northwest bicyclists for almost two decades, I have noticed a trend: You never see two people smiling on a tandem bike ride. However, while researching bicycle facts for this book, I learned that the longest tandem bike ever built was 67-feet long and could seat 35 people. Surely at least two of them must have been smiling.
Directions: The festival is about 30 miles outside of Seattle. To get there by car, head east on I-90 and take exit 27 toward Snoqualmie. Turn left onto Winery Rd, then turn left on to Meadowbrooke Way SE. Find Parking at Mt. Si High School or Snoqualmie Elementary.

Seattle Hempfest
Seattle, King County
Third weekend in August

In 2012, Washington state voters approved Initiative 502 making simple possession of 1-oz. of cannabis legal for adults in Washington State. The law went into effect in 2013, which gave Hempfesters a reason to celebrate. The festival also received press that year because the Seattle Police Department handed out bags of Doritos to the munchie-riddled crowd that were emblazoned with informational stickers detailing the legal parameters of the new law. Hempfest strives to educate the public on the myriad of potential benefits offered by the Cannabis plant, including medicinal, industrial, agricultural, economic, and environmental. Hempfest also hopes to advance the public image of the Cannabis advocate or enthusiast through example—sort of a "we're not Spicoli" campaign. Hempfest is reportedly the world's largest event advocating cannabis law reform, in a unique "protestival" environment. The three-day event also includes six stages of music, speakers, and hundreds of food, art, craft, and political booths. Although smoking of cannabis is not legal in public areas, there are designated non-public smoking areas for adults 21 and older.

Address: Myrtle Edwards Park, 3130 Alaskan Way
Admission: Free, donations accepted
Parking: There is no parking at Myrtle Edwards Park. There are pay parking lots nearby in downtown and on Queen Anne. Street parking is free after 6 pm in most areas and all day on Sunday. Access the north entrance from Elliott Avenue by crossing the DNA pedestrian bridge at Prospect Street. Limited unmetered parking can be found along Elliott Avenue W, or on lower Queen Anne near the West Thomas Street overpass. Event organizers strongly suggest carpooling, taking the Metro Bus, riding your bike, or walking to Hempfest. Take metro bus #18 to the north entrance, or #15 to the south entrance. Downtown Seattle has several parking garages. More direction and transportation information: www.hempfest.org/festival/attendees
Accessible: Yes
Pets: No
Lodging: www.hempfest.org/festival/attendees/#sleeping_in_seattle
Website: www.hempfest.org
Facebook: www.facebook.com/seattlehempfest
Attractions: Pike's Place Market, Museum of History and Industry, Lake Union, Seattle Children's Museum, Burke Museum of Natural History and Culture
Trivia: The 15-ft. tall, 50-ft. wide Market Theater Gum Wall is in Post Alley near Pike's Place Market. Since 1993, visitors have been plastering the wall with their used chewing gum, which now measures several inches thick in some places. The tradition began when patrons of a local improvisational comedy company stuck coins to the wall using gum. The gum wall was deemed a tourist attraction in 1991, and in 2009, it was named by TripAdvisor as one of the germiest tourist attractions, second only to the Blarney Stone.
Directions: From I-5 N, take exit 165 on the left for Seneca St. Make a slight right on to 6th Ave. Travel almost a mile, then turn left on to Denny Way. Make a slight right on to Western Ave W, then turn right onto 3rd Ave W. Take the 1st left onto W Thomas St and then turn left

onto Elliott Ave W. Take a slight right to stay on Elliot Ave, then turn right on Thomas St, which ends at Myrtle Edwards Park. From I-5 S, take exit 166 for Stewart St toward Denny Way. Turn right on to Denny Way, travel 1.2 miles, and make a slight right on to Western Ave W. Turn right onto 3rd Ave W, take the first left on to W Thomas St, then turn left onto Elliott Ave W. Make a slight right to stay on Elliott Ave W, then turn right onto W Thomas St, which ends at Myrtle Edwards Park.

Tacoma Maritime Fest
Tacoma, Pierce County
August or September

Even if you're not an avid boater or sailor, the Tacoma Maritime Fest includes lots of pretty cool hands-on activities for landlubbers. The city of Tacoma contains more than 46 miles of shoreline, and the Port of Tacoma is the largest port in Washington State. As such, a majority of the city's history centers on the waterway, from shipping and industry to food and recreation. The Tacoma Maritime Fest invites you to board and explore tug boats, local work boats, military craft, tall ships, recreational craft, and historical vessels. You can also catch a free guided boat tour for a ship-side view of one of North America's largest container ports, or get tickets to take a ride on a tall ship, or on a sailboat in Walker Bay. Activities for kids (and kids at heart) include a hands-on marine science lab, a catch-and-release tank, musicians and magicians on a kids' stage, human-sized hamster balls (for humans, not for human-sized hamsters—that would be terrifying), and a pond for remote control miniature boats. You'll find plenty to keep you busy, but whatever you're doing, don't miss the Quick and Dirty boat-building competition. The competition pits 10 teams of three people against each other, who are all given the same materials and six hours to build a boat. At the end of the six hours, teams race their boats (provided they stay afloat) in the Theta Foss Waterway. This entertaining race is described by the festival as "buffoonery at its finest." Delightful!

Address: Thea Foss Park and the Foss Waterway Seaport, 705 Dock Street
Admission: Free
Parking: Parking in downtown Tacoma is only $2 for all day on Saturdays, and free all day on Sundays. If you park anywhere near 11th Street,

you can access Dock Street via the stairs or elevator on Murray Morgan Bridge. If you park further away, you can catch the free Sound Transit Tacoma Link to the Commerce Street Station (between 11th and 13th streets). You can access Dock Street via the stairs or elevator on Murray Morgan Bridge. You can also walk down to Dock Street from Pacific Ave and 7th Street. Walk against traffic on the sidewalk right outside the old City Hall—it takes you along Schuster Parkway briefly. Cross at the first crosswalk you come to onto the 4th Street Bridge, which takes you right to the entrance of Maritime Fest. Also, a free Maritime Fest Shuttle runs from the Tacoma Dome Station Parking Lot. Parking in the Dome Station is also free.

Accessible: Many attractions, but not all of the boats, are handicap accessible.
Lodging: www.traveltacoma.com/where-to-stay (Includes boat slip information.)
Website: http://maritimefest.org
Facebook: www.facebook.com/#!/maritimefest?fref=ts
Attractions: Point Defiance Park, Wright Park Arboretum, Museum of Glass, Fort Nisqually
Trivia: Cartoonist and creator of *The Far Side* cartoon series, Gary Larson was born and raised in University Place, a suburb of Tacoma. *The Far Side*, which is known for its surreal and twisted situations often used animals as his humorous subjects. In 1989, biologist Dale Clayton was the first to describe a species of chewing louse found only on owls. He named the species *Strigiphilus garylarsoni* in honor of Larson, because of the enormous contribution that his comic strips had made to the study of biology. Larson considered this "an extreme honor." Larson also has an Ecuadorian butterfly named after him—*Serratoterga larsoni*.
Directions: From I-5 S, take exit 133 for I-705 N/WA-7 S toward City Center. Keep right to continue toward I-705 N. Follow signs for I-705 N/City Center. Drive on I-705 N for 1.3 miles, then take the Schuster Pkwy exit on the left. Turn right onto S 4th St. Theya Park is on your left and the Foss Waterway Seaport is down the road on your left. From I-5 N, take exit 132 for S 38th St and keep left, following the signs for Washington 16 W/Gig Harbor/Bremerton. Keep right at the fork, and follow signs for Interstate 705 N/Washington 7 S. Keep left, and follow signs for City Center. Continue on to I-705 N. Take the Schuster Pkwy exit on the left, and follow the instructions given previously.

Renton River Days
Renton, King County
Fourth weekend in July

Renton River Days is an annual multi-day family festival and celebration of community pride that hosts a wide variety of events. Activities include tennis, soccer, and golf tournaments; a senior day barbecue picnic; the Renton Annual Art Show; an art market; outdoor films; a quilter's exposition; a pancake breakfast; a sidewalk sale; a BMW car show; live music and entertainment; and a rubber ducky derby. Make sure to sign up for the 6K, 11K, or 14K fun walks—you need the calorie-burning exercise after visiting the "Nibble of Renton," where food vendors serve up tasteful delights such as smoked salmon wraps, Mongolian Chicken, barbecue pork, humbao, Thai, teriyaki, burgers, corn dogs, barbecue ribs, chowder, fish and chips, grilled salmon caesar salads, roasted corn, gyros, polish dogs and kielbasas, elephant ears, funnel cakes, strawberry shortcake, smoothies, waffle cones, and ice cream (phew!). Plenty of children's events are also on tap, such as human-sized hamster balls, mobile gaming theater, putt-putt golf, a climbing wall, a petting zoo, photo ID cards, board games of the world, a caricaturist, hula hooping, a LEGO play zone, Dizzy's Tumble Bus, a chalk art contest, and craft-making booths.

Address: Liberty Park is located at 1101 Bronson Way North, and Cedar River Park is located at 1717 Maple Valley Hwy. Both parks are in close proximity to each other.
Admission: Most events are free.
Parking: Continuous shuttle service offers pick-up and drop-off at two locations: Renton Memorial Stadium (Logan Avenue N) and Liberty Park (Bronson Way N) near the tennis courts.
Accessible: Yes
Lodging: http://rentonchamber.chambermaster.com/list/category/hotels-motels-279
Website: www.rentonriverdays.org
Facebook: www.facebook.com/RentonRiverDays
Attractions: Renton History Museum, Jimi Hendrix memorial and grave site, Gene Coulon Memorial Beach Park, Mt. Rainier
Trivia: Legendary guitarist and Seattle native Jimi Hendrix was buried on October 1, 1970 in Greenwood Memorial Park in Renton. At the time, his grave was marked by a simple headstone with an etching of his favorite

guitar, a Fender Stratocaster. However, the etching is incorrect—it shows a right-handed guitar, but Jimi was left-handed, and would play his guitar upside down. Because of all of the foot traffic to the Hendrix gravesite, and the possible damage to other graves in the cemetery, his father created a new granite memorial in a different part of the cemetery, away from the other graves. Hendrix is buried underneath the monument, as are other Hendrix family members, and his original gravestone is embedded on a pedestal in the center.

Directions: From I-405 N (from I-5 and the Southcenter area) and from Hwy 167, take exit #4 Bronson Way (the Maple Valley Hwy exit, follow the Bronson Way off ramp). At the end of the ramp turn right, stay in the middle lane going under the freeway. Proceed straight approximately two blocks and Liberty Park is on your left. From I-405 S (from I-90 and Bellevue), take exit #4, Maple Valley/Enumclaw exit and follow the off-ramp merging with Sunset Blvd to the second light. Take a right onto Bronson Way and Liberty Park is on your left.

Seafair
Seattle, King County
June through August

Seafair is not one particular event, but rather a collection of many neighborhood events (some of which have been covered in this book) as well as several major city-wide celebrations. The event's website describes it as "a month-long, region-wide barbecue that brings an entire community together in celebration." Seafair, itself, is widely known because of a couple of signature events: the Torchlight Parade (and Torchlight Run) and hydroplane racing. The evening Torchlight Parade includes giant helium balloons, drill teams representing local communities, equestrian units, clowns, pirates, and bands. Other events covered under the Seafair umbrella include a pirate landing (at which a motley group of scallywags, heralded by cannon booms, storm Alki beach), a July 4th celebration, a milk carton derby (where 100 boats of all shapes and design, made entirely out of milk cartons, take to Green Lake), a stand-up paddleboard competition, triathlons (one for kids and one for adults), a marathon and half marathon, fleet week, a vintage hydroplane exhibition, and an air show put on by the Blue Angels.

Address: Various
Admission: Many events are free. July 4th celebration costs $25. Miss Seafair coronation costs $25. Seats at the Torchlight Parade cost $20–$50. For other ticket prices, see the Seafair website: http://seafair.ticketmob.com/Upcoming-Events
Parking: Mostly paid parking.
Accessible: Most events are accessible
Lodging: http://visitseattle.org/Visitors/Stay.aspx
Website: www.seafair.com
Facebook: www.facebook.com/Seafair
Attractions: Chihuly Garden and Glass, Space Needle, Pacific Science Center, Seattle Art Museum, Kerry Park
Trivia: Seattle was named after a local Duwamish tribal leader, Si'ahl, who proved to be a friend to white settlers in the mid-1800s. Around 1950, Si'ahl was baptized in the Roman Catholic Church and given the name Noah. He died in 1866, and was probably close to 80 years old.
Directions: Various locales in the city

Snoqualmie Railroad Days
Snoqualmie, King County
Mid-August

On July 4, 1889 the inaugural run of a train carrying passengers in Washington was a day trip from the foot of Western Avenue in Seattle to Snoqualmie Falls. More than 100 years later, the Northwest Railway Museum continues the tradition of train excursions to Snoqualmie Falls. Railroad Days is the annual community festival celebrating Snoqualmie's spirit and origin as a railroad and logging town, and the home of the Snoqualmie Indian Tribe. The event is held in Historic Snoqualmie, in and around the Northwest Railway Museum, which incorporates the Snoqualmie Depot, a functioning, restored 1890 Victorian train depot listed on the National Register of Historic Places. Railroad Days features traditional favorites such as train rides, a Grand Parade, fun runs, music and entertainment on three stages, the Legends Car Club Show, and plenty of food and craft vendors. Visitors also enjoy Art in the Park, featuring artists in action, the Plein Air Paintout, Kids' Paint Junction, wine and beer gardens, timbersports, living history displays, and free wagon rides. You also get a chance to see historic equipment demonstrations, including motor cars, a tie spacer, an automatic spiker, a ballast regulator, and even special cranes that travel on both the railroad and the road. The 2014 event provided a special chance to ride a 1909-built Porter locomotive. The museum is currently working on restoration of more steam locomotives, some of which should be operational in 2015, so expect more chances to ride one of these historical trains.

Address: Snoqualmie Depot, 38625 SE King Street
Admission: Most events are free. Train excursions cost around $10–$20.
Parking: Free street and parking lot parking. There is diagonal parking on Railroad Avenue and parallel parking on side streets. There is an additional railroad parking lot off of Fir Street, one block north of the Depot.
Accessible: Yes
Lodging: http://business.snovalley.org/list/QL/lodging-travel-15
Website: www.railroaddays.com
Facebook: www.facebook.com/SnoqualmieRailroadDays
Attractions: Snoqualmie Falls, Snoqualmie Historic Log, Meadowbrook Farm Interpretive Center, Snoqualmie Casino, Mt. Si
Trivia: The Salish Lodge and Spa in Snoqualmie was used as the setting for the television show *Twin Peaks*. Shots of nearby Snoqualmie Falls were also used in the show's opening credits.
Directions: Traveling on I-90 E, take exit 27 for Snoqualmie and North Bend (there is only one ramp). Turn left at the foot of the exit ramp and pass under the freeway. You are now on North Bend Way. Proceed for approximately 3/4 of a mile. (Stay in the right-hand lane to go through the roundabout at the Snoqualmie Casino.) Turn left on Meadowbrook Way and proceed for approximately 1/2 mile, crossing over the railroad tracks. Turn left on Railroad Ave (SR-202). (This intersection is signalized and features a local landmark called the Milkbarn.) Proceed approximately 1/2 mile into downtown Snoqualmie (follow the Museum's railroad tracks). The Snoqualmie Depot is on the left at the intersection of King St. Traveling on I-90 W, take exit 31 "North Bend" (there is only one ramp) and turn right at the stop. You are now on SR-202 (Bendigo St) and in North Bend. Follow SR-202 for approximately 6 miles to Snoqualmie. The Snoqualmie Depot is on the left at the intersection of King St.

Food & Agricultural Festivals

Rhubarb Days
Sumner, Pierce County
Mid-July

As the self-professed "rhubarb pie capital of the world," the town of Sumner takes a couple of weeks every summer to celebrate the tart "fruitegetable" that was an agricultural staple of the region in the early 1900s. In fact, a good portion of rhubarb in the U.S. is still grown around Sumner in the Puyallup Valley. The festival celebrates all things rhubarb. It provides a pie walk, antique tractors and a car show, a scavenger hunt, a rhubarb dish bake off, food and craft vendors, game and contest booths, a photo contest, Doug McDonald's Farmers Market, a petting zoo, a children's art center, lots of live music, a beer garden, and a strawberry-rhubarb pie eating contest, at which you can pretend you are eating a whole pie for the sake of competition.

Address: Heritage Park, Cherry and Kincaid Avenue
Admission: Free
Parking: Street and parking lot parking
Accessible: Yes
Lodging: www.puyallupsumnerchamber.com/communities/lodging
Website: http://sumnerdowntown.com/rhubarb_days.html
Attractions: Meeker Mansion, Mt. Rainier National Park, Sumner Historic Walking Tour, Tacoma Rainiers baseball
Trivia: Rhubarb is technically a vegetable, and was considered so in America until the 1940s. In 1947, a New York court reclassified rhubarb as a fruit, because that's how it was used. Science be damned!
Directions: Sumner is located 12 miles east of Tacoma via I-5 N and Valley Ave E.

Daffodil Festival
Puyallup and other towns in Pierce County
Early April

The Daffodil Festival promotes the tradition and history of Pierce County through a royalty program, parades, and other community events. Twenty-four senior ladies from participating high schools in the county make up the royalty court for the year. The court princesses spend thousands of hours throughout the year promoting education, community pride, and volunteerism throughout the county. The yearly Queen's Coronation at the festival determines who will reign over the many festival activities that occur in the upcoming year. The Princess Tea is a chance for little princesses (as well as moms and grandmas) to meet and mingle with the royal court of all 24 Daffodil Princesses. A themed party on one of the festival evenings includes food, skills contests, and music for kids and their families. The crowning glory of the Daffodil Festival is the Grand Floral Parade, which spends seven hours traveling through four cities (Tacoma, Puyallup, Sumner, and Orting). The parade consists of more than 150 entries, including floats, bands, and mounted units. The floats are decorated with thousands of freshly cut daffodils. Other festival events include a 5K fun run, a Most Magnificent Mutt show, a junior daffodil parade, and a marine parade, which includes Daffodil royalty, and dozens of yachts and marine vessels.

Address: Various locations
Admission: Prices vary for individual events. Coronation tickets cost $10 for adults, $5 for students and seniors 65 and older. Tickets cost $20 for the Princess Promenade where each member of the royal court is introduced and crowned as a Daffodil Princess.
Parking: Varies by location
Accessible: Yes
Lodging: www.puyallupsumnerchamber.com/communities/lodging
Website: http://thedaffodilfestival.org
Facebook: www.facebook.com/daffodilfestival
Attractions: Northwest Trek, Foothills Trail, Karshner Museum, Emerald Queen Casino, Muckleshoot Casino
Trivia: The daffodil is the official flower of March, the traditional flower for a 10th wedding anniversary, and the national flower of Wales.
Directions: Puyallup is situated at the junction of two major transportation routes—SR 167 and Hwy 512—with easy access to I-5.

Issaquah Salmon Days Festival
Issaquah, King County
First full weekend in October

The Issaquah Salmon Days Festival, centered at the city's historical fish hatchery, celebrates the miraculous annual return of the salmon to spawn. The festival has been "celebrating shagging salmon" since 1970. During the event, the hatchery provides live streaming hot salmon-spawning action, fish ladder viewing, exhibits, displays, eco- and fish-friendly info, docents, special events, and plenty of free activities. Outside of the hatchery, Veteran's Memorial Park is populated with more than 500 art and craft vendors, 60 food booths, and multiple entertainment stages. The Kiwanis club barbecues almost two tons of salmon each year for the 180,000 festival attendees. The event also features the Dock Dogs competition, a carnival, live music and entertainment, and the Grand Parade.

Address: Veteran's Memorial Park, at Front Street N and W Sunset Way
Admission: Admission is free. Individual carnival tickets may be purchased for $1 each with most rides costing between 3–4 tickets. An unlimited-ride wristband costs $25.
Parking: You can park in various paid parking lots around downtown Issaquah. Three park and ride locations are also available: Issaquah Transit Center (exit 15 S, located at SR-900 and Newport Way), festival parking lot (exit 15 N located at 5150 220th Avenue SE), and Issaquah Highlands (exit 18 N, located at 1755 Highlands Drive NE). Shuttle service is provided to these three lots. Shuttles run every 15 minutes from 9 am until 7 pm and cost $3 round trip per person (the cash-only fee is charged on the return trip). Kids age 8 and under travel free on the shuttle.
Accessible: Yes
Lodging: Several local hotels provide specials for the festival. Additional information at the festival website: www.salmondays.org/spend-the-night.html
Website: www.salmondays.org
Facebook: www.facebook.com/SalmonDays?fref=ts
Attractions: Cougar Mountain Zoo, Gilman Village, Triple XXX root beer restaurant, Lake Sammamish State Park, Squak Mountain
Trivia: Ten miles outside the town of Issaquah is an opportunity to try a unique overnight experience. Treehouse Point, on the banks of the Raging River is a bed and breakfast, where you stay in treehouses. The

property currently houses seven treehouses that were all built by property owner, and experienced treehouse builder, Pete Nelson. In case you get bit by the treehouse bug during your stay, and decide you just can't live without one on your property, Nelson also runs Nelson Treehouse and Supply, which offers supplies, plans, consulting and site visits. The website www.nelsontreehouseandsupply.com shows a portfolio of the cool treehouses Nelson has helped design. Tours of Treehouse Point are available by appointment only.

Directions: Issaquah is located 20 miles east of Seattle via I-90 E.

Ballard Seafood Fest
Seattle, King County
July

Ballard was founded as a Scandinavian fishing community, and if there's one thing fisherman know how to do, it's cook seafood. So, in 1974, the community held its first Ballard Seafood Fest to celebrate these Nordic roots with neighbors and visitors. These days, the festival invites you to eat, play, and plunder at the annual event, which includes plenty of yummy food and desserts, live music, a Festi-Bowl skateboard competition and exhibition, lots of kids' activities including a family stage with special presentations for kids, and a salmon dinner that still uses the same salmon recipe that originated with the event in 1974. The longest-running event, and one of the biggest crowd-pleasers at the festival, is the Lutefisk eating contest. Lutefisk, if you haven't had the pleasure, is dried cod, soaked in a lye solution for several days, then often cooked before being served to those who have massive control over their gag reflexes. It has the consistency of Jell-O and is very pungent. So crowds generally aren't rooting for those who can eat the most lutefisk, they are rooting for those who can eat lutefisk. In 2013, the festival introduced a new event, BeerFest, which proved to be a phenomenal success because, well . . . beer. As an added bonus, you can get your pillage on by purchasing a Viking helmet at the event.

Address: Downtown Ballard
Admission: Free entry. Food and drink available for a fee. BeerFest charges $5 for a 14-oz. beer and $7 for wine. The salmon barbecue costs $12.
Parking: Street and parking lot
Accessible: Yes

Lodging: For information about lodging in the Ballard neighborhood, see: www.visitseattle.org/visitors/discover/neighborhoods/ballard.aspx. Other Seattle: http://visitseattle.org/Visitors/Stay.aspx
Website: www.seafoodfest.org
Facebook: www.facebook.com/pages/Ballard-SeafoodFest/134234436639757?ref=hl
Attractions: Nordic Heritage Museum, Golden Gardens Park, Hiram M. Chittenden Locks, Ballard Farmers Market
Trivia: Once its own thriving, self-governing city, Ballard ran into a problem in the early 1900s when it was unable to supply its citizens with an adequate water supply. Ballard citizens voted, begrudgingly, to approve annexation by the city of Seattle in 1906. Not ones to give up a fight, to this day, many residents of the neighborhood would like to see Ballard secede from Seattle. So, don't be surprised if you see a "Free Ballard" bumper sticker in your travels around Seattle.
Directions: From 1-5, take the 45th St exit. Go west on 45th and continue to follow it as it changes to 46th, and then to Market St. Follow Market to 20th and you're there.

Taste Washington
Seattle, King County
Last weekend in March

Featuring 200 Washington wineries and 60 local restaurants, Taste Washington bills itself as the nation's largest single-region wine and food event. Offering an opportunity to treat your palate and experience new wine and savory food, the annual weekend in March is packed with activities. Top national wine personalities and sommeliers lead wine seminars on both Saturday and Sunday covering topics that showcase various aspects of Washington wine, and include wine and food pairing demonstrations by renowned chefs. The Grand Tasting on Saturday and Sunday afternoon and evening bring all of the elements together. Sample wines from the hundreds of wineries and enjoy food from top Pacific Northwest Restaurants. Top local and national chefs also provide educational cooking demonstrations on the show floor in a state-of-the-art kitchen.

Address: CenturyLink Field Event Center, 800 Occidental Avenue S
Admission: Seminar tickets range from $45–$85. Grand Tasting tickets

range from $80 for a one-day pass to $125 for a two-day pass. VIP tickets cost $145 for one day and $185 for two days. VIP tickets allow you one-hour early entrance to the event, access to the barrel room and the exclusive VIP lounge, and a VIP swag bag.

Parking: CenturyLink Field Event Center has two adjacent parking lots—CenturyLink Field Event Center Garage and the North Lot (on the north end of the football field). Parking is $12 per day.

Accessible: Yes

Pets: No

Lodging: Taste Washington has several participating hotel partners, including Best Western Plus Executive Inn (bestwesternwashington.com), Best Western Loyal Inn (bestwesternwashington.com), Executive Hotel Pacific (executivehotels.net), Fairmont Olympic Hotel (fairmont.com/Seattle), Grand Hyatt Seattle (grandseattle.hyatt.com), Hotel Vintage (hotelvintagepark.com), Hyatt at Olive 8 (olive8.hyatt.com), Inn at the WAC (wac.net), Mayflower Park Hotel (mayflowerpark.com), Quality Inn & Suites Seattle Center (qualityinn.com), Renaissance Seattle Hotel (marriott.com), and Springhill Suites Downtown/South Lake Union (marriott.com). You can search for hotel packages directly on the event's website.

Website: http://tastewashington.org

Facebook: www.facebook.com/TasteWashington

Attractions: Space Needle, Woodland Park Zoo, Olympic Sculpture Park, Seattle Art Museum, Carl S. English, Jr. Botanical Gardens

Trivia: With 800+ wineries, Washington state is the second largest premium wine producer in the U.S. (California is the largest).

Directions: I-5 and the Alaskan Way Viaduct both have exits near CenturyLink Field and CenturyLink Field Event Center. I-5 has exits at James St, 4th Ave, and Airport Way that all place visitors in close proximity to the facility. CenturyLink Field and CenturyLink Field Event Center can also be reached by both I-90 and SR-520 from the east. From I-90, follow the signs to 4th Ave S and turn right. Turn right on to South Royal Brougham Way. From SR-520, take I-5 S, then take either the James St, 4th Ave, or Airport Way exits to place you in proximity to the facility.

Music

Laid Back Attack
Seattle metro area, King County
July

The Laid Back Attack is the brainchild of the local chapter of the Parrotheads in Paradise network of Jimmie Buffett devotees. The goal of the Parrotheads is to engage in activities that are charitable, educational, and contribute to the betterment of the community. And if they can do it while sharing their love of Buffett-esque "trop rock" (tropical rock), even better. The festival assembles the biggest names in tropical rock, including Don Middlebrook and the Pearl Divers, Jim Morris, Thom Sheppard, and "Mexico Mark" Mulligan for a four-day "party with a purpose." In 2014, 100% of the event proceeds (which totaled $27,000) went to USO Northwest. Who wouldn't want to take the opportunity to don their tiki attire and take a relaxing trip to Margaritaville?

Address: Different location in Puget Sound every year
Admission: $80 for the weekend
Parking: Varies depending on venue
Accessible: Yes
Pets: No
Lodging: http://visitseattle.org/Visitors/Stay.aspx
Website: http://laidbackattack.com
Facebook: www.facebook.com/LaidBackAttack
Attractions: Discovery Park, Seattle Aquarium, Center for Wooden Boats, Klondike Gold Rush National Historic Park, Museum of Flight
Trivia: Himank is a project that is responsible for the construction and maintenance of roads in the inhospitable Himalayas in northernmost India. Oddly enough, the project places humorous road signs along the routes that they maintain, presumably to divert drivers' attentions from the fact that they could careen to their deaths at any moment. One of these signs displays Jimmy Buffet's quote "Without geography, you're nowhere." So, next time you're in the Himalayas, you should go check it out.
Directions: Varies

Bumbershoot

Seattle, King County
September/Labor Day weekend

Bumbershoot is a massive international art and music event that takes place every Labor Day weekend. One of the largest such events of its type in North America, Bumbershoot stretches across the 74-acre Seattle Center beneath the city's iconic Space Needle. The three-day festival, which includes indoor theaters as well as outdoor stages, offers a diverse array of arts including live music, comedy, words and ideas, theatre, film, visual arts, children's programming, and the Indie Market featuring urban crafts. Past performers have included Emmylou Harris, Chuck Berry, Etta James, The Eurythmics, James Brown, Spinal Tap, Martin Mull, and Tina Turner, as well as internationally known Pacific Northwest-grown bands such as Modest Mouse and Death Cab for Cutie. Other entertainments have included the Grand Kabuki Theater of Japan, a film festival, poetry slams, break dancing, circus performers, contortion and aerial acts, and street theater, as well as many other oddities. Plenty of food vendors are on hand, as well as several beer gardens.

Address: Seattle Center, 305 Harrison Street
Admission: Ticket prices range from $62 for a single-day ticket, to $575 for a three-day platinum pass. Children age 10 and younger get in free.
Parking: Seattle Center is surrounded by lots of public and private parking spots. However, because of the popularity of the festival, parking can sometimes be difficult to find, especially in the afternoon. Consider using public transportation, coming on foot or bike, or carpooling. Some of the pay lots are cash only and some are unattended, so come prepared with cash in all bill sizes. If you want to skateboard to the event, a skateboard valet checks your board for $5.
Accessible: Yes
Pets: No
Lodging: http://visitseattle.org/Visitors/Stay.aspx
Website: http://bumbershoot.org
Facebook: www.facebook.com/BumbershootFestival
Attractions: Seattle Underground Tour, Seattle Aquarium, Space Needle, Seattle Mariners, Seattle Seahawks, Seward Park
Trivia: The first Bumbershoot was called Festival '71. The two-day event starred Sheb Wooley, best known for the novelty hit "The Purple People Eater." It also included a logging show, indoor motorcycle races in the

Coliseum (now Key Arena), horseback rides for kids and 'the world's first electronic music instrument jam.' The Miss Hot Pants Contest was one of the biggest draws. Local rock bands and dance troupes were featured. The festival was a hit, attracting the largest crowds to Seattle Center since the 1962–63 World's Fair.

Directions: To get to Seattle Center from I-5 N, take exit 165 on the left for Seneca St. Take a slight right onto 6th Ave, travel for nearly a mile, then turn left on to Denny Way. Seattle Center is on your right. To reach Seattle Center from I-5 S, take exit 167 for Mercer St toward Seattle Center. Continue on Mercer St for approximately 0.7 miles. Seattle Center is on your left.

Decibel Festival
Seattle, King County
Late September

Founded in 2003, Decibel Festival has become a unique platform that presents leading-edge multimedia art from around the globe. The five-day event includes more than 150 artists across 12 venues, and it focuses on live performance, interactive multimedia art, state-of-the-art sound, and technology-based education. In addition to performances, the event also hosts the three-day Decibel Conference, with artist talks, panel discussions, and sessions discussing music and gaming. The conference also includes an exhibition of cutting-edge digital tools, along with workshops.

Address: Various venues
Admission: Individual performances tickets generally range from $10–$25. All-access ticket prices are $160 for tier-one tickets, $185 for tier-two tickets, and $225 for three-tier tickets.
Parking: Varies by venue
Accessible: Yes
Pets: No
Lodging: The W Seattle (206.264.6000) has been the official host hotel for the festival. Other lodging: http://visitseattle.org/Visitors/Stay.aspx
Website: http://dbfestival.com
Facebook: www.facebook.com/DecibelFestival
Attractions: Ye Olde Curiosity Shop, Walker Rock Garden, Alki Beach, Seattle Aquarium

Trivia: Viretta Park, in the Denny-Blaine neighborhood of Seattle, is located just south of the home where Nirvana front man Kurt Cobain was found dead from a self-inflicted gunshot wound in 1994. Since his death, Nirvana fans have gathered in the park every year on the date of his death (April 5) and on his birthday (Feb. 20) to pay tribute. In a makeshift memorial for Cobain, fans from all over the world have written graffiti messages to the musician on the park's wooden benches.
Directions: Varies

Seattle Chamber Music Festival
Seattle, King County
January and July

Each year, Seattle Chamber Music Society (SCMS) presents a winter festival in January and a summer festival in July, which aim to foster the appreciation of chamber music by bringing audiences of all ages in close contact with world-class musicians and their music through informal, accessible, and enjoyable formats. Concerts typically last around two hours, including one 15-minute intermission. Bar service is available before the concert and during intermission, along with dessert service provided by Wolfgang Puck. One hour prior to each concert, a 30-minute recital features one or two artists from the main concert playing a piece of their choice. Recitals are free to attend. After the recital is over, ushers clear the hall and begin seating for the main concert.

Address: Benaroya Hall, 200 University Street
Admission: Single ticket seats are $48 for each concert. Tickets for patrons 30 years and younger, or students with ID cost only $16. Senior Rush Tickets are $30 for patrons (65 years and older) available only at the box office starting 90 minutes before the concert. A full-series ticket costs $270 and gets you in to all concerts. A four-concert pass costs $180, and a three-concert pass costs $135. All of the multi-ticket packages provide guaranteed priority seating.
Parking: Parking is available in the Benaroya Hall parking garage. The entrance is located on 2nd Avenue, just south of Union Street.
Accessible: Yes
Pets: No
Lodging: http://visitseattle.org/Visitors/Stay.aspx
Website: www.seattlechambermusic.org/concerts/concert-

series/?series_id=37&display=performances
Facebook: www.facebook.com/pages/Seattle-Chamber-Music-Society/14800801126
Attractions: EMP (Experience Music Project) Museum, Seattle Great Wheel, Seattle Art Museum, Space Needle
Trivia: The Space Needle was built for the 1962 World's Fair. When it was constructed, at 605 feet, it was the tallest building west of the Mississippi River. The Committee Hoping for Extra-Terrestrial Encounters to Save the Earth (CHEESE) claims that they have proof from the 1962 World's Fair that the Space Needle was constructed to send transmissions to advanced beings in other solar systems.
Directions: From I-5 S, take the Union St exit (#165B). Continue onto Union St and proceed approximately five blocks to 2nd Ave. Turn left onto 2nd Ave. The Benaroya Hall parking garage is on your immediate left. The garage entrance is on 2nd Ave, just south of Union St. From I-5 N, exit left onto Seneca St (exit #165). Proceed two blocks and turn right onto 4th Ave. Continue two blocks. Turn left onto Union St. Continue two blocks. Turn left onto 2nd Ave. The Benaroya Hall parking garage is on your immediate left. The garage entrance is on 2nd Ave, just south of Union St.

Earshot Jazz Festival
Seattle, King County
October–November

Earshot Jazz Festival brings jazz greats from around the world to creatively collaborate with area audiences and artists, inviting everyone to engage more deeply with today's jazz music. The festival also celebrates Seattle's place in the world of jazz with main stage concerts by award-winning local student ensembles and a strong representation by renowned resident artists. The event includes more than 50 concerts and events in venues all around Seattle.

Address: Various locations
Admission: General Admission tickets range from $5–$50 for individual events. Earshot members and seniors receive a $2 discount on most shows. Students and veterans generally get in for half price. An all-access pass costs $350 for general admission, $300 for Earshot members, and gets you preferred seating at most events.

Parking: Varies with location
Accessible: Yes
Pets: No
Lodging: http://visitseattle.org/Visitors/Stay.aspx
Website: www.earshot.org/Festival/festival.html
Facebook: www.facebook.com/#!/EarshotJazz
Attractions: Seattle Center, Space Needle, Pike Place Market, Museum of Flight, EMP (Experience Music Project) Museum
Trivia: Seattle band Soundgarden named itself after a wind-channeling pipe sculpture, "A Sound Garden," located on National Oceanic and Atmospheric Administration property next to Magnuson Park in Seattle.
Directions: Varies

Seattle/South Puget Sound County Fairs

King
Enumclaw
www.thekingcountyfair.com

Pierce
Graham
www.piercecountyfair.com

Washington State Fair
Puyallup
www.thefair.com

Northwest Region

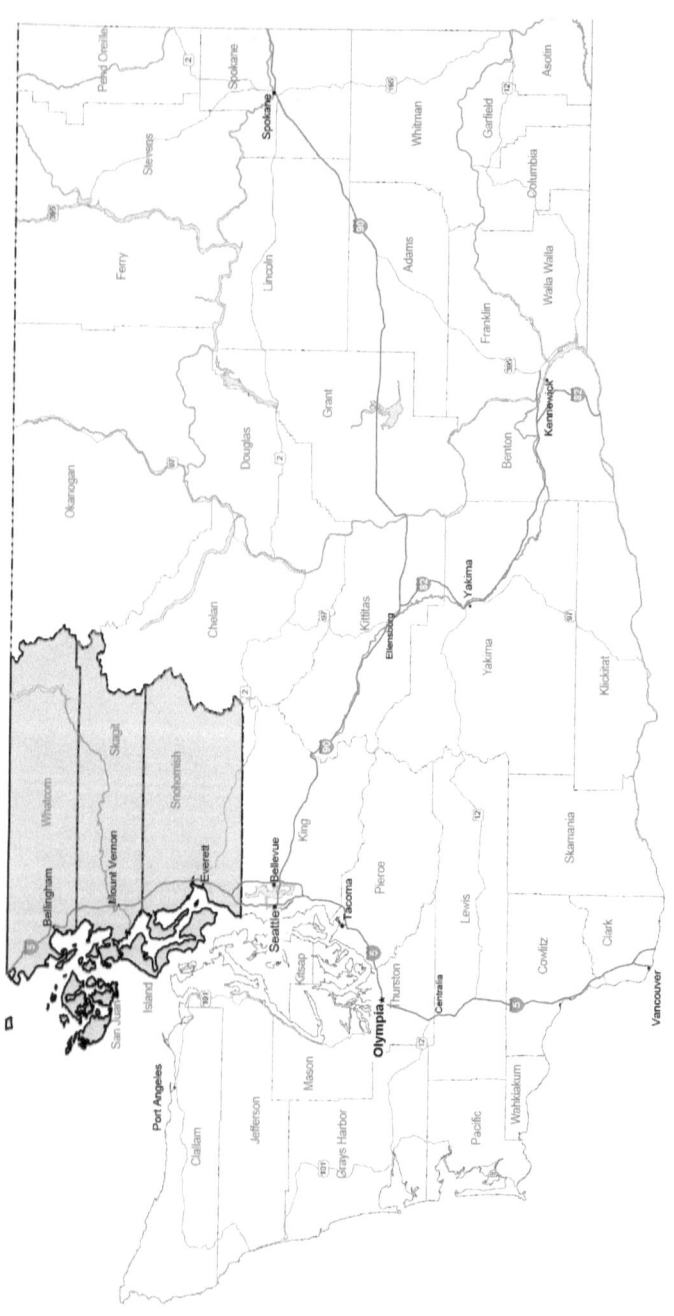

Northwest Washington

Northwest Washington is an outdoor-enthusiast's paradise. The North Cascades Region, also known as the "American Alps," is home to some of the state's most dramatic scenery. Its glaciated volcanoes and plentiful mountain views make it a premium hiking and mountaineering area. The Skagit River winds its way through the peaks and valleys, providing ideal habitat for salmon, and it hosts one of the largest wintering bald eagle populations in the continental United States. The Skagit River Salmon Festival commemorates the return of the spawning salmon, and their importance to the region. The yearly "must-see" event in the area is the Skagit Valley Tulip Festival each May, where visitors are delighted by the blooming of the millions of colorful tulips and daffodils that thrive in this climate.

The San Juan Islands operate at a mellower pace, and offer lots of artsy towns and funky boutiques to peruse. Friday Harbor hosts an annual film festival, as well as the San Juan Island Summer Arts Fair, and the town of Langley (on Whidbey Island) annually hosts its celebrated Island Shakespeare Festival. The San Juans comprise 172 named islands and reefs, and San Juan County has more shoreline than any other county in the U.S., so the area, understandably, attracts adventurers who enjoy boating, sailing, kayaking, and whale watching.

The local area delicacies are lauded at events such as Bellingham's Dirty Dan Seafood Festival and Coupeville's Penn Cove Musselfest. The towns of Lynden and Marysville invite visitors to enjoy the delicious bounty of this large berry-producing region at the Northwest Raspberry Festival and the Marysville Strawberry Festival. Everett's Craft Beer Festival and the Snohomish on the Rocks Distillery Festival give you a taste of the area's best spirits and brews.

Music festivals abound in Northwest Washington. The variety of genres offered at multiple venues such as Bellingham Festival of Music, Birch Bay Music Festival, Darrington Bluegrass Festival, and Langley's Django-Fest NW, ensure that everyone will find something they will enjoy. And events like Bellingham's Steampunk Festival, Sedro Woolley's Loggerodeo, and Everett's Snohomish Pumpkin Hurl and Medieval Faire are just plain fun.

Art Events

Island Shakespeare Festival
Langley, Whidbey Island, Island County
Thursdays, Fridays, and Saturdays throughout August and the beginning of September.

The organizers of the Island Shakespeare Festival believe strongly that everyone should be able to see quality theatre for free. The goal of the festival is to make great classics, particularly Shakespeare, accessible, understandable, physical, alive, visceral, and real through passionate and quality performances. That is what has been attracting thousands of guests from all over the world to Whidbey Island since 2009. All of the performances take place under a 2400-square-foot custom-built vintage circus tent affectionately dubbed "Henry." After the performances, the venues are often open to musicians. Guests are welcome to bring their own food and beverages. Langley has a number of great places to buy these items before the show.

Address: Whidbey Island, behind Langley Middle School, 723 Camano Avenue
Admission: Free
Parking: Abundant parking can be found close to the venue and it's just a short walk from downtown Langley. The festival site is on the bus line. Buses are free and run daily (except Sunday).
Accessible: Yes
Pets: No
Lodging: www.langleywa.org/visitors/lodging.php
Website: www.islandshakespearefest.org
Facebook: www.facebook.com/pages/Island-Shakespeare-Fest/143121522369250
Attractions: Whale watching, kayaking in Puget Sound, Deception Pass State Park, Fort Casey State Park, Fort Ebey, Meerkerk Rhododendron Gardens, Island County Historical Society Museum, Blue Fox Drive-in Movie Theater
Trivia: Since the mid-1980s, every February Langley hosts a Mystery Weekend, in which town residents and visitors are invited to help solve a fictional murder. The coroner's report is delivered on early Saturday afternoon, and for the next 24 hours, amateur gumshoes have the opportunity to hunt down clues provided by local businesses, interview

costumed characters, and use their sleuthing skills to determine who committed the dastardly deed. The mystery is solved and the culprit arrested on late Sunday afternoon at the middle school. This is reportedly the world's longest running annual mystery event.

Directions: From Seattle, take the 15-min ferry voyage from Mukilteo to Clinton on Whidbey Island. From there, it's a 15-min drive north on WA-525 to Langley. From Oak Harbor, take WA-20 south, which turns into WA-525. Turn left at Bayview Rd. From Port Townsend, take the Port Townsend/Keystone Ferry to Whidbey Island. Turn right out of the ferry terminal onto WA-20 (Engle Rd), then turn right onto WA-525. Turn left at Bayview Rd.

San Juan Island Summer Arts Fair
Friday Harbor, San Juan Island, San Juan County
Third weekend in July

Festival organizers call the San Juan Island Summer Arts Fair the largest and longest-running art show on the San Juan Islands. This annual tradition takes place on the lawn of the historic San Juan County courthouse. Organizers block off Court Street with rows of white tents where around 50 regional artists show and sell their works, which include pottery, textiles, jewelry, paintings, photography, sculpture, soaps, and furniture. Each artist is on site at their booth and ready to answer your questions. Buy a lunch from one of the food vendors and have a picnic on the lawn while enjoying local live music. The Chalk it Up event allows kids of all ages to decorate the courthouse sidewalks. The event also has a children's craft tent.

Address: Court Street, Friday Harbor
Admission: Free
Parking: Street and parking lot parking
Accessible: Yes
Lodging: www.visitsanjuans.com/accommodations
Website: www.sanjuanisland.org/summer-arts-fair.htm
Attractions: Sailing and kayaking in Puget Sound, whale watching, Whale Museum, Spring Street Landing Aquarium, art galleries, zip line tour
Trivia: Friday Harbor is home to the "World's Skinniest Latte Shop," also known as Tight Squeeze, located at 127 Spring Street. It was built in a narrow alley between two buildings, and is only slightly wider than the

entryway door. Because of its tiny size, you have to get your coffee to go.
Directions: From I-5 N in Seattle, take exit 230 to Burlington/Anacortes (or exits 221 or 226 through scenic Skagit Valley). At the first light, turn left toward Anacortes onto Hwy 20 west. Follow Hwy 20 west to Anacortes, merge right into the traffic circle, and take another right onto Commercial Ave. Take a left at 12th St, where signs point you to the San Juan Islands ferry, and follow for about 2 miles to the terminal. Allow a 1.5–2 hours to enjoy the drive and the scenery from Seattle or Vancouver B.C. to the Anacortes ferry terminal.

Friday Harbor Film Festival
Friday Harbor, San Juan Island, San Juan County
October/November

The annual Friday Harbor Film Festival is a documentary-only film festival whose goal is to entertain, enlighten, and inspire. The three-day festival includes films that cover people, cultures, and environments that make up the area known as the Pacific Rim. The event includes 25+ films, and takes place in four venues around Friday Harbor. In addition to film screenings, festival events also include presentation of a local hero/lifetime achievement award, a Young Filmmakers Project that showcases films submitted by student filmmakers, a filmmakers forum where visiting filmmakers discuss the documentary production process, a filmmakers soiree that is an exclusive party for filmmakers and holders of the all-access pass, and awards presentations for best short film, best full-length feature by theme (explorers and adventurers, local heroes, things to consider, and tales from the heart), as well as the audience choice award.

Address: Various locations in downtown Friday Harbor
Admission: The price to view one film is $15 for adults, $12 for students. Four films cost $50 for adults, $40 for students. Eight films cost $88 for adults, $72 for students. Twelve films cost $120 for adults, $96 for students. An all-access pass costs $150 for both adults and students.
Parking: Street and parking lot parking
Accessible: Yes
Pets: No
Lodging: www.fhff.org/friday-harbor-lodging
Website: www.fhff.org

Facebook: www.facebook.com/pages/Friday-Harbor-FILM-Festival/341386545960297
Attractions: Kayak tours, whale watching tours, San Juan Islands Museum of Art, farmers market, bicycle rentals
Trivia: According to the Internet Movie Database, the top five highest-U.S.-grossing documentaries are *Farenheit 9/11* (2004, $119 million), *Jackass 3D* (2010, $117 million), *Space Station 3D* (2002, $91.2 million), *March of the Penguins* (2005, $77.4 million), and *Everest* (1998, $76.4 million). We won't continue because #6 on the list is *Justin Bieber: Never Say Never*, and it is already depressing enough that a *Jackass* movie appears on this list.
Directions: From I-5 N in Seattle, take exit 230 to Burlington/Anacortes (or exits 221 or 226 through scenic Skagit Valley). At the first light, turn left toward Anacortes onto Hwy 20 west. Follow Hwy 20 west to Anacortes, merge right into the traffic circle, and take another right onto Commercial Ave. Take a left at 12th St, where signs point you to the San Juan Islands ferry, and follow for about 2 miles to the terminal. Allow a 1.5–2 hours to enjoy the drive and the scenery from Seattle or Vancouver B.C. to the Anacortes ferry terminal.

Anacortes Arts Festival
Anacortes, Skagit County
First full weekend in August

The organizers of the Anacortes Arts Festival are committed to producing a first-class festival that features art in all its forms. Begun in 1962, the festival attracts visitors and artists from throughout the region and beyond. The festival features 250 diverse booth artisans who transform six blocks of historic downtown into an open-air showcase. The event also includes a youth art exhibition, artist demonstrations, and hands-on youth activities. You can purchase regional and ethnic foods at the Island Eatery food court and throughout the festival. Wine, beer, and spirits are available at three locations. Entertainment takes place on three stages and includes rock, country, jazz, and world music, as well as performance art. An Art Dash fun run takes place on Saturday morning.

Address: Commercial Avenue, from 4th St to 10th Street, downtown Anacortes
Admission: Free, but some events may have a fee

Parking: Street and paid parking
Accessible: Yes
Lodging: www.anacortes.org/explore.cfm?s=accommodations
Website: www.anacortesartsfestival.com
Facebook: www.facebook.com/anacortesartsfestival
Attractions: Anacortes Museum and Maritime Heritage Center, Tommy Thompson Trail, Cranberry Lake, Heart Lake, Whistle Lake.
Trivia: From 1989 until his death in 1995, actor, writer, and folk music singer Burl Ives made Anacortes his home.
Directions: Take I-5 to exit 230, go west on SR-20 and Spur 20 to downtown Anacortes.

Sorticulture, Everett's Garden Art Festival
Everett, Snohomish County
Early June

This garden-arts festival features distinctive hand-crafted garden art and nurseries displaying a wide variety of plants to transform your back yard. Learn tips and tricks from top regional gardening experts. Sorticulture also features display gardens, a food fair, a wine garden, live music, and free activities for the kids.

Address: Legion Park, 145 Alverson Blvd.
Admission: No info
Parking: Parking is limited to people with a Disabled Parking Permit at Sorticulture, so take the bus. Parking is free in the Everett Community College Broadway parking lot, N Broadway in between 10th Street and Tower Street (900 N Broadway) and jump on the Sorticulture shuttle (adult fare is $1).
Accessible: Yes
Lodging: http://experienceeverett.com. Check the event Website to see the various hotels offering festival specials.
Website: www.everettwa.org/default.aspx?ID=1228
Facebook: www.facebook.com/sorticulture
Attractions: Schack Art Center, Flying Heritage Collection, Imagine Children's Museum, Everett Art Walk, Jetty Island, Spencer Island, Legion Memorial Park, Boeing Tour, Forest Park Animal Farm
Trivia: The Boeing Everett Factory, at Paine Field, is an airplane assembly building owned by Boeing. It is the largest building in the world by vol-

ume at 472,370,319 cubic feet (98.3 acres). It is where wide-body 747s, 767s, 777s, and the 787 Dreamliner are assembled.

Directions: From I-5 S, take exit 198 and follow Hwy 529 south into Everett as it becomes Broadway Ave N to Tower St and turn left. Park in the Everett Community College North Broadway parking lot. From I-5 N, take exit 195 and turn left onto E Marine View Dr. Go 0.5 miles to 16th St and turn left. Follow 16th St to Broadway. Turn right onto Broadway and continue to Tower St and turn right. Park in the Everett Community College North Broadway parking lot.

International Art Festival
Blaine, Whatcom County
June

Peace Arch Park stands on the international boundary between Blaine, Washington, and Douglas, British Columbia. The Peace Arch was constructed to commemorate the centennial (1814–1914) of the signing of the Treaty of Ghent on December 24, 1814. The Treaty of Ghent ended the war of 1812 between the United States and Great Britain, a conflict that was waged in North America and involved Canadians, as well as Americans and British. The International Art Festival is a juried fine arts festival that is held on the U.S. side of the park. It is a gathering of visual artists from the greater northwest and beyond, representing a rich cultural tapestry. Organizers strive to provide a unique art display with a touch of sophistication within the beautiful park setting. In addition to visual arts, textiles, sculpture, music, and dance, the event includes live music, gourmet food, and a wine and beer garden.

Address: Peace Arch State Park, 19 A Street
Admission: Free. Art is duty free into Canada
Parking: Free parking is available in the north half of parking lot closest to the park; should the free portion fill up, a Washington State Park Discover Pass is required. A Discover Pass can be purchased at the park and provides access to the extensive Washington State Parks system for one year from the date of purchase. Parking is also available on the street outside of the park.
Accessible: Yes
Lodging: www.blainechamber.com/lodging.html
Website: http://scottsusank.wix.com/peacearchart

Facebook: www.facebook.com/pages/International-Art-Festival-at-Peace-Arch-Park/429013377147903

Attractions: Blaine Marine Park, Great Washington State Birding Trail, Historic Plover Ferry, Drayton Harbor Maritime Museum, kayaking in Drayton Harbor

Trivia: Built in 1920–21, construction used in the Peace Arch was ahead of its time. It stands 67 feet high and is made of concrete and reinforced steel. The foundation consists of 76 14-in pilings driven 25–30 feet into the earth. The Arch is said to be one of the first structures in North America to be earthquake-proof.

Directions: From I-5 N, take exit 276, go around the traffic and turn off at 2nd St. Follow 2nd St to the entrance to Peace Arch Park.

Everett, Washington is the site of Boeing's final assembly plant and the world's largest building by volume.

It is illegal to display a hypnotized person in a store window in Everett.

Beer, Wine & Spirits

Anacortes Spring Wine Festival
Anacortes, Skagit County
Second Saturday in April

The annual date of the Anacortes Spring Wine Festival was carefully chosen to coincide with the blooming of the Skagit Valley tulip fields. So, even before visitors arrive at the festival, they will have already experienced a visual treat of amazing colors and scenic vistas. The Anacortes Spring Wine Festival brings together 30 wineries and six gourmet restaurants for an event to delight the palate and senses. Sample all varieties of wine and pick your favorites. You can take home a bottle or a case at special discounted rates. Enjoy live music and sweet and savory bites from local restaurants. The event concludes at 4:30 pm., so you have plenty of time afterward to stroll through historic downtown Anacortes.

Address: Port Transit Shed Event Center, 100 Commercial Avenue
Admission: General Admission is $45. Designated driver admission is $25. Attendees must be 21+ and ready to present ID at the door. Tickets include tasting glass, unlimited wine tasting, bites from six restaurants, and musical entertainment. Advance purchase ticket prices are $40 for general admission, and $20 for a designated driver.
Parking: Street and parking lot parking
Accessible: Yes
Pets: No
Lodging: www.visitskagitvalley.com/stay. Many local area hotels offer wine packages for the festival weekend, so when you make reservations, make sure to tell them you are there for the event.
Website: www.anacortes.org/spring-wine-fest
Facebook: www.facebook.com/anacortesspringwinefestival
Attractions: Mt. Erie Park, Washington Park, Deception Pass State Park, ferry trips to other San Juan Islands
Trivia: Anacortes was historically the center of the fishing and canning industry in the Puget Sound area. The city pays tribute to this history with an artistic set of trash cans, throughout downtown and at Cap Sante Marina, that are decorated to look like cans of salmon with vintage labels.
Directions: From I-5, take exit 230 (SR-20). Go west to downtown Anacortes.

Skagit Wine and Beer Festival
Mount Vernon, Skagit County
Mid-November

Delight in wines and microbrews from regions throughout Washington, including local Skagit County wineries, breweries, and distilleries. Pair your tastings with gourmet appetizers, divine chocolate, and delectable cheese samplings made right in Skagit County. A VIP pass gets you access to an exclusive sampling hour, access to the VIP lounge where you can visit with the wine and beer reps, additional food samplings, and entry for a prize.

Address: Best Western Plus Skagit Valley Inn and Convention Center, 2300 Market Street
Admission: Admission is $40 per person, $70 per couple. This includes wine tastings, a glass, food, chocolate, and cheese samplings. VIP tickets cost $60 per person or $110 per couple.
Parking: Street and parking lot parking
Accessible: Yes
Pets: No
Lodging: www.visitskagitvalley.com/stay
Website: www.mountvernonchamber.com/events/annual-chamber-events/skagit-wine-festival
Facebook: www.facebook.com/skagitwinefestival
Attractions: Children's Museum of Skagit County, Skagit Valley tulip farms, Birch Bay Water Slides, Skagit Wildlife Area, Skagit River Bald Eagle Natural Area, Rasar State Park, North Cascade Scenic Hwy, Whidbey Scenic Isle Way, Tulip Country Bike Tours
Trivia: Lenning Farms/Berry Barn in Mount Vernon is home to what owners call the "biggest hedge maze in North America." The farm-themed maze incorporates a viewing platform, a giant slide, and eight stations within that provide farm and berry facts. The maze comprises more than 2,500 hedge-type trees (grown at Lenning Farms), which took three years to plan and plant.
Directions: From I-5 N, take exit 227 WA-538 E/E College Way. Turn right, then take the first left onto E College Way. E College Way becomes Market St.

Everett Craft Beer Festival
Everett, Snohomish County
Mid-August

Everett Craft Beer Festival is a celebration of seasonal craft beers that features 30 Washington breweries pouring more than 70 different beers. Each brewery brings at least two of their locally produced selections to downtown Everett for tasting. The event features live music throughout the day, and a select number of food trucks offer food for purchase. For other food options, visit one of the many terrific Everett downtown eateries. You must be 21 or older to attend this event.

Address: Hoyt Avenue and Hewitt Avenue
Admission: $20 in advance, $25 at the door, and $15 for military with valid ID. Entry includes a tasting cup and six tokens. Each token is good for a 5-oz taste. Additional tokens may be purchased at $1.50 each or four for $5. Designated Driver admission is $5, which includes free water and soft drinks. Paid attendees may re-enter the event by showing their wristband and ID.
Parking: In addition to signed street parking, free parking is available at the Everpark Garage located at 2823 Hoyt Avenue in downtown Everett.
Accessible: Yes
Pets: No
Lodging: http://experienceeverett.com
Website: http://washingtonbeer.com/everett-craft-beer-festival
Facebook: www.facebook.com/EverettCraftBeerFestival
Attractions: Schack Art Center, Flying Heritage Collection, Imagine Children's Museum, Nishiyama Garden, Jetty Island, Spencer Island, Legion Memorial Park, Boeing Tour, Forest Park Animal Farm
Trivia: Navy Commander James Kyes was born in Everett. Kyes was posthumously awarded the Navy Cross for the extraordinary heroism he showed during action against German submarines in the North Atlantic on December 23, 1943. After his ship Leary had been hit with three torpedoes, he ordered all hands to abandon ship. On his last walk-through to make sure no personnel was still on board, he discovered that a kitchen worker's life jacket was torn and useless. Kyes removed his own jacket and gave it to the boy, thus sacrificing himself. In 1945, the destroyer USS James E. Kyes was named in his honor. Kyes was also a member of the first climbing party to summit Goblin Peak in the Cascade Mountain. He brought down a sapling from the peak, which he

planted in the town of Monte Cristo, WA (which is now a ghost town). Because of his bravery, Goblin Peak was renamed to Kyes Peak shortly after the war, and the sapling that he planted still grows in the same place. A plaque and a letter beside the tree explain the events of 1943, when Kyes lost his life.

Directions: From the south, use I-5 exit 193, Pacific Ave. From the north, use I-5 exit 194, Everett Ave/City Center. From the east, take Hwy 2 across the Hewitt Ave Trestle and follow the exit to Hewitt Ave.

Snohomish on the Rocks Distillery Festival
Snohomish, Snohomish County
February/March

Snohomish on the Rocks is an event that celebrates the growing local distillery industry, and showcases distinctive spirits from many local distilleries. Come meet the distillers, sample their products, and learn about the art of creating spirits. Each distiller offers their spirit straight, which you can purchase with your tasting tickets, and the Signature Bar features a signature cocktail from each participating distillery. Beer, wine, and soda are also available for purchase. Distilleries at previous events have included 3 Howls Distillery, Bainbridge Organic Distillers, Batch 206 Distillery, Bellewood Distilling, Black Sam Distillery, Bluewater Distilling, Copperworks Distilling Co., Dark Moon Artisan Distillery, Dry County Distillery, Eastside Distilling, Ellensburg Distillery, Heritage Distilling Company, House Spirits Distillery, It's 5 LLC, Letterpress Distilling, Mt. Index Distillery, Pacific Distillery, Port Steilacoom Distillery, River Sands Distillery, Sidetrack Distillery, Skip Rock Distillers, Sodo Spirits Distillery, Sound Spirits Distillery, Square One, Swede Hill Distilling, Valley Shine Distillery, Westland Distillery, and Woodinville Whiskey Co.

Address: Location varies
Admission: VIP ticket package is $50/person (includes one-hour early entrance to afternoon tasting session, eight tasting tickets, commemorative shot glass, $5 food truck coupon, 10% off of one bottle purchase, and a VIP tote). General admission is $25/person (includes five tasting tickets, commemorative shot glass, and $5 food truck coupon).
Parking: Varies by venue/year
Accessible: Yes
Pets: No

Lodging: Inn at Snohomish (www.snohomishinn.com) provides a special rate for festival attendees. Other lodging information: http://reservations.snohomish.org/6121_hotel-list_m2977_r308268.html
Website: http://snohomishrocks.com
Facebook: www.facebook.com/SnohomishRocks
Attractions: Old Snohomish Village, Snohomish River, Blackman House Museum, local area wineries
Trivia: In a Pacific Northwest adaptation of Ground Hog Day, the town of Snohomish celebrates its yearly Ground Frog Day. As a northwest counterpart to Punxsutawney Phil in Pennsylvania, every February, a bullfrog named Snohomish Slew comes to the microphone and determines whether or not the Pacific Northwest will have six more weeks of winter. If he remains silent, that means six more weeks of wet wintry weather. If he croaks, that means spring is on its way.
Directions: Snohomish is 30 miles north of Seattle via I-5 N.

The Grand Coulee Dam, which was completed in 1941, stands as tall as a 46-story building, stretches the length of a dozen city blocks, and has a spillway nearly twice as high as Niagara Falls.

Ethnic & Cultural Celebrations

Gold Dust Days
Gold Bar, Snohomish County
Fourth weekend in July

Begun as a prospectors' camp in 1889, the town of Gold Bar celebrates its annual Gold Dust Days heritage festival, which pays tribute to the rich gold-panning history of the town. Precious metals are still being harvested from the rich mineral deposits in the valley, and this festival gives you the unique opportunity to try your hand at panning and learn all the tricks of the trade from local professionals. The event also includes a Civil War encampment, live music, handcrafted-only street fair, a car show with a classic pin-up girl contest, a parade, a motorcycle poker run, gunny sack races against the firefighters, a theatrical performance by the Red Hat Ladies, and plenty of food and live music. It also includes free activities for children, including a bouncy house, as well as a bike-decorating session, followed by a bike parade.

Address: Downtown
Admission: Free
Parking: Free street and parking lot parking
Accessible: Yes
Pets: Yes
Lodging: www.snohomish.org/explore/lodging
Website: www.skyvalleychamber.com/events-and-attractions/2014-gold-dust-days
Facebook: www.facebook.com/GoldDustDays
Attractions: Whitewater rafting on the Skykomish River, Wallace Falls State Park, Reiter Foothills, Cascade Loop Scenic Hwy, Index town wall, Wild Sky Wilderness Area
Trivia: In 1981, Dennis "Slick" Lilly escaped from Kansas State Prison, where he was doing time for assault and theft charges, as well as charges related to previous prison escapes. Within a couple of hours, he was captured after a shootout with police. He was then transferred to the Missouri State Penn, where he spent his time slowly collecting pieces of prison guard uniforms. In 1986, he had enough pieces to assemble a complete uniform, which he donned, and then simply walked out of the prison on a guard shift change. Since 1986, Lilly has been on the FBI's most wanted list, and his story has twice appeared on the *America's*

Most Wanted television show. Fast-forward almost 30 years. Gold Bar resident Amanda Murray files an application with an online stock trading firm, but is denied because her birthdate and social security numbers don't match up. A compliance officer at the firm becomes suspicious, and refers the matter to the FBI. The number and birthdate belong to a Mary Lilly—Dennis Lilly's wife. In January 2014, the FBI visited Amanda Murray in nearby Monroe, WA, at the mail service business that she ran as a respected Gold Bar resident. Soon thereafter, Amanda admitted that she was actually Mary Lilly, and her husband was the fugitive Dennis Lilly. She claimed that Dennis had died of pancreatic cancer in 2012, and as proof, revealed his final resting place: the back yard of their home, where she dug a hole and buried him. She feared that a formal burial would attract the attention of authorities.
Directions: The town of Gold Bar is located one hour northeast of Seattle on Hwy 2.

Lummi Stommish Water Festival
Bellingham, Whatcom County
Second weekend in June

In 1946, when World War II veterans were coming home, the Lummi tribe's World War I veterans decided to gather in celebration of their safe return. They decided to call this event Stommish, which is a Cowichan word meaning "warrior." The yearly Stommish is a multicultural contemporary Coast Salish gathering that includes activities and entertainment for the entire family. The festival features athletic events, such as the exciting war canoe races and a Sla-hal bone game. It also features a film festival, a parade, a talent show, traditional singing and dancing (including a pow wow honoring all veterans), a traditional Lummi-style salmon barbecue, a carnival, a fireworks show, and a moonlight concert series featuring Native comedians and local musicians.

Address: Lummi Stommish Grounds, Stommish Lane
Admission: Free
Parking: Parking on-site
Accessible: No info
Pets: No info
Lodging: www.bellingham.org/lodging
Website: www.stommish.com/events2011.php

Facebook: www.facebook.com/pages/Lummi-Stommish-Water-Festival/194097253959259
Attractions: Whatcom Museum, Bellingham Railway Museum, Spark Museum of Electrical Invention, Mt. Baker Ski Area, Larrabee State Park
Trivia: In 2007, the Lummi hosted their first potlatch since the 1930s. Sixty-eight families paddled hand-made canoes to the Lummi Reservation from parts of Washington and British Columbia.
Directions: From I-5, take the Slater Rd exit #260 and follow the signs toward Lummi Island. At the stop light, turn left onto Haxton Way, and continue for one mile past the ferry terminal. The Stommish grounds is on your right.

Bridge of Aloha Festival
Ferndale, Whatcom County
May or June

The Bridge of Aloha festival honors the Hawaiian culture, and shares traditions, educates, and builds friendship between communities and cultural groups. This event features Hawaiian music, hula and Polynesian dancing, art and craft vendors, children's activities, raffle drawings, workshops, live music, and, of course, lots of island food.

Address: Ferndale Events Center, 5715 Barrett Road
Admission: General Admission $7. Seniors (65 and older) $5. Children under age 8 get in free.
Parking: Parking available on-site at the event center
Accessible: Yes
Pets: No
Lodging: The Silver Reef Casino Hotel (866.383.0777) offers a discounted group rate for festival attendees. Other lodging options: http://bridgeofaloha.webs.com/lodging.htm
Website: http://bridgeofaloha.webs.com
Attractions: Pioneer Park, Hovander Park, Tenant Lake, Centennial Riverwalk Park
Trivia: Ferndale was originally called Jam because it was situated next to a large log jam on the Nooksack River. It was renamed to Ferndale by a schoolteacher who thought it needed a better name.
Directions: From I-5, take exit #262, and head east on W Axton Rd. Turn left (north) on Barrett Rd, then turn left (west) into the first parking lot. The building is the second building on the left.

Bellingham Scottish Highland Games
Ferndale, Whatcom County
First full weekend in June

This "Country Fair with Scottish Flair" has a little something for everyone. The weekend begins on Friday with a Blessing of the Games, and the tapping of the firkin. These are followed by live music and a talent show. The main events begin on Saturday morning, and continue throughout Sunday. These include Scottish highland and country dancing, heavy athletics, piping and drumming, Celtic music showcases, food and merchandise vendors, kids' games, an ale and wine garden, and the popular Massing of the Bands on the great field. Just before the closing ceremonies, watch the athletes turn the impressive caber.

Address: Hovander Homestead Park, 5299 Nielsen Avenue
Admission: Friday's ceiligh (featuring the Blessing of the Games) is free. Tickets for Saturday and Sunday cost $15 each day for adults, $10 each day for children and seniors. Admission for both days is free if you are a veteran or are in active military (ID required).
Parking: Street parking and parking lot parking available on site
Accessible: Yes
Pets: No
Lodging: www.bellingham.org/lodging
Website: www.bhga.org
Facebook: www.facebook.com/scottishhighlandgames
Attractions: Western's Outdoor Sculpture Collection, Whatcom Museum, Bellingham International Maritime Museum, Fairhaven Pharmacy Museum, Birch Bay State Park
Trivia: The Bellingham Wig Out, held each year the Friday before Memorial Day, is a celebration of fun and an irreverent welcome to spring. Events include the Wig Walk, a promenade of wig wearers through the downtown business district, a wig competition, complete with categories from Wee Wigster to the Best Handmade Wig, and a Wig Out Party held at various locations that evening.
Directions: From I-5 take the Ferndale exit (#262). Turn west on Main St. Immediately after the railroad underpass turn left. Turn right on Nielson Ave and follow the signs to the park.

Oktoberfest
Friday Harbor, San Juan Island, San Juan County
Early October

This fun and crazy annual family event features San Juan's original Blaskapelle Oompah Orchestra, Bavarian menu and drinks (including brats, German potato salad, schnitzel, and locally made apple strudel), professional polka instruction, and kids' activities. Break out the lederhosen and dirndl skirts for the costume contest, where you can win a collectible San Juan Island Oktoberfest stein.

Address: San Juan Island
Admission: Oktoberfest is free to anyone in costume. Otherwise, admission costs $5. Kids get in free whether or not they are in costume.
Parking: Parking available on site at the fairgrounds
Accessible: Yes
Pets: No
Lodging: www.visitsanjuans.com/accommodations
Website: www.visitsanjuans.com/events/san-juan-island/san-juan-island-oktoberfest
Attractions: Kayak tours, whale watching tours, San Juan Islands Museum of Art, farmers market, bicycle rentals
Trivia: In 1859, a hungry pig on the island of San Juan caused an international incident. Because of boundary ambiguity, both American settlers and British Hudson's Bay Company staked out their territory on San Juan. One day, Lyman Cutler, an American farmer, found a large black pig rooting in his garden, which he subsequently shot. Turns out, the pig belonged to an employee of the Hudson's Bay Company. Tempers flared on both sides, and before you knew it, Captain George Pickett was sent with a regiment to San Juan, and the British retaliated with three warships. For several days, the British and U.S. soldiers attempted to goad the other into firing the first shot, but no shots were fired. When leaders in London and Washington D.C. were fully apprised of the situation, they were shocked and appalled that two nations were about to go to war over a pig. The conflict was resolved and the Pig War remained a bloodless conflict.

Directions: From I-5 N in Seattle, take exit 230 to Burlington/Anacortes (or exits 221 or 226 through scenic Skagit Valley). At the first light, turn left toward Anacortes onto Hwy 20 west. Follow Hwy 20 west to Anacortes, merge right into the traffic circle, and take another right onto Commercial Ave. Take a left at 12th St, where signs point you to the San Juan Islands ferry, and follow for about 2 miles to the terminal. Allow a 1.5–2 hours to enjoy the drive and the scenery from Seattle or Vancouver B.C. to the Anacortes ferry terminal.

The San Juan Islands host the greatest concentration of bald eagles (Haliaeetus leucocephalus) in the continental United States.

Family Fun

Steampunk Festival and the Fantastical Mr. Flip's Carnival of Wonders and Curiosities
Bellingham, Whatcom County
July

The Steampunk Festival provides a spectacular showcase of music, art, and literature. It celebrates the "strange and wondrous" through a menagerie of music and entertainment including buskers, tumblers, fencing demos, sword handling, and steampunk bicycles. The event also includes discussions with authors and informational booths by the Whatcom Museum, SPARK Museum, and the Bureau of Historical Investigation. Enjoy food and art and craft vendors, and participate in a costume contest.

Address: In the Fairhaven district at two locations: Village Books at 1200 11th Street, and Fairhaven Village Inn at 1200 10th Street
Admission: Free
Parking: Street and paid parking lot parking
Accessible: Yes
Pets: No
Lodging: www.bellingham.org/lodging
Website: www.fairhaven.com/events/detail/7190
Facebook: www.facebook.com/pages/Fairhaven-Steampunk-Festival-Mr-Flips-Carnival-of-Wonders-Curiosities/1388670034681483
Attractions: Whatcom Falls Park, Larrabee State Park, Lake Padden, Lake Samish, Bellis Fair shopping mall.
Trivia: Bellingham is currently the home of retired competitive female bodybuilder Yolanda Hughes-Heying. While competing as an amateur, she won the World Amateur Championship title in 1992 and the Ms. International titles consecutively in 1997 and 1998. She retired from body building in 1999, and opened up a fitness studio in Bellingham called Fitness Exotica, which specialized in pole dancing and striptease fitness.
Directions: From I-5 N, take exit 250, which is the exit for Connelly Ave/Old Fairhaven Pkwy/SR-11 S. Turn left onto Connelly Ave/Old Fairhaven Pkwy/SR-11 S. Continue on this road to 10th St.

Snohomish Pumpkin Hurl and Medieval Faire
Everett, Snohomish County
Mid-September

The Snohomish Valley Festival of Pumpkins is a September/October series of harvest-related events held by an association of seven family owned pumpkin farms. One of the most exciting is the Snohomish Pumpkin Hurl and Medieval Faire, which offers the opportunity to view a true rarity in nature as the normally passive and pudgy pumpkin sheds its awkward façade and becomes a graceful soaring beauty, as it flies away to . . . S-P-L-A-T! Contestant teams build and bring their very own pumpkin hurling machines (trebuchets) to compete for the title of Champion of the Northwest Regional Pumpkin Hurl. If you don't want to build your own punkin' chunkin' machine, you can still take a turn at launching one of the gourds using an air cannon or a mini trebuchet. The Seattle Knights—the Pacific Northwest's premiere sword fighting and jousting theatrical troupe—has also performed at the event. Enjoy many hands-on activities, black-powder demonstrations, live music, costume contests, pony rides, mock battles (for adults and kids), artisans, and entertainment. Learn the rules of chivalry. Meet royalty, fairies, and the Seattle Garden Gnome. Learn about medieval times as historical experts the Knights of Veritas share real relics and reveal true history. Enjoy craft vendors and a wide variety of food, as well as spirits and mead tasting.

Address: Alexander Farm, corner of 43rd Avenue SE and Ebey Island Road
Admission: $8 per person. Children aged 4 and under. Spirit and wine tasting costs $5 for three tastes.
Parking: $5 per car
Accessible: Event takes place on farm grounds
Pets: No
Lodging: http://ci.snohomish.wa.us/321/Places-to-Stay
Website: www.festivalofpumpkins.org/#!pumpkin-hurl/c13ud
Facebook: www.facebook.com/SnohomishPumpkinHurl
Attractions: Blackman House Museum, Snohomish River, Old Snohomish Village
Trivia: Pumpkins are grown on every continent of the world, except for Antarctica. The world's heaviest pumpkin weighed in at 2,096.6 pounds. The record was set in 2014 by Beni Meier, a Swiss gardener.

Directions: From I-5, take exit 194 to merge onto US-2 E toward Snohomish/Wenatchee. Take the exit off the trestle toward Ebey Island/Homeacres Rd. Merge onto 20th St SE and turn right onto 51st Ave SE. Turn left onto 43rd Ave SE/Home Acres Rd. Drive 1.5 miles. The entrance is on your left. From the north on SR-9, turn right on WA-204 W and take ramp onto the US-2 trestle. Take the exit on the left toward Ebey Island/Homeacres Rd. Merge onto 20th St SE and turn left onto 51st Ave SE. Turn left onto 43rd Ave SE/Home Acres Rd. Drive 1.5 miles. The entrance is on your left. From Snohomish, head north on SR-9. Turn left onto 56th St SE. Continue on to Fobes Rd, then turn left onto 83rd Ave SE. Take the first right onto 60th St SE/John Mack Rd. Continue to follow 60th St SE. Turn right onto Home Acres Rd and continue onto 52nd St SE/Ebey Island Rd. Arrive at corner 43rd Ave SE and turn into parking entrance.

Puget Sound Bird Fest
Edmonds, Snohomish County
Mid-September

Puget Sound Bird Fest is a yearly celebration of birds and nature found on the beautiful shores of Puget Sound. The three-day event includes speakers, guided walks, land- and water-based field trips, exhibits, and educational activities for children and adults. Tour local sites such as Edmonds Marsh, Willow Creek, Point Edwards, Yost Park, Pine Ridge Park, and beaches, as well as Edmonds Wildlife Habitat Native Plant Demonstration Garden. So, bring your binoculars and spend the weekend birding and meeting other birders, naturalists, photographers, and people engaged in fascinating bird research projects. Bird Fest is eagerly anticipated by Edmonds locals, so expect to see bonus activities and entertainments around town.

Address: Frances Anderson Center, 700 Main Street
Admission: General Admission is free. Guided walks and field trips require registration and a fee.
Parking: Parking is free on Edmonds streets and in public parking lots, but some in downtown have a three-hour limit.
Accessible: Yes
Pets: No
Lodging: www.edmondswa.gov/visiting/visitors-guide/shopping-dining-lodging.html

Website: www.pugetsoundbirdfest.org
Attractions: Edmonds Underwater Park, Brackett's Landing Park, murals tour, Edmonds Historical Museum, Great Washington State Birding Trail
Trivia: Rick Steves, European-travel aficionado and host of the American Public Television series *Rick Steves' Europe*, was born in and currently resides in Edmonds, WA. His production company, Back Door Productions, is also headquartered in Edmonds.
Directions: Edmonds is 30 miles north of Seattle via I-5 N.

Aquafest
Lake Stevens, Snohomish County
Last full weekend in July

Aquafest began as an afternoon waterski tournament between friends in 1960. It is now a three-day festival, drawing crowds from throughout the northwest and Canada, and boasting 60 events such as a 10K/5K/1K Aquarun; boat, children, and grand parades; a carnival; sidewalk chalk art; a classic car show; a diaper dash; a duck race; fireworks; a firefighter's pancake breakfast; horse drawn wagon rides; a Miss Aquafest pageant; a pizza eating contest; a Proud Pet Show; a quadrathon (swim, bike, run, paddle-boat); a Family FunFest (with plenty of kids' activities and inflatables); a teen dance; an Aquafest Idol competition; a chance to try your hand at rowing a racing shell with the Lake Stevens Rowing Club; and basketball, disc golf, softball, volleyball, and water ski/wakeboard tournaments. Many of the Aquafest events are offered at no charge, such as the Family FunFest, movies in the park, rowing introduction, ambush makeovers, and North Cove entertainment. The goal of the $50 Boat Race is to build a boat at minimum cost, and earn the fastest finishing time while sailing it 200 yards to the finish line. Many of the boats are constructed of recyclables and require some finesse to finish the race. Trophies for this competition are given for the first place finisher, and for winners of other categories such as "Looks like a real boat" or "Should have been first." Lots of arts, crafts, and food vendors are on site, as well as a beverage garden.

Address: Downtown
Admission: Free general admission, but some activities require a separate fee. The beverage garden has a $5 cover charge. Carnival tickets cost $1.25 each (rides generally cost 3–4 tickets per person), or get a

book of 24 tickets for $24. Unlimited-ride wristbands cost around $25.

Parking: Limited parking is available at the festival site. Event organizers highly recommend you avoid the trouble of downtown parking and take the free shuttle. Many roads are closed for different events. The shuttle runs from Lake Stevens High School to downtown Lake Stevens throughout the weekend.

Accessible: No info

Pets: Leashed pets allowed, but no animals in the food court

Lodging: www.snohomish.org/travel/lodging

Website: www.aquafest.org

Facebook: www.facebook.com/pages/Lake-Stevens-Aquafest/256816687742086?hc_location=timeline

Attractions: Centennial Trail, Lake Stevens Historical Museum, activities on Lake Stevens

Trivia: Actor Chris Pratt, best known for his roles as Andy Dwyer in the NBC sitcom *Parks and Recreation* and as lead Peter Quill in *Guardians of the Galaxy*, was raised in Lake Stevens. As a wrestler at Lake Stevens High School, he placed fifth at state in his senior year in 1997. Pratt is married to actress Anna Faris, who is best known for her portrayal of Cindy Campbell in the *Scary Movie* film series, and who graduated from the University of Washington.

Directions: Lake Stevens is 40 miles north of Seattle via I-5 N.

Loggerodeo

Sedro Woolley, Skagit County
First week in July

Loggerodeo is an annual celebration, around the 4th of July, that fills a week with many exciting activities and fun for the entire family. In addition to the actual rodeo, the event also includes a carnival, a street dance, logger sports competitions (choker setting, axe throwing, and chainsaw bucking), a blues jamboree, a grand parade, a beard contest, a car show, and a barbecue. But what sets the Loggerodeo apart from other Fourth of July celebrations is that it hosts the longest running international, invitation-only, chainsaw carving competition. Armed with a chainsaw, axe, and a few tools, chainsaw carvers whittle an 8-ft. high, 3-ft. wide piece of cedar into amazing works of art. This select group of men and women have gone on to become national and world champions.

Address: Many activities occur downtown. The rodeo takes place at the rodeo grounds at Hwy 20 and Polte Road
Admission: Rodeo: Adults $10; military/seniors 55+/youth 7–15 $8; kids aged 6 and under get in free. Some other activities require a fee.
Parking: Parking is available in the Municipal Parking Lot on Metcalf and Warner, in the gravel area of Eastern, or other parking spaces in town. Riverfront Park has adequate parking for the carnival and fireworks show.
Accessible: Yes
Pets: Pets allowed at some events
Lodging: Three Rivers Inn (360.855.2626), is the official hotel of Loggerodeo. Other lodging information: www.sedro-woolley.com/things-to-do/accommodations
Website: www.loggerodeo.com
Facebook: www.facebook.com/Loggerodeo
Attractions: Sedro-Woolley Museum, Skagit River, North Cascades National Park, Children's Museum of Skagit County
Trivia: In May 1922, when the Al G. Barnes Circus rolled in to Sedro-Woolley, little did the townsfolk know that the circus cavalcade would bring more than big-top entertainment. Touted as the largest elephant ever in captivity, circus performer Tusko, "The Mighty Monarch of the Jungle," was 10-feet-2-inches tall, 7.5 tons, and had 7-ft. long tusks. Apparently bored with the whole performance scene, Tusko escaped and hightailed it out of the animal tent just before show time, then spent the next 13 hours stomping and trumpeting his way around the town and the surrounding area, destroying chicken coops, uprooting trees, ripping out fences, munching on pilfered hay bales, and generally having a wonderful pachyderm frolic, whilst being pursued by dozens of townsfolk (in varying stages of sobriety), keepers, and attendants (a couple of whom pursued mounted on other elephants from the circus). The beast was finally cornered between two boxcars, and taken back into custody the following morning. No one was hurt during the escapade, but circus owner Al Barnes ended up paying $20,000 in damages.
Directions: The festival is conveniently located off I-5. Coming from I-5, take exit 232, Cook Rd/Sedro-Woolley. Turn east on to Cook Rd and follow it into town (approximately 4 miles). Continue on Cook Rd until you reach the stoplight with the "Welcome to Sedro-Woolley" sign and the train. This is the Hwy 20/Cook Rd intersection. Continue straight through the intersection traveling east, and Cook Rd becomes Ferry St.

Ring of Fire and Hope
Birch Bay, Whatcom County
December/New Year's Eve

On New Year's Eve, the shoreline of half-moon shaped Birch Bay becomes a spectacular light display during the Ring of Fire and Hope celebration. Revelers begin bringing in the New Year early by lighting road flares along the Birch Bay shoreline. The flare-lighting starts at 7 pm and anyone can participate in the festivities, which are said to signify hope for the coming year. You can bring your own (spikeless) flares, or some free flares are available on a first come, first-served basis. Enjoy the beautiful sight as the flares burn for 15–30 minutes, then continue on with your New Year's celebration. And if one of your resolutions is to get more exercise, consider joining in with hundreds of other hung-over souls to participate in the Birch Bay Polar Bear Swim at noon on New Year's Day.

Address: Birch Bay Waterfront (Birch Bay State Park to Birch Bay Village)
Admission: Free
Parking: Street parking
Accessible: No info
Lodging: www.birchbayvillage.com/bus_dir_lodging.html
Website: http://birchbaychamber.com/december
Attractions: Alaska Packers Association Cannery Museum, Birch Bay Waterslides, Historic Plover Passenger Ferry, Chuckanut Drive, Miniature World Family Fun Center, and birding in Drayton Harbor, Semiahmoo Spit, and Bondary Bay
Trivia: In nearby Blaine, Semiahmoo Spit protrudes in to Drayton Harbor. The spit was once the location of a large Lummi Nation village, and artifacts are still being recovered from the area. In the late 1800s, the spit housed the world's largest salmon cannery, operated by the Alaska Packer's Association. Some of the cannery buildings remain as part of Semiahmoo Park, and as part of the Alaska Packers Association Cannery Museum. The tip of the spit is now home to the Semmiahmoo Resort.
Directions: Birch Bay is located between Seattle and Vancouver, British Columbia, just north of Bellingham. Birch Bay is minutes off of I-5 at exit 270. After you exit, head west on Birch Bay-Lynden Rd for approximately 4 miles to the Birch Bay waterfront.

Food & Agricultural Festivals

Marysville Strawberry Festival
Marysville, Snohomish County
Third weekend in June

During the Roaring Twenties, the city of Marysville earned the nickname "The Strawberry City" in recognition of the area's abundance of the sweet, fruity berries, which are regularly celebrated and devoured in the annual Strawberry Festival. Begun in 1932, the Strawberry Festival is one of the longest ongoing festivals in Washington State. Events include the Berry Run, Kids Party in the Park, a fashion show, a talent show, a carnival, a rose-planting ceremony, a market, a beer garden, a kid's parade, the Twilight Grand Parade, fireworks, and, of course, a strawberry-shortcake eating contest.

Address: Downtown
Admission: Free
Parking: Street parking
Accessible: Yes
Pets: Yes
Lodging: www.maryfest.org/Accomodations
Website: www.maryfest.org
Facebook: www.facebook.com/MarysvilleStrawberryFestival
Attractions: Seattle Premium Outlets, Mountain Loop Hwy, Centennial Trail, Tulalip Casino
Trivia: The average strawberry has 200 seeds.
Directions: Marysville is 34 miles north of Seattle via I-5 N.

Northwest Raspberry Festival
Lynden, Whatcom County
Third weekend in July

Lynden invites you to celebrate in one of the greatest raspberry producing regions of the world. Mid-July is the peak time to get your share of Lynden's bountiful crop of red raspberries (reportedly more than half of the nation's total production) while enjoying the summer sunshine and a variety of family friendly activities at the downtown celebration that attracts around 25,000 visitors each year. Festivities include kids' games, face painting, sand art, a 3-on-3 basketball tournament, and live concerts. Dine on luscious raspberry and ice cream sundaes for only $2, as well as smoothies, pies, and other treats made from local products, or purchase a flat of raspberries to take home that are picked fresh daily from nearby farms. Shop at Lynden's downtown merchants and street vendors at the "Berry Fair" street market. On Sunday, enjoy the Razz & Shine cruise-in car show, race in the fun run, and enjoy an all-you-can-eat raspberry pancake breakfast. Good thing raspberries only clock in at about one calorie per berry.

Address: Downtown
Admission: Free
Parking: Street and parking lot
Accessible: Yes
Lodging: http://lynden.org
Website: http://lynden.org/northwest-raspberry-festival
Facebook: www.facebook.com/pages/Northwest-Raspberry-Festival/328339560562995
Attractions: Pioneer Museum, Hovander Homestead Park, Tennant Lake Natural History Interpretive Center, Raspberry Ridge Golf Course
Trivia: Raspberries come in more than 200 species, including yellow, purple, and black raspberries.
Directions: Lynden is located 100 miles (2 hours) north of Seattle via I-5 N, just on the U.S. side of the U.S./Canadian border.

Skagit Valley Tulip Festival
Mount Vernon and Skagit Valley, Skagit County
Month of April

Every spring hundreds of thousands of people come to the Skagit Valley to enjoy the millions of tulips that burst into bloom. The month-long Skagit Valley Tulip Festival is a driving tour, rather than a one-site event. The farmers in the area raise tulips as an agricultural crop and the hundreds of acres of blooming flowers are scattered throughout the Skagit Valley. Events and activities occur throughout the area during the month of April, including art shows, gala celebrations, concerts, tours of local shellfish and cheese operations, a parade, a downtown Mount Vernon street fair, kids' activities, a Kiwanis salmon barbecue, a fun run, a Tulip Ride for bicyclists, and a youth basketball tournament. To get a full appreciation of the glorious panorama, consider taking a helicopter tour from Mount Vernon with Sky Flyn' Helicopter (360.377.4115). One caveat: The tulips bloom according to Mother Nature's schedule. Festival organizers cannot guarantee that all tulips will be in bloom on the date you choose to visit. The good news is, if you happen to do your tour before the tulips are in full bloom, you get a fantastic display of daffodils. To obtain a map of the tulip field area, check out the festival website before you go, or pick up a copy at any official information station in the valley, or at the Tulip Festival Office (311 W Kincaid Street, Mount Vernon), at Cascade Mall (201 Cascade Mall Drive, Burlington), at Conway Foods (18707 Main Street, Conway), Skagit River Produce (19193 SR-534, Mount Vernon), or at I-5, exit 230 (Hwy 20) at Skagit's Own Fish Market (18042 SR 20, Burlington) or Holiday Inn Express Hotel and Suites (900 Andis Road, Burlington)

Address: Various locations
Admission: Varies by venue
Parking: Parking is available at designated lots in the Tulip Field area. There is plenty of free parking at Tulip Town and RoozenGaarde. Look for the RoozenGaarde logo for other official parking areas. These lots are operated by Washington Bulb Company/RoozenGaarde. Parking in official lots is $5 per car; the ticket you receive from the parking attendant also admits one person to RoozenGaarde on the same day. Private individuals sometimes operate their own lots. Fees paid to private parties do not work for admission to RoozenGaarde.
Accessible: Most venues are working farms
Pets: Pets are not allowed in gardens
Lodging: www.visitskagitvalley.com/stay
Website: www.tulipfestival.org
Facebook: www.facebook.com/SkagitValleyTulipFestival
Attractions: Lincoln Theater, Little Mountain Park, Padilla Bay National Estuarine Research Reserve, Breazeale Interpretive Center, La Conner Sculpture Tour, outlet shopping malls
Trivia: Pioneer snowboarder Craig Kelly grew up in Mount Vernon. Kelly was known as the "Godfather of Freeriding," which means he loved to snowboard over natural, ungroomed terrain. In 1988, he appeared in a Wrigleys Gum commercial, doing a 540. He also appeared in several Warren Miller films, and was the first snowboarder to appear in an IMAX movie. During his 15-year career, he won four world championships and

three U.S. championships. Kelly died at the age of 36 in an avalanche near Revelstoke, British Columbia. The documentary film Let it Ride is a chronicle of Kelly's life and his snowboarding career.

Directions: Skagit Valley is located 60 miles north of Seattle along I-5 and 70 miles south of Vancouver, BC, Canada. The tulips are generally grown in a 15-mile triangle bordered by Hwy 20, the Skagit River, and the Swinomish River Channel. The festival is designed as a driving tour because many events and attractions are miles apart, scattered throughout the lower Skagit Valley.

Penn Cove Musselfest

Coupeville, Whidbey Island, Island County
First full weekend in March

Penn Cove, located in historic downtown Coupeville, is home to the Penn Cove Mussel, which is known for being particularly tender (not chewy), sweet, and meaty. These world-famous mussels are the centerpiece of two days of festivities, including chowder tasting and mussel-eating competitions, mussel farm tours, and activities for all ages. Start your visit at the MusselFest Headquarters in the heart of historic downtown Coupeville. Enjoy mussel cooking demonstrations, and purchase tickets for the mussel farm boat tour, and tickets to the festival favorite mussel chowder tasting competition, which pits more than a dozen local restaurants against each other for the best mussel chowder. MusselFest Headquarters is also the place where you can compete (or cheer on your favorite contestant) in the mussel eating contest, where you try to be the quickest to down three 16-oz. cups of mussels. During the festival, the merchants of Coupeville offer extended hours for art walk shopping. The Waterfront Wine and Beer Garden provides locally crafted brews, with nearby family outdoor dining. On Saturday, the wine and beer garden entertains the crowd with live music, as well as fresh mussels and great beverages. The event also coincides with "Mussels in the Kettles" Mountain Bike Poker Ride and the Spring Art Tour, featuring artists at studios from Greenbank to Oak Harbor.

Address: Whidbey Island, Coupeville, Coupeville Recreation Hall, 901 NW Alexander Street
Admission: Admission is free. Chowder tasting costs $10, mussel farm tours cost $10, and competing in the mussel eating competition costs $5.

Parking: Parking is available for $3 on Alexander Street, next to the Coupeville Sno-Isle Library. Free parking, with free shuttle service to the festival, is available at Coupeville Elementary (6th S Main Street), Island County Campus (1 NE 7th Street), Coupeville United Methodist Church (608 N Main Street), and St. Mary's Catholic Church (207 N Main Street)
Accessible: Yes
Lodging: www.cometocoupeville.com/coupeville_lodging.html
Website: http://thepenncovemusselsfestival.com
Facebook: www.facebook.com/pages/Penn-Cove-MusselFest/257283287674?sk=timeline
Attractions: Ebey's Landing National Historical Reserve, Island County Historical Museum, Admiralty Head Lighthouse, Meerkerk Rhododendron Gardens, skeleton of Rosie the whale
Trivia: Established in 1853, Coupville is one of the oldest cities in the state of Washington. The city, which has a population of 1,800, has nearly 50 structures registered on the National Register of Historic Places.
Directions: From Seattle, take I-5 N to exit 182 toward Mukilteo. Take a slight right onto WA-525 and continue on to WA-525/Ferry Lanes. Take the Clinton-Mukilteo ferry to Clinton (Whidbey Island). Continue onto WA-20 E toward Coupeville. At the Coupeville overpass, take a right onto Main St. Continue toward Coupeville's historic downtown waterfront and take a left on to Coveland. MusselFest Headquarters is on your right (901 NW Alexander St). From Vancouver, BC, take BC-99 S toward the U.S. Border. Continue on to I-5 S and take exit 230 toward Burlington/Anacortes/WA-20. Turn left to stay on WA-20 W toward Oak Harbor. Turn right onto WA-20 W toward Coupeville and continue on to WA-20 E toward Coupeville. At the Coupeville overpass, take a right onto Main St. Continue toward Coupeville's historic downtown waterfront and take left onto Coveland. MusselFest Headquarters is on your right (901 NW Alexander St).

Skagit River Salmon Festival
Anacortes, Skagit County
Early September

The Skagit River Salmon Festival is a family event that celebrates the return of the salmon and the mighty Skagit River. The festival features youth activities and crafts, pony rides for the kids, recreational and educational booths, live music and cultural performances (including Native storytellers), great food, a salmon barbecue, a beer and wine garden (featuring local breweries), commercial art and craft vendors, a silent auction and raffle, and fly-fishing and -tying lessons. The 2014 festival introduced the Puget Sound DockDogs competition, where canines from Washington, Oregon, and Canada compete in aquatic events such as big air, extreme vertical, and speed retrieve. The day's activities and events are designed so that participants leave with a greater understanding and appreciation of the Skagit River, the area's salmon resources, and the many communities that are sustained by the river.

Address: Waterfront Park, Swinomish Casino and Lodge, 12885 Casino Drive
Admission: Free
Parking: Parking lot parking at the casino
Accessible: Yes
Pets: No info
Lodging: www.skagitriverfest.org/visit/lodging.html
Website: www.skagitriverfest.org
Facebook: www.facebook.com/pages/Skagit-River-Salmon-Festival/163269223803491
Attractions: Whale watching, Museum of Northwest Art (MONA), Skagit County Historical Museum, North Cascades Hwy, Sternwheeler W.T. Preston
Trivia: Two-week old Bobo, a Western Lowland Gorilla in French Equatorial Africa, was captured in 1951 after his mother was killed. He was so young that no zoo would take him. Luckily, Washington resident Bill Lowman was looking for a chimpanzee to purchase as a present for his parents, who lived in Anacortes. Bobo soon came to live with the Lowman family. They raised him as a human until he was two, at which point, his size, strength, and destructive behavior became an issue. Bobo then went to live at Woodland Park Zoo in Seattle, where he became a huge tourist attraction. Bobo died in 1968 after an apparent pulmonary embolism. Shortly afterward, his remains were transferred to the Burke Museum in Seattle, but a graduate student quickly discovered that Bobo's head was missing. The skull had been taken by Merrill Spencer, a physician who attended Bobo's autopsy. Spencer refused to give back the skull. After Spencer's death in 2006, however, the skull was returned to the museum and reunited with the rest of the body.
Directions: From I-5, take exit 230 and head west on SR-20 (Hwy 20) approximately nine miles. After crossing over the Twin Bridges turn right on to S March Point Rd. Take the first right onto Casino Dr and arrive at

the Skagit River Salmon Festival on the waterfront park at the Swinomish Casino and Lodge. From Anacortes, head east SR-20 E/WA-20 E. Take a right onto Padilla Heights Rd, then take the first left onto Knudson Ln. At the traffic circle, take the first exit and stay on Knudson Ln. Follow signs for festival parking.

Dirty Dan Day Seafood Festival
Bellingham, Whatcom County
Last Sunday in April

This festival is Fairhaven's annual celebration of seafood and community founder (and all-around smelly guy) Dirty Dan Harris. The festival features food and games, live music, a fish fillet contest, a salmon toss, cupcake- or donut-eating contests, toy boat building, interactive fish art, an 1800s costume contest (for both humans and pets), a beer garden, and cooking demos. As the story goes, when Dirty Dan sold the Fairhaven Hotel in 1890, the new owner refused to pay extra for the piano that was housed there, so Dan walked into the lobby, pushed the piano out the door and down the hill into the bay. In homage to this historical bout of fit-throwing, the festival hosts what may be the world's only piano race, where teams of four runners push and race pianos uphill. At the Dan Harris Challenge, rowers, pullers, and paddlers race each other for nine miles along the Fairhaven and Chuckanut shorelines in a challenging, and generally unpredictable, competition. For the chowder cook-off, 10 restaurants each prepare 20 gallons of their best chowder (clam, crab, salmon, corn, or other). Ticketholders get a 1-oz. taste of each chowder. Once you've picked your favorite, you give your ticket to that restaurant in exchange for an 8-oz cup of chowder and a piece of bread. The restaurant with the most tickets wins the People's Choice Award.

Address: Fairhaven Village Green, Mill Avenue and 10th Street
Admission: Admission is free. A ticket for the chowder cook-off costs around $10.
Parking: Street and parking lot parking
Accessible: Yes
Lodging: www.bellingham.org/lodging
Website: www.fairhaven.com/events/detail/6387
Attractions: Fairhaven Historic District, Whatcom Falls Park, Lake Padden Park, Spark Museum of Electrical Invention, Glen Echo Garden

Trivia: In 1854, Dan Harris arrived on the shore of Bellingham Bay as a 21-year-old adventurer. He became a legend as a homesteader, land owner, smuggler, rum-runner, hotel owner, and seaman, who founded Fairhaven in 1883. He was known to sport a top hat and a frock overcoat over a red long undershirt, which he never, ever washed. Because of this and his infrequent bathing, he earned the colorful nickname Dirty Dan. One of his amazing feats was regularly traveling by rowboat between Fairhaven and Victoria, B.C., a distance of around 50 miles one way.
Directions: Fairhaven is 90 miles north of Seattle via I-5 N.

The popular games Pictionary, Pickle-ball, and Cranium were invented in Washington.

Music

Oak Harbor Music Festival
Oak Harbor, Whidbey Island, Island County
September/Labor Day weekend

The Oak Harbor Music Festival is a free event held annually on Labor Day weekend in Historic Downtown Oak Harbor. The festival includes two main stages and 30 bands playing throughout the weekend, featuring all types of musical genres. Enjoy two beer gardens, a variety of food vendors and sidewalk cafes, and art and craft vendors as you stroll from one stage to the other.

Address: Whidbey Island
Admission: Admission is free, but donations are appreciated. Funds raised at the festival go to a scholarship for students interested in pursuing a career in music.
Parking: Parking costs $5 for the day. Parking is located in the empty lot on the southeast end of Bayshore.
Accessible: Yes
Lodging: Camping and RV sites are available in the empty lot on the southeast end of Bayshore. Spots cost $25 per night. Other lodging information: www.oakharborcomeashore.com
Website: www.oakharborfestival.com
Facebook: www.facebook.com/OakHarborMusicFestival
Attractions: PBY Memorial Foundation Naval Heritage Center, Windjammer Park, Pioneer Way and historic downtown Oak Harbor, Joseph Whidbey State Park, Fort Ebey State Park
Trivia: Built in 1959, Oak Harbor's family-owned Blue Fox Drive-In is one of the four operating drive-in theaters remaining in the state of Washington (others are in Port Townsend, Shelton, and Bremerton). Visitors can enjoy double features on a gigantic movie screen, food and beverages from a 1950s style snack bar, arcade games, and go-karting.
Directions: To reach the festival via freeway, take I-5 N to Burlington (about 1.5 hours north of Seattle) and exit on the Burlington exit 230 toward Anacortes/San Juan Ferry. Continue west on Hwy 20, approximately 15–20 minutes, towards Anacortes until you see the Oak Harbor/Whidbey Island cut off. Turn left at this intersection, continuing on Hwy 20 for approximately 20–25 minutes. Go through town and instead of turning right toward Coupeville on Hwy 20, turn left onto Pioneer

Way. Proceed one block and you are here. To reach the festival via the Mukilteo to Clinton ferry, get on the ferry at Mukilteo. The ride takes approximately 20 minutes, plus loading and unloading. Drive on Hwy 525 to Oak Harbor (approximately 45 minutes). Hwy 525 becomes Hwy 20 between the cities of Coupeville and Oak Harbor. As you come into Oak Harbor proceed straight ahead onto Pioneer Way instead of turning left and continuing on Hwy 20. The festival is one block ahead. From the ferry from Port Townsend to Coupeville, once you are off the ferry, head northwest on Engle Rd toward Fort Casey. Engle Rd becomes South Main St. Turn left at the stoplight on to Hwy 20. Travel 9.5 miles to Oak Harbor. Go straight at the second stop light onto Pioneer Way. The festival is one block ahead.

Doe Bay Festival
Olga, Orcas Island, San Juan County
Second weekend in August

Doe Bay Festival is the brainchild of the owners of Doe Bay Resort. This four-day festival features music, food, drink, camping, and activities in a unique, relaxed setting. The event's Facebook page describes it as "a festival which is basically musicians on vacations with their friends at one of the coolest places in the world for a holiday." Doe Bay Resort owns more than 30 acres of pristine waterfront property on Orcas Island, and it offers a variety of accommodations in a rustic, down-to-earth environment. Although festival tickets are hard to come by, if you stay at the Doe Bay Resort in the winter, you get the opportunity to purchase tickets to the upcoming festival.

Address: Orcas Island, Doe Bay Resort and Retreat, Olga
Admission: Admission runs $100 for all three days. The event is open only to ticket holders, and tickets are non-transferrable. No tickets are sold at the event. You have to be on your toes, though—tickets sell out extremely quickly.
Parking: Parking available on site
Accessible: Yes
Lodging: The Doe Bay Resort and Retreat (360.376.2291) hosts the festival. For information about other lodging options on Orcas Island: http://orcasislandchamber.com/lodging
Website: www.doebayfest.com

Facebook: www.facebook.com/doebayfest
Attractions: Orcas Island kayak tours, Moran State Park, Orcas Island Historical Museum, Doe Bay Hot Springs
Trivia: Orcas is the largest of all 172 named San Juan Islands, and it has the highest peak (Mt. Constitution, 2,400 feet). Orcas Island has no stoplights.
Directions: From Seattle, drive 60 miles north on I-5 and take exit 226. Continue on WA-536 W to WA-20 W to Anacortes, then take a ferry to the Orcas ferry landing, which is 20 miles from Doe Bay. For the most convenience, drive your car on to the boat. Alternatively, you can arrange ahead for a Doe Bay shuttle to pick you up (charge is $20/person one way, when available). For early-morning or later-evening pick-ups, taxi service on the island can take you to and from Doe Bay.

Bellingham Festival of Music
Bellingham, Whatcom County
Month of July

The Bellingham Festival of Music is one of America's premier virtuoso orchestra festivals. Each summer the festival features a repertoire of the finest symphonic music. Members of the orchestra all hold artistically prestigious positions elsewhere, and many of them are principal players in major North American symphony orchestras. The festival also features world famous guest artists and young rising stars.

Address: Western Washington University Performing Arts Center, 516 High Street
Admission: Tickets for individual events range from $30–$50. Students receive a substantial discount, as do faculty and staff members of Western Washington University. A full season pass gets you in to all events and costs $242–$319, depending on seating location. Orchestra-only season tickets cost $144–$210.
Parking: Parking is free for all concert goers in lot 14G on High Street. Metered parking is available in the other WWU Lots. No shuttle service is available from any of the WWU parking lots.
Accessible: Yes
Pets: No
Lodging: www.bellinghamfestival.org/visit/index.shtml
Website: www.bellinghamfestival.org

Facebook: www.facebook.com/bellingham.festival
Attractions: Fairhaven Historic District, North Bellingham Golf Course, Pickford Film Center, Whatcom Museum, Bellingham Railway Museum
Trivia: Gene Savoy, world renowned explorer, author, religious leader, and theologian, was born in Bellingham in 1927. Savoy rose to prominence in the 1960s for his research and discovery of numerous ancient and mysterious stone cities in Peru. In 1969 he built and captained the Kuviqu (also known as the Feathered Serpent I), a totora-reed raft of ancient design, along 2,000 miles of coastline from Peru to Mesoamerica in an effort to prove that Peruvians and Mexicans could have maintained contact in ancient times. To study ocean and wind currents, he then captained the Feathered Serpent II, which he sailed from the United States to the Caribbean, to Central and South America, and to Hawaii. In 1997 (at the age of 70, no less) he sailed a 73-foot wooden catamaran from Peru to Hawaii to demonstrate that ancient Peruvians could have done so. His diverse talents and swashbuckling ways led *People Magazine* in 1985 to declare him the *real* Indiana Jones.
Directions: From I-5, take the Lakeway St exit #253. Head west on Lakeway toward the city center. At the three-way intersection, continue west as Lakeway turns into Holly St. Turn left on to N Garden St and follow as it veers left and heads up the hill turning into W Campus Way. Make a sharp left onto Highland Dr, the first left-hand turn as you go up the hill. The first large brick building on the left is the Performing Arts Center.

Birch Bay Music Festival
Birch Bay, Whatcom County
First weekend in August

The Birch Bay Music Festival combines the love of animals and music in one location. The main goal of the event is to raise funds for local non-profit animal rescues though sponsorships, vendor fees, and a raffle. Event organizers hope to bring animal awareness and responsibility to the community through the greatest universal language of all—music. The event features live bands and singers/songwriters (all who donate their valuable time for the event), art and craft vendor booths, a children's train ride and bouncy house, local food offerings, pet nail trimming, pet photographs, and a beer and wine garden. Enjoy an alpaca petting area and K-9 demonstrations by law enforcement agencies. Don't forget to buy your raffle tickets. Past prizes have included a custom Cronk guitar.

Address: Corner of Birch Bay Drive and Alderson Road
Admission: Admission is free. Vendor booth proceeds, sponsorship fees, and a percentage of the sales from the sponsors are donated to an animal cause.
Accessible: Yes
Pets: Yes
Lodging: www.birchbayvillage.com/bus_dir_lodging.html
Website: www.birchbaymusicfestival.com
Facebook: www.facebook.com/musicfestivalinbirchbay
Attractions: Point Whitehorn Marine Park, Peace Arch State Park, clamming and crabbing in Birch Bay, Drayton Harbor Maritime Museum
Trivia: The ASPCA website estimates that 70–80 million dogs and 74–96 million cats are owned in the United States. Approximately 37%–47% of all households in the United States have a dog, and 30%–37% have a cat.
Directions: Birch Bay is located between Seattle and Vancouver, British Columbia, just north of Bellingham. Birch Bay is minutes off of I-5 at exit 270.

Darrington Bluegrass Festival
Darrington, Snohomish County
Third weekend in July

Billing itself as one of the biggest and premiere bluegrass festivals in the northwest, the Darrington Bluegrass Festival takes place at the base of Whitehorse Mountain that rises 6,200 feet and has a year-round glacier. The setting is so appealing, that the festival opens up its camping area a week prior to the event so that people can come and enjoy the area. The three-day festival includes awesome music, vendor booths, great food (breakfast, lunch, and dinner), and 24-hour jam sessions, some even at the campground. The rules for the festival say that a band has to be made up of at least four people, musicians can play in one band only, and no drums or electric instruments are allowed, except the electric bass.

Address: Darrington Bluegrass Music Park, Hwy 530
Admission: Admission for all three days is $45 if purchased before July 1, or $55 if purchased after July 1. At the gate, tickets cost $20 for Friday, $25 for Saturday, and $20 for Sunday. Children age 12 and under get in free with an adult.

Accessible: Yes
Pets: Dogs allowed at campground only
Lodging: Camping costs $35 a night and is available for both RVs and tents. The Medallion Hotel in Arlington (www.medallionhotel.net) provides a discount for festival attendees.
Website: www.darringtonbluegrass.com
Facebook: www.facebook.com/pages/Darrington-Bluegrass-Festival/309713789447
Attractions: Sauk River, Mt Baker-Snoqualmie National Forest, Stillaguamish River, Sam Strom Mines trail, Mountain Loop Hwy, Monte Cristo and Goat Lake ghost towns
Trivia: At one point called The Portage, the town was renamed Barrington in 1895 following a community meeting. The U.S. Postal Department mistakenly changed the first letter to a D, resulting in the current name of Darrington.
Directions: From I-5 take exit 208, the Arlington Darrington exit. Go east on Hwy 530 for approximately 30 miles following the Darrington signs. The Darrington Bluegrass Music Park is three miles before you come into the town of Darrington on the left. Follow the signs.

DjangoFest Northwest
Langley, Whidbey Island, Island County
Begins third Wednesday in September

DjangoFest is a series of music festivals celebrating the music of Django Reinhardt and other forms of gypsy jazz and traditional gypsy music. DjangoFest Northwest is one of North America's premier showcases of gypsy jazz, having presented some of the biggest names in the genre to thousands of enthusiastic participants. Whidbey Island Center for the Arts is proud to host this fabulous festival, bringing local and international musicians to the rural island community. Workshops and presentations by artists invite not only guitarists and violinists, but the general public as well. In the past, workshops have covered gypsy jazz rhythm, picking, finding your style, right-hand technique, the art of ensemble playing, swing fiddle, and sound, style, and technique.

Address: Whidbey Island, Whidbey Island Center for the Arts (WICA), 565 Camano Avenue and Langley Middle School Auditorium, 723 Camano Avenue

Admission: Individual concert admission prices range from $25–$70. Weekend passes run from $275–$314. Complete festival passes cost $342–$380. Festival passes do not include admission to workshops. Participating in a workshop at the main stage costs $50, and offsite workshops cost $40. Audience tickets for the main stage workshops run $20.
Parking: Street and parking lot parking
Accessible: Yes
Pets: No
Lodging: Camping with RV hookups is located next door to WICA at the Island County Fairgrounds for $10/night (no reservations needed). Other lodging information: www.visitlangley.com/lodging
Website: www.wicaonline.org/djangofest-northwest
Facebook: www.facebook.com/pages/DjangoFest-NW/175127719172627
Attractions: Earth Sanctuary, Langley Whale Center, sea kayaking, Fort Casey State Park, Langley History Museum
Trivia: It is believed that Langley, in 1919, was the first municipality in the nation to elect an all-woman council. The mayor elected was Miss Helen Coe, and with the rest of her council, she immediately set to work "cleaning up the town."
Directions: From downtown Seattle, travel time to Langley is approximately 1 hour, 18 minutes. Distance is 35 miles. From I-5 N, take exit 182 (in Lynnwood), merge left onto WA-525 west towards Mukilteo. Stay on WA-525 until you reach the WA State Ferry Terminal. Take the ferry across Puget Sound to Clinton. Once off of the ferry, continue north on WA-525. Turn right on to Langley Rd (it's the second traffic light on WA-525). From downtown Oak Harbor, travel time is about 58 minutes. Distance is 36 miles. Take WA-20 south, and continue south as WA-20 turns into WA-525. Turn left at Bayview Rd. Stay on Bayview Rd as it turns into Brooks Hill Rd, and then turns into 3rd St. Take 3rd St through Langley. From downtown Port Townsend, travel time is about 1 hour, 21 minutes. Distance is 30 miles. From Port Townsend, take the Port Townsend/Keystone Ferry to Whidbey Island. Turn right out of the ferry terminal onto WA-20 (Engle Rd). Turn right onto WA-525, then turn left at Bayview Rd. Stay on Bayview Rd as it turns into Brooks Hill Rd, and then turns into 3rd St. Take 3rd St through Langley.

Northwest Washington County Fairs

San Juan
Harbor
www.sjcfair.org

Skagit
Mt. Vernon
www.skagitcounty.net/Departments/Fair

Snohomish/Evergreen
Monroe
www.evergreenfair.org

Whatcom/Northwest Washington
Lynden
http://nwwafair.com/default.aspx

Whidbey Island
Langley
www.whidbeyislandfair.com

Mount Rainier is the highest point in Washington at a heigh of 14,410 feet. Named after Peter Rainier, a British soldier who fought against the Americans in the Revolutionary War, it has more glacial ice than any other peak in the United States. The first climers to scale Mount Ranier were P.B. VanTrump and General Hazard Stevens in 1870.

Central Region

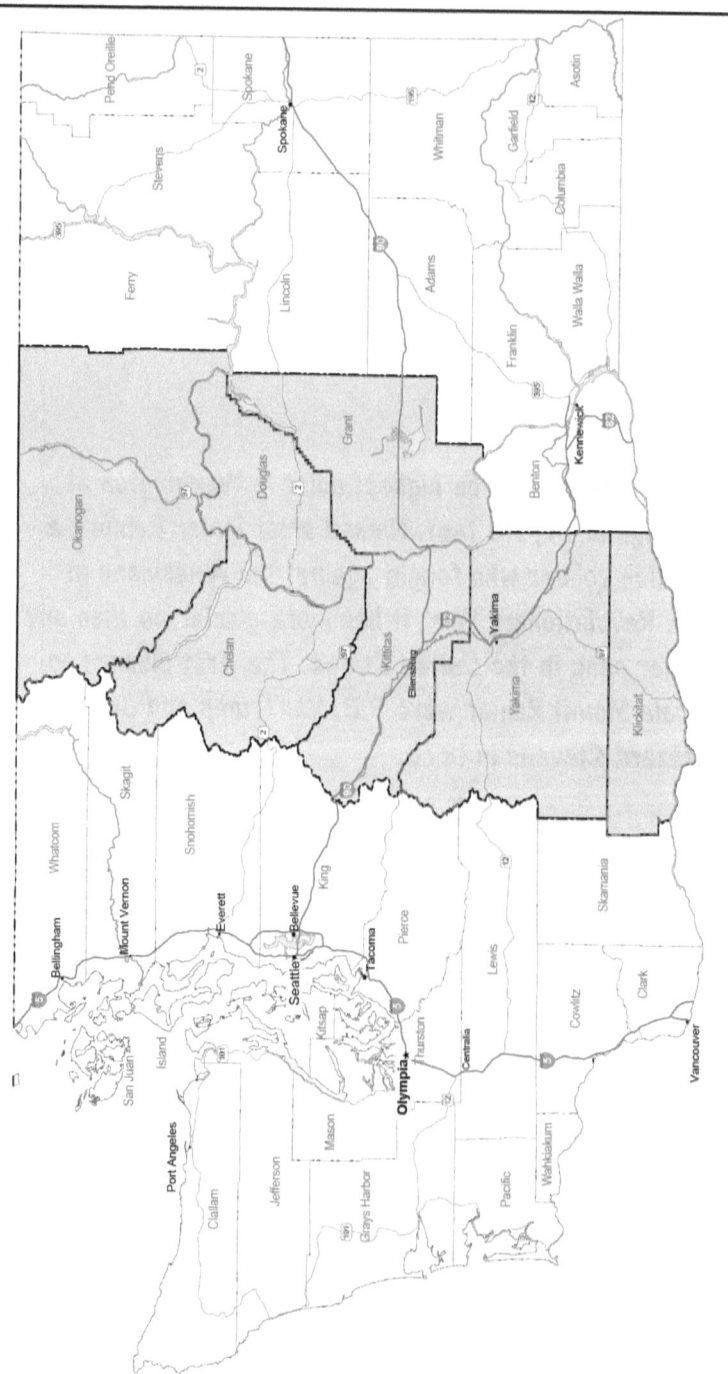

Central Washington

Central Washington is the perfect place to go if you want a great drink. The area surrounding the Yakima Valley is a veritable cornucopia of all the ingredients necessary for a really great party. The valley, which lies roughly on the same latitude as the French Bordeaux and Burgundy wine regions, is the second largest premium wine producer in the country. If you are so inclined, and have a designated driver in tow, you can get your tasting fill at any of the area's 160 wineries—most within an hour's drive of each other. Contrary to the perception that Washington is an extremely damp state (which is true on the western side), Central Washington, which lies in the rain shadow of the Cascade Mountain Range, boasts 300 days of sunshine each year. This fact, along with the fertile soil that permeates central and eastern Washington, means that vineyards thrive. Wine-related events occur year-round, and vintages are celebrated with grape stomps, wine tours, and festivals like Quincy's Hot Air Balloon and Wine Festival, White Salmon's Art and Wine Fusion, and Lake Chelan's Mahogany and Merlot Vintage Boat Show.

As if it weren't enough that Central Washington is a major wine mecca, the region is also responsible for 75% of the hops produced in America. Events like the Fresh Hop Ale Festival in Yakima, and the WinterHop BrewFest in Ellensburg provide great venues for sampling the area's best craft beers and microbrews.

And let's not forget about apples (and cherries, grapes, and pears). Smack dab in the middle of the state sits Wenatchee, the Apple Capitol of the World. Washington produces around 70% of the nation's apples (as well as half of the nation's pears), and a good portion of them come from this area. This hearty fruit is celebrated at Wenatchee's Washington State Apple Festival, Selah's Skewered Apple BBQ Competition, and Pateros' Apple Pie Jamboree.

The Baviarian-themed village of Leavenworth will charm your Germanic-loving socks off with year-round festivities, including a massive Oktoberfest in the fall and its Bavarian Ice Fest in January.

The spirit of the old west is celebrated annually at the Omak Stampede and at Ellensburg's Spirit of the West Cowboy Gathering. Wapato's Tamale Festival and Sunnyside's huge Cinco de Mayo festival celebrate the culture of the hard-working Hispanic people who helped this agricultural region become what it is today.

Art Events

Art and Wine Fusion
White Salmon, Klickitat County
Last Saturday in July

Art and Wine Fusion celebrates the many artists and fine wines of the Mt. Adams region of the Columbia River Gorge. Each year, the town of White Salmon (located 65 miles east of Portland) closes down the state highway that runs through the town center to create a pedestrian-only zone. Carefully chosen regional artists line the streets with booths that feature clothing, jewelry, paintings, drawings, photographs, pottery, wood craft, fabric arts, literature, furniture, and cement lawn art. The event includes two large tasting tents on either end of the street where you can sample wine and cider from more than 20 local and regional vintners. Wineries also set up tasting stations in local businesses if you want a more personal wine experience. The event also includes a beer garden. The main stage is set up in the middle of the action, and several bands perform throughout the day. Food booths are located amongst the artist booths, and serve up unique flavors of the Gorge. In addition, the event hosts a salmon cook-off. Children's activities include an art corral and a bike parade.

Address: Downtown
Admission: Entrance is free, but for wine and cider tasting you must be 21 or older and purchase a tasting package. Two tasting packages are available. The Classic Package costs $18 and includes five tasting tokens and an embossed wine glass. The economy package includes five tokens and a plastic wine cup.
Parking: Free street parking
Accessible: Yes
Pets: Yes
Lodging: The area includes several boutique inns, B&Bs, and historic hotels. Lodging information can be found at http://mtadamschamber.com/stay. Camping is also possible at commercial RV parks and campgrounds, as well as in national forest, state, and county campgrounds in Mt. Adams Recreation Area and in Gifford Pinchot National Forest. Camping information can be found at http://mtadamschamber.com/camping-in-the-gorge.
Website: www.artwinefusion.com

Facebook: www.facebook.com/ArtWineFusion
Attractions: Mt. Adams Recreation Area, Gifford Pinchot National Forest, Columbia River Gorge National Scenic Area
Trivia: The city of White Salmon takes its name from the nearby White Salmon River, which was named by the Lewis and Clark Expedition when they observed the river teeming with salmon whose color had turned white after spawning.
Directions: White Salmon is located 65 miles east of Portland, OR and Vancouver, WA via I-84 E and WA-14.

National Western Art Show and Auction
Ellensburg, Kittitas County
Third weekend in May

For more than 40 years, this three-day event has gathered together local and nationally acclaimed artists, talented new artists, and art collectors from around the country to share their love of the art of Western America. The presented artwork shows what you might see while traveling through the West of yesterday, today, or tomorrow. The 14,000 ft2 artist exhibition hall provides you the opportunity to meet the artists and watch them work. One of the crowd-pleasing activities is the Quick Draw, where you can cheer on your favorite artist as they produce works of art, from start to finish, in one hour. The Quick Draw pieces are then immediately auctioned off. Friday's schedule includes wine tasting, light hors d' oeuvres, a no-host bar, and the Quick Draw auction. Saturday's events include an artists' autograph session, wine tasting, a buffet dinner, and the main event auction, at which you can bid on original works of art, including works completed during the art show. Sunday also includes a live event and an auction.

Address: Kittitas Valley Event Center at the Kittitas County Fairgrounds, junction of Hwy 97 and Interstates 90 and 82.
Admission: The artist exhibition hall is open free to the public. Ticketed events occur on Saturday, and include a buffet dinner, a Quick Draw demonstration, and the main art auction.
Parking: Free parking at the event center
Accessible: Yes
Pets: No
Lodging: www.myellensburg.com/stay

Website: http://westernartassociation.org/art-show-and-auction
Facebook: www.facebook.com/WesternArtAssociation/info
Attractions: Ginkgo Petrified Forest/Wanapum Recreational Area, L.T. Murray Wildlife Area, Ellensburg Frontier Village, Olmstead State Park.
Trivia: In the late 1800s, Ellensburg was one of the cities considered for Washington's state capitol. Unfortunately, a fire destroyed the town in 1890, removing it from contention.
Directions: Ellensburg is located 108 miles (2 hours) east of Seattle on I-90 E; 120 miles (2 hours) northwest of the Tri-Cities; and 170 miles (2.5 hours) west of Spokane on I-90 W.

Ellensburg Film Festival
Ellensburg, Kittitas County
First full weekend in October

Started in 2004, the three-day Ellensburg Film Festival has grown into a major Northwest film and arts festival that attracts more than 2,000 attendees. Considering that the town of Ellensburg has a population of only 18,000, that's quite an influx of avid movie fans. The festival is noted for its selection of critically acclaimed films, numerous screenings and venues, and diverse offerings. And, as is typical with the Northwest, does so all in a relaxed, fun atmosphere. The goal of the festival is to expose audiences to the artistry, issues, and perspectives in current independent film. Festival films have also been featured at Cannes, Toronto, Berlin, and New York festivals. Film categories include feature film (longer than 40 minutes), documentary, short subject (shorter than 40 minutes), and animation.

Address: Gallery One Visual Arts Center, 408 N. Pearl Street
Admission: Single tickets cost $6 or $3 for students with a valid ID. Choose any six films with the festival's SixTix Deal, which costs $30. An all-festival pass costs $50, and includes admission to all screenings, events, and ceremonies, as well as a festival t-shirt.
Parking: Street parking is available at most of the venues. Public parking is also available on 4th and Pearl.
Accessible: Yes
Pets: No
Lodging: Two hotels in Ellensburg—Holiday Inn Express (509.962.9400) and Hampton Inn (509.933.1600) offer discounts for film festival at-

tendees. Quality Inn (509.925.9800) provides another option for lodging close to the festival.
Website: http://ellensburgfilmfestival.com
Facebook: www.facebook.com/ellensburg.filmfestival
Attractions: Ginkgo Petrified Forest/Wanapum Recreational Area, L.T. Murray Wildlife Area
Trivia: The nearby town of Cle Elum was one of the last cities in the country to still use manual telephone switchboards, finally changing over to automatic dialing in the mid '60s. The city has established the Cle Elum Historical Telephone Museum, which is the oldest complete telephone museum west of the Mississippi.
Directions: From Seattle: Take I-90 East to Ellensburg exit #106. Merge onto US-97 S and follow 0.5 miles until it turns into West University Way. Travel 2.1 miles on West University Way to Main St, turn right, and travel 0.3 miles. Turn left on 4th Ave and go to the stop sign on North Pearl. Turn left on North Pearl and travel 150 feet. Gallery One is on the right side of the block. From Spokane: Take I-90 West to Ellensburg exit #109. Turn right off the exit ramp on to Canyon Rd/Main St. Travel 1.6 miles on Canyon Rd/Main St to 4th Ave. Turn right on 4th Ave and go to the stop sign on North Pearl. Turn left on North Pearl and travel 150 feet. Gallery One is on the right side of the block.

Trout Lake Festival of the Arts
Trout Lake, Klickitat County
Second weekend in July

Billing itself as "Fine Art, Music, and Food with a Mountain View," the Trout Lake Festival of the arts features more than 50 juried artists displaying their works outdoors, surrounded by fir and pine trees, beneath a spectacular backdrop of Mt. Adams. In addition to the display of fine arts, the festival includes a Literary Corner where local authors can share their works, as well as a Kids Corner for budding artists ages 2–10 to experience art and music hands-on. While you peruse the fine artwork, take a break to sit down, eat some good festival food, and sip a lemonade or a cold beer while enjoying music from local and non-local musicians throughout the weekend.

Address: On the lawn at Trout Lake School, 2310 Hwy 141
Admission: Free
Parking: Free

Lodging: The area includes several boutique inns, B&Bs, and historic hotels. Lodging information at http://mtadamschamber.com/stay. Camping is also possible at commercial RV parks and campgrounds, as well as in national forest, state, and county campgrounds in Mt. Adams Recreation Area and in Gifford Pinchot National Forest. Camping information at http://mtadamschamber.com/camping-in-the-gorge
Website: http://troutlakefestivalofthearts.wordpress.com
Facebook: www.facebook.com/pages/Trout-Lake-Festival-of-the-Arts/256840884502371
Attractions: Local area wineries, Columbia River Gorge National Scenic Area, Ice Caves, Pacific Crest Trail
Trivia: The town of Trout Lake is located 13 miles from the Pacific Crest Trail, and members of the local Pacific Crest Trail Association regularly make arrangements to transport weary hikers to and from the trail when they are in need of amenities.
Directions: From Hood River: I-84, exit 64, cross the bridge to Washington and Hwy 14. Turn left and go 1.5 miles. Turn right on to WA-141 Alt and go 2.5 miles. Turn left on to WA-141 and drive north 18 miles to Trout Lake. The festival site is just before mile post 23. Follow the signs.

The Ginkgo Petrified Forest in Vantage, Washington is one of the largest petrified forests in the world.

Beer, Wine & Spirits

Lake Chelan Crush Festival
Lake Chelan, Chelan County
First two weekends in October

The annual Crush Festival takes place on back-to-back weekends amidst the spectacularly colored October countryside. Experience first-hand the steps involved in the grape harvest. Taste the raw juice that comes from the press, and learn from the master or wine maker how the wine will taste at bottling time. And those who don't mind getting a little messy can participate in stomping grapes the old-fashioned way.

Address: Downtown
Admission: Wine tasting fees vary by winery.
Parking: Street, parking lot
Accessible: Yes
Lodging: Information can be found at www.lakechelan.com/where-to-stay
Website: www.lakechelanwinevalley.com/events/lake-chelan-crush.html
Attractions: Boating, jet skiing, tubing, skiing, swimming on Lake Chelan; Lake Chelan State Park, Bear Mountain Ranch Golf Course
Trivia: Every October, the Sonoma County Harvest Fair in Santa Rosa, California holds the World Championship Grape Stomp, where teams of two compete to see how much juice they can produce from a barrel full of grapes. The winning team receives $1,500. The 2014 champions squeezed out 26.11 pounds of juice in five minutes.
Directions: From Seattle via Snoqualmie/Blewett: Travel time is approximately 3 hours/173 miles. From I-5, take I-90 east. Take the second exit (Cle Elum to Wenatchee). Head north on Hwy 97 to Hwy 2 east. Off of Hwy 2, take the exit for East Wenatchee/Spokane. Take Lake Chelan exit on to 97 Alt. From Seattle via Stevens Pass: Travel time is approximately 3 hours/166 miles. From Everett, head east on Hwy 2. Take East Wenatchee/Spokane exit. Take exit for Lake Chelan on 97 Alt. From Spokane via McNeil Canyon: Travel time is approximately 2.5 hours/153 miles. Take Hwy 2 west to Coulee City. Continue west to Hwy 17. Drive north on Hwy 17 to Hwy 172. Drive through Mansfield. Following signs to Lake Chelan, continue to McNeil Canyon/Beebe Bridge Park. Taking a right on Hwy 97, cross Beebe Bridge. Take an immediate left after crossing the Columbia River over the Beebe Bridge. Hwy 150 becomes

Woodin Ave in downtown Chelan. From Spokane via Pine Canyon: Travel time is approximately three hours/173 miles. On Hwy 2, head west to Hwy 97. Continue North on Hwy 97, then take an immediate left after crossing the Columbia River over Beebe Bridge. Hwy 150 becomes Woodin Ave into downtown Chelan.

WinterHop BrewFest
Ellensburg, Kittitas County
Third Saturday in January

For more than a decade, WinterHop BrewFest has been featuring a taste of the Northwest's finest microbreweries, including Ellensburg's own Iron Horse Brewery, best known for its dark ale Quilter's Irish Death. Samples from more than 20 brewers are served at various venues scattered throughout the historic downtown. Bundled-up beer fans enjoy live music including jazz, blues, and classical, as well as great food from local venues while sampling the varied brews.

Address: Downtown
Admission: Tickets cost $30 and include a souvenir glass and five tastings. Tickets go on sale the first business day of December and sell out quickly.
Parking: Plenty of parking is available in downtown Ellensburg.
Accessible: Yes
Pets: No
Lodging: Holiday Inn Express in Ellensburg (509.962.9400) offers BrewFest attendees a package deal that includes tickets.
Website: www.myellensburg.com/events/brewfest
Facebook: www.facebook.com/pages/WinterHop-Brew-Fest/129737553743333
Attractions: Ginkgo Petrified Forest, Wanapum Recreational Area, Ellensburg Frontier Village, Olmstead State Park.
Trivia: Old English pubs served ale in pints and quarts. Unruly customers would invariably roust the bartender to yell at them to settle down and mind their own pints and quarts. Thus the phrase "mind your Ps and Qs" was born.
Directions: Ellensburg is located 108 miles (2 hours) east of Seattle on I-90 E; 120 miles (2 hours) northwest of the Tri-Cities; and 170 miles (2.5 hours) west of Spokane on I-90 W.

Great Grandview Grape Stomp
Grandview, Yakima County
September

The Great Grandview Grape Stomp provides a fun time to celebrate the fall grape harvest deep in the heart of the Yakima wine valley, and to channel your inner Lucille Ball, ala the "Lucy's Italian Movie" episode. The Grape Stomp is a competition in which three-member teams vie to stomp out the most juice (based on weight). Each member stomps with their bare feet for one minute while another team member holds the juice container. Wacky team names and costumes are highly encouraged. The event also includes food, art, and craft vendors, and activities for kids.

Address: Yakima Valley Community College Grandview Campus, 114 Grandridge
Admission: Spectators get in free. For stompers, early registration is $35 per team, which includes a Grape Stomp t-shirt for each team member. Day-of-the-event registration is $45, which includes a t-shirt (until supplies run out).
Parking: Free parking on the college campus.
Accessible: Yes
Pets: No
Lodging: Information can be found at: www.visityakima.com/newSite/yakima-valley-accommodations.asp
Website: www.visitgrandview.org/events/grandview-grape-stomp
Facebook: www.facebook.com/pages/The-Great-Grandview-Grape-Stomp/246837618681173
Attractions: Fort Simcoe State Park, Yakima Valley wineries, Yakama Nation Museum, Toppenish Murals, Meadowbrook Family Fun Center, Cowiche Canyon
Trivia: In October 2014, the Lucy Desi Center for Comedy hosted the Welch's World Record Grape Stomp in Jamestown, NY (Lucille Ball's home town) where 1,232 people stomped 60 tons of grapes in honor of the famous comedy grape-stomping scene from the *I Love Lucy* television show. The event set the new Guinness World Record for "most people treading grapes." The previous record of 977 people was set in Spain in 2010.
Directions: Grandview is located 50 miles west of the Tri-Cities via I-82 W.

Fresh Hop Ale Festival

Yakima , Yakima County
First Saturday in October

The Yakima Valley produces nearly 75% of the total U.S. hop crop, so it's only natural that Yakima hosts the annual Fresh Hop Ale Festival. Depending on the timing of each year's hop harvest, fresh hop ale is generally produced throughout the month of September. The festival defines "fresh hop ale" as beer that is produced with hops that were picked no more than 24 hours prior to brewing. Fresh hop ale is typically pale- or IPA-style beer that is milder in flavor and less bitter than beers made from dried hops. The festival features ales from more than 30 breweries, wine, food booths, and music on a festival stage. Proceeds from the Fresh Hop Ale Festival go to support Yakima Valley art organizations.

Address: Millennium Arts Plaza, South 3rd Street & Yakima Avenue
Admission: Tickets cost $30 pre-sale or $35 at the gate. Admission includes a commemorative beer glass and $9 scrip (used instead of cash for beer and wine). Please note: Traditionally, food purchases at the event have been cash only. So make sure you bring plenty with you.
Parking: If you arrive early, free on-site parking is available. Otherwise, street parking and parking lots are available within walking distance.
Accessible: Yes
Pets: No
Lodging: Several local inns provide package deals that include lodging and tickets. Information at: www.freshhopalefestival.com/lodging.html
Website: www.freshhopalefestival.com
Facebook: www.facebook.com/FreshHopAleFestival
Attractions: Fort Simcoe State Park, Yakima Valley wineries, Yakama Nation Museum, Toppenish Murals, Meadowbrook Family Fun Center, Cowiche Canyon
Trivia: In addition to being the nation's largest producer of hops, the Yakima Valley region is one of the world's leading producers of apples. The area is also known for growing more than 30 varieties of fruits and vegetables such as cherries, peaches, pears, nectarines, mint, asparagus, hay, berries, and eggplant.
Directions: Yakima is located 142 miles (2.5 hours) southeast of Seattle via I-90 E and 85 miles (1.5 hours) northwest of the Tri-Cities via I-82 W.

Snake in the Glass Passport Party
Zillah, Yakima County
August

Wine and dine with the winemakers of the Rattlesnake Hills Wine Trail, dance under the stars, and enjoy the beauty of a warm summer evening in wine country. This annual Passport Party is hosted by the 13 wineries in Rattlesnake Hills. A Passport Party requires the pre-purchase of a Rattlesnake Hills Passport (no expiration date), which secures you an invitation to the annual Snake in the Glass event, as well as benefits and discounts at all 13 Rattlesnake Hills wineries. Party attendees enjoy heavy appetizers that are paired with some of the Yakima valley's award-winning wines. Enjoy live music and, of course, the company of winemakers, grape growers, and other wine lovers.

Address: Maison de Padgett Winery, 2231 Roza Drive
Admission: Rattlesnake Hills Passport costs $10, event tickets cost $35.
Parking: Free
Accessible: Yes
Pets: No
Lodging: Many B&Bs, hotels, and camping spots are available in or around the Rattlesnake Hills Wine Trail. Information at: www.rattlesnakehills.org/rattlesnake-wine-trips.php
Website: www.rattlesnakehills.org/passport-party.php
Facebook: www.facebook.com/RattlesnakeHillsWineTrail
Attractions: Silbury Hill Alpaca Farm, Yakima Valley fruit and produce stands, Fort Simcoe State Park, Yakama Nation Museum, Toppenish Murals, Meadowbrook Family Fun Center, Cowiche Canyon
Trivia: On 1st Avenue in Zillah stands the Teapot Dome Service Station, a former service station constructed in the shape of a teapot. Built in 1922, the teapot was a reminder to the public of the Teapot Dome Scandal that happened during the Warren G. Harding administration. No longer in service, the tiny building is listed on the U.S. National Register of Historic Places.
Directions: From Seattle, Ellensburg, Yakima, and points west: From the Tri-Cities, take I-182 to I-82. Then take the right exit to Yakima and Seattle. The Wine Trail can be accessed from exit 63 to exit 44. From Portland, OR, Toppenish, WA and points south: Proceed east from Portland on I-84 to Biggs Junction, OR (US-97). Exit right to the stop sign (US-97). Turn left across the Columbia River on US-97 toward Goldendale and

Yakima. Proceed about 60 miles to Toppenish to the stop light. (Hwy 22/Hwy 97). At the light, proceed straight into Toppenish on Elm St, past the second light, across the railroad tracks and out of town (now Buena Way). Cross the Yakima River to I-82. You are now at exit 50 of I-82. The Wine Trail can be accessed from exit 44 to exit 63. From Spokane and Northern Idaho: Either go to Ellensburg on I-90 or go to Pasco on US-395. Follow previous directions from there.

In Washington, it is illegal to paint polka dots on the American flag.

Ethnic & Cultural Celebrations

Maifest
Leavenworth, Chelan County
May/Mother's Day weekend

Maifest is a German tradition in which villagers gathered to celebrate the arrival of spring by planting flowers, playing music and games, and raising a maipole in the local square. They would decorate the pole with flowers, ribbons, and food, and dance around it, believing that it would bring good luck and wealth to the village. The Leavenworth Maifest festival captures this spirit of spring, and Mother's Day, in a weekend filled with music and dance, a parade and Grand March, traditional German dance lessons and performances, art in the park, a display of medieval antiques and replicas, and even a 60-minute longsword battle presentation and a mini trebuchet demonstration. Come dressed in your best Bavarian outfit and compete in Bavaria's Best Dressed contest. If mom enjoys the town's famous hanging flower baskets, then she will delight in making one of her own.

Address: Front Street
Admission: Free
Parking: Street, parking lot
Accessible: Yes
Pets: No
Lodging: Many hotels, motels, cabins, B&Bs, vacation homes, and camping spots are available in Leavenworth and the surrounding area. Information at: www.leavenworth.org/lodging
Website: www.leavenworth.org/event/Maifest-2014
Attractions: Sleeping Lady Mountain Resort Art Walk and Organic Garden, Icicle Junction Activity Center, Nutcracker Museum, Cashmere Museum and Pioneer Village, Hidden Lake, Icicle River, Lake Minotaur, Waterfront Park.
Trivia: During a particularly dry summer in 1994, after eight years of drought, out-of-control wildfires forced Leavenworth residents to evacuate. As many as 2,400 firefighters from 24 different states worked to save the town. No one was injured, but 14 homes were destroyed in Icicle Creek canyon during the fire. The fire burned a total of 180,000 acres in Chelan County. Again in 2014, homes in the Leavenworth area were evacuated because of lightning-sparked wildfires that amassed and

became one of the worst wildfires in Washington state history, eventually consuming 360,000 acres.

Directions: Leavenworth is easily accessible from the west coast via US-2, and the drive through the Cascades has been voted one of the most scenic drives in the United States.

Spirit of the West Cowboy Gathering
Ellensburg, Kittitas County
Mid-February/President's Day weekend

The Spirit of the West Cowboy Gathering celebrates and preserves the heritage of the American Cowboy and the pioneer values that distinguish America's history. The Gathering brings the best traditional cowboy musicians, poets, and artists together to celebrate the western tradition of ranching and cowboy life. Attendees hear local and regional cowboy and cowgirl poets and crooners share rhymes, stories, and songs. Other events include a gear and art show, a gospel music show, a ranch roping competition, Dutch Oven cooking, the annual Spirit of the West Fiddle Contest, a Saturday evening concert and dance, cowboy church on Sunday, and a Sunday afternoon concert. Workshops and presentations highlight local people who keep alive the skills and spirit of the western and native ways. On Sunday afternoon, kids learn how to rope using a real lariat and race stick horses around a barrel pattern.

Address: Various venues
Admission: All of the events are free and open to the public except for main stage concerts and western dance and music workshops. Main stage concert tickets range from $30 to $100. Tickets for the Friday night gospel concert cost $8, and the Saturday night dance costs $5.
Parking: Free street and parking lot parking
Accessible: Yes
Pets: No
Lodging: The host hotel for the Cowboy Gathering has been the Quality Inn and Conference Center, 509.925.9800. Other lodging can be found at: http://ellensburgcowboygathering.com/?page_id=270
Website: http://ellensburgcowboygathering.com
Facebook: www.facebook.com/SpiritOfTheWestCowboyGathering
Attractions: Ginkgo Petrified Forest/Wanapum Recreational Area, L.T. Murray Wildlife Area, Ellensburg Frontier Village, Olmstead State Park.

Trivia: The grunge/alternative rock band Screaming Trees hails from Ellensburg.
Directions: Ellensburg is located 108 miles (2 hours) east of Seattle on I-90 E; 120 miles (2 hours) northwest of the Tri-Cities; and 170 miles (2.5 hours) west of Spokane on I-90 W.

Cinco de Mayo Festival
Sunnyside, Yakima County
Weekend closest to May 5th

Sunnyside is host to the largest Cinco de Mayo festival in the Pacific Northwest. Because of its agricultural heritage, the Yakima Valley has drawn many migrant workers from Mexico, Texas, and California, resulting in a large Hispanic population. Over the years, many migrant families have settled in the area, bringing their native culture—and cuisine—with them. So if you're in the mood for fantastic authentic Mexican food, you can't do any better than this festival. Enjoy the colorful parade; live entertainment; dancing horses; a car show; a carnival; softball, soccer, and half-court basketball tournaments; and the Miss Cinco de Mayo Pageant. Plus, the event includes more than 100 street vendors, and lots of live music and mariachi bands.

Address: Downtown
Admission: Free. Carnival ticket prices vary
Parking: Street and parking lot parking
Accessible: Yes
Pets: Yes
Lodging: Information at: www.sunnyside-wa.gov/DocumentCenter/View/658.
Website: http://visityakima.com/cinco-de-mayo/
Attractions: Yakima Valley wineries, Yakima's historic Front Street, Toppenish murals, Yakama Nation's Legends Casino, White Pass Scenic Byway, whitewater rafting on the Tieton River
Trivia: Sunnyside, deep in the heart of Yakima's agricultural community, has its own down-home take on a Christmas light parade. Every first Saturday of December, the town hosts its annual Lighted Farm Implement Parade. In addition to regular parade entrants, the event features combines, sprayers, grape pickers, and all types of tractors decorated with thousands of colorful lights. First held in 1989, the parade was fea-

tured on A&E's *Ultimate Holiday Town USA* and is considered by many to be one of the premier lighted parades in the Pacific Northwest.
Directions: Sunnyside is located 35 miles southeast of Yakima and 45 miles east of the Tri-Cities.

Yakima Folklife Festival
Yakima, Yakima County
Third weekend in July

The Yakima Folklife Association was formed to promote broader community awareness of cultural and folk traditions such as music, dance, crafts, and other folk arts. Thus, the Yakima Folklife Festival was born. The annual festival takes place at the Yakima Valley Museum and adjacent Franklin Park. The three-day festival has craft and food vendors, extensive children's activities, a Saturday night Contradance (a partnered folk dance), and more than 50 music and dance performances (including the Yakama Nation Dance Troupe) on five outdoor stages.

Address: Yakima Valley Museum and adjacent Franklin Park, 2105 Tieton Drive, and various locations downtown
Admission: Free
Parking: Street and parking lot parking
Accessible: Yes
Lodging: http://visityakima.com/newSite/yakima-valley-accommodations.asp
Website: www.yakimafolklife.com
Facebook: www.facebook.com/pages/Yakima-Folklife-Association/120265111317613
Attractions: Yakima Valley wineries, Yakima's historic Front Street, Toppenish murals, Yakama Nation's Legends Casino, White Pass Scenic Byway, whitewater rafting on the Tieton river
Trivia: In the mid-1990s the Yakima Nation renamed itself to "Yakama," more closely reflecting the proper pronunciation in their native tongue. There is disagreement on what "Yakama" means. Possibilities include "growing family," "pregnant ones," "black bear," or "runaway."
Directions: Yakima is located 142 miles (2.5 hours) southeast of Seattle via I-90 E and 85 miles (1.5 hours) northwest of the Tri-Cities via I-82 W.

Oktoberfest

Leavenworth, Chelan County
First three Fridays and Saturdays in October

This three-weekend-long family-friendly event celebrates German heritage and all of its wonderful music, cuisine, art, and of course, beer. Set in Leavenworth's Bavarian village, this festival has been ranked one of the top Oktoberfests in the nation. Guests are entertained with four venues of continuous live entertainment including Bavarian dancing, as well as oompah and polka music from bands hailing from Germany, Canada, and the U.S. Children can participate in activities at Kinderplatz, which includes a rock climbing wall, bouncy toys, and clowns. Following the parade every Saturday afternoon, Leavenworth's mayor hosts a ceremony honoring the Bavarian tradition of tapping the keg. Oktoberfest's hours are generally 6 pm–12 am on Fridays and 12 pm–12 am on Saturdays. Minors are allowed inside the gates until 9 pm. Don't forget to pick up an Oktoberfest stein, which features a new design each year.

Address: Festhalle and Tent, Front Street
Admission: Friday admission is $10 and Saturday admission is $20. Children under age 12 are free. Active military (with ID) are free at the gate. Tickets can be purchased in advance or at the gate.
Parking: Street and parking lot. Free shuttle transportation is available within Leavenworth. Shuttles are available outside Leavenworth for a fee, with routes extending as far as Wenatchee.
Accessible: Yes
Pets: No
Lodging: With more than a million tourists visiting each year, many hotels, motels, cabins, B&Bs, vacation homes, and camping spots are available in Leavenworth and the surrounding area. www.leavenworth.org/lodging
Website: www.leavenworthoktoberfest.com
Facebook: www.facebook.com/oktoberfestWA
Attractions: Icicle Junction Activity Center, Nutcracker Museum, Cashmere Museum and Pioneer Village, Hidden Lake, Icicle River, Lake Minotaur, Waterfront Park.
Trivia: Germany's Oktoberfest began in Munich in 1810 as a celebration of the marriage of Prince Ludwig I to Princess Therese from Saxony-Hildburghausen. It started as a wedding feast on the outskirts of Munich where the guests ate, drank, and celebrated. It was such a success that

it became an annual tradition now enjoyed by more than 10 million people per year worldwide.

Directions: Leavenworth is easily accessible from the west coast via US-2, and the drive through the Cascades has been voted one of the most scenic drives in the United States.

Spring Barrel Tasting
Yakima, Yakima County
Mid to late April

Spring Barrel Tasting is your chance to get a jump on tasting and purchasing some of the best wines in wine country. Droves of people gather in the Yakima Valley for the largest wine festival in the Pacific Northwest to experience the new vintages straight from the barrel. Winemakers are on hand to mingle with visitors, conduct tours, and answer questions. More than 50 wineries participate, spanning the area from Yakima to the Tri-Cities, and offer appetizers, live music, and various festivities. Brush up on your wine-tasting etiquette, bring a wine glass (or be prepared to purchase one at a winery—most require a wine glass during the event weekend), and enjoy samples of the new wines that taste very different from what you are used to from a bottle.

Address: Various wineries in the Yakima Valley
Admission: If you purchase a Premier Pass, you receive exclusive weekend benefits, which include a signature wine glass, library tastings, waived tasting fees at some locations, and access to special events. Cost for a Premier Pass is $30 in advance or $35 at the door.
Parking: Free parking available at participating wineries
Accessible: Yes
Pets: No
Lodging: www.visityakima.com/newSite/yakima-valley-accommodations.asp
Website: www.visityakima.com/find-spring/spring-barrel-wine-tasting.asp
Facebook: www.facebook.com/winedivasllc/timeline
Attractions: Yakima Area Arboretum, Fort Simcoe, Yakima Electric Railway Museum, Indian Painted Rocks
Trivia: Washington's first wine grapes were planted at Fort Vancouver by

the Hudson's Bay Company in 1825. It wasn't until 1903 that irrigation enabled the cultivation of grapes in Eastern Washington.
Directions: Yakima is located 142 miles (2.5 hours) southeast of Seattle via I-90 E and 85 miles (1.5 hours) northwest of the Tri-Cities via I-82 W.

Summer White Party
Yakima, Yakima County
Late June

Men: Fire up the barbecue, and invite your manly-men friends over to catch a baseball game. This wear-white-only event is for women only. Women: Bring your girlfriend (21 and older) to an evening of wine tasting, hors d'oeuvres, shopping, on-site pampering services, live entertainment, and door prizes. The event features local premium wines and local business owners as vendors. Partial proceeds from the event benefit a local charity.

Address: 4th Street Theater, 14 South 4th Street
Admission: $30 in advance, $35 at the door
Accessible: Yes
Pets: No
Lodging: Various lodging facilities are located in Yakima.
Website: www.winedivasllc.com/#!just-wear-white-party/c24hy
Facebook: www.facebook.com/winedivasllc
Attractions: Yakima Valley wineries, Yakama Nation Legends Casino, Yakima Greenway, Hillside Desert Botanical Gardens, American Hop Museum, McAllister Museum of Aviation
Trivia: Actor Kyle MacLachlan (*Twin Peaks*, *Portlandia*) was born and raised in Yakima. He graduated from Eisenhower High School in 1977. In collaboration with Dunham Cellars in Walla Walla, Washington, MacLachlan has developed his own brand of wine, called Pursued by Bear (which is a reference to the stage direction "Exit, pursued by a bear" from Shakespeare's *The Winter's Tale*).
Directions: Yakima is located 142 miles (2.5 hours) southeast of Seattle via I-90 E and 85 miles (1.5 hours) northwest of the Tri-Cities via I-82 W.

Family Fun

Maryhill Festival of Speed
Goldendale, Klickitat County
Last Wednesday in June

Maryhill Festival of Speed is the largest North American gravity sports festival, and is known throughout the world as one of the best downhill skateboarding venues. Each year, approximately 3,000 spectators witness the thrills and spills that are part of the Festival of Speed, which brings more than 200 top international competitors to the Columbia River Gorge for the Downhill Skateboarding World Cup, as well as street luge and classic luge events. Skateboarders from 24 countries battle it out for their share of a $10,000 prize purse on the 2.2-mile, 22-corner historic Maryhill Loops Road. The course, which often sees racers traveling at around 50 mph, features two spectator areas, as well as action sports exhibits, food, and musical entertainment. The festival also includes a daily half-pipe competition and best trick competitions.

Address: Maryhill Museum of Art, 35 Maryhill Museum Drive
Admission: Free for spectators
Accessible: Yes
Pets: Yes
Lodging: Nearby Goldendale offers accommodations. www.maryhillfestivalofspeed.com/location-info/accomodations
Website: www.maryhillfestivalofspeed.com
Facebook: www.facebook.com/johnozman1
Attractions: Goldendale Observatory, Maryhill Museum, Maryhill Stonhenge, Presby Museum, Local Wineries
Trivia: The world record for fastest skateboard speed from a standing position is 129.94 km/h (80.74 mph) set by Canadian Mischo Erban on a downhill run on a road in Les Éboulements, Quebec that reaches an 18% grade in some spots.
Directions: Maryhill Museum of Art overlooks the Columbia River on Washington's SR-14, just west of US-97 and across the Biggs Rapids-Sam Hill Bridge from I-84.

Quincy Hot Air Balloon and Wine Festival
Quincy, Grant County
Second weekend in September

The beauty and open space of Quincy make it an ideal place to enjoy the colorful Quincy Valley Hot Air Balloon and Wine Festival. Although event balloon rides are reserved for sponsors and volunteers only, spectators are invited to bring lawn chairs, blankets, and cameras to take advantage of the fantastic photo opportunity. The festival begins with a sunrise launch at around 6 am. On Saturday evening, enjoy food vendors, a beer and wine garden, and live entertainment. At dusk, tethered balloons light up for a Night Glow to illuminate the nighttime sky. The evening ends with a dazzling fireworks display.

Address: Twin Firs Turf, 7737 Road L.5 NW
Admission: Free
Pets: No
Lodging: www.quincyvalleytourism.org/accommodations.html
Website: www.partiesonthegreen.com/id56.html
Facebook: www.facebook.com/pages/Parties-on-the-Green/446278485098
Attractions: Quincy Lakes, local area wineries, Gorge Amphitheater, Crescent Bar Recreation Area, Columbia River Gorge
Trivia: The book *Fateful Harvest: The True Story of a Small Town, a Global Industry, and a Toxic Secret* is about Quincy, Washington. It details the reality of corporations recycling toxic industrial byproducts and relabeling them as fertilizer.
Directions: The event is located at Twin Firs Turf Farm, 6 miles outside of Quincy, half way between Wenatchee and Moses Lake, just off Hwy 28. From I-90 eastbound go to exit 151. At the stop sign, turn right toward Ephrata/Grand Coulee on Hwy 283. Go four miles, then turn left on Adams Rd. Go four miles and turn right on Rd 8 NW. Go 1/2 mile, turn right on L.5 NW, then go 1/4 mile to the first driveway on the left. From I-90 westbound: take exit 154, Adams Rd. At the stop sign, turn left and go 7 miles to Rd 8 NW. Turn right and go 1/2 mile. Turn right on L.5 NW, and go 1/4 mile to the first driveway on the left. From Hwy 28: three miles east of Quincy, turn south on Adams Rd. Go two miles to Rd 8 NW, turn left. Go 1/2 mile, turn right on L.5 NW, and go 1/4 mile to the first driveway on the left.

Mahogany and Merlot Vintage Boat Show
Lake Chelan, Chelan County
First weekend in October

Mahogany and Merlot Vintage Boat Show is an on-the-water boat show that showcases vintage unlimited hydroplanes from the Hydroplane and Raceboat Museum in Kent, WA; vintage inboard limited class hydroplanes; and antique and classic mahogany runabouts from the golden era of pleasure boating. In addition to the boats, the Pacific Northwest chapter of the Classic Car Club of America exhibits Kaisers, Bentleys, Rolls Royces, Woodys, and other classic cars restored to their original condition. Hydro exhibition races begin early Saturday morning. The event also includes vintage-item vendors, a classic-boat-parts swap meet, wine barrel furniture, food booths, and a beer and wine garden featuring local wines and ales.

Address: Chelan Waterfront Park and Marina
Admission: Free
Parking: Street, parking lot
Accessible: Yes
Pets: Yes
Lodging: www.mahoganyandmerlot.com/where-to-stay.html
Website: www.mahoganyandmerlot.com
Attractions: Boating, jet skiing, tubing, skiing, swimming on Lake Chelan; Lake Chelan State Park, local area wineries, Bear Mountain Ranch Golf Course
Trivia: The Mahogany and Merlot Vintage Boat Show is presented by the Hydroplane and Raceboat Museum in Kent, WA. The museum is unique in that is has a fully equipped boat restoration shop, and has restored seven Gold Cup and Harmsworth winners to full running condition.
Directions: Lake Chelan is 200 miles (4 hours) northeast of Seattle via I-90 E and US-97 N; 160 miles (3.5 hours) north of Yakima via US-97 N; and 182 miles (4 hours) east of Spokane via US-2 W.

Omak Stampede

Omak, Okanogan County
Second weekend in August

The western town of Omak, in the heart of cattle country, started its small-town rodeo in 1933. Soon, the rodeo began to attract world-famous cowboys such as Stub Bathlemay, world champion at the Calgary Roundup; Norman Stewart, winner of both Pendleton Roundup and Cheyenne Wyoming Roundup and the world's best bronc rider; Bert Evans, winner of the north central Washington championship in 1932, and Ralph Sutton, winner at Waterville's 1933 rodeo. From humble beginnings, the Omak Stampede has grown into one of the largest rodeos in the Northwest. From the Thursday morning ride-in to the Sunday running of the World Famous Suicide Race (in which horses race 225 feet down a 62-degree sloped Suicide Hill, and swim across the Okanogan River), the action-packed weekend includes a carnival, Wrangler Kids Night, a western and native art show, rodeo dances, a demolition derby, and plenty of food and craft vendors. Also, the event hosts the annual Indian Encampment and Pow Wow, sponsored by the Colville Confederated Tribes. The encampment features an authentic teepee village, dancing, drumming and singing competitions, and stick games, Native American games of chance.

Address: 21 Stampede Drive East
Admission: Rodeo tickets generally range from $10–$25, although more expensive box seats are available. On Thursday—Family Night—two children (aged 12 and under) can attend the rodeo at no charge with the purchase of an adult ticket in the family section of the arena. Tickets for ages 3 and under (on a lap) are free for Thursday, Friday, and Sunday performances. Ages 1 and under (on a lap) are free on Saturday.
Parking: Paid parking
Accessible: Yes
Pets: No
Lodging: Many hotels, motels, inns, B&Bs, and RV and camping spots are available in Omak and the surrounding area. www.omakstampede.org/?page=accomodations
Website: www.omakstampede.org
Facebook: www.facebook.com/pages/Omak-Stampede-Inc/275480242478035

Attractions: Okanogan National Forest, Conconully State Park, Bridgeport State Park and Osoyoos Lake State Park, Okanogan County Historical Museum

Trivia: The community adopted the name Omak from the Salishan term Omache—which means "good medicine" or "plenty," referring to the region's favorable climate.

Directions: Omak is located 237 miles (4 hours) northeast of Seattle via I-90 E and US-97 N; 140 miles (3 hours) northwest of Spokane via US-2 W and WA-155; and 195 miles (3.5 hours) north of Yakima via WA-17 N.

Bavarian Ice Fest
Leavenworth, Chelan County
Third weekend in January

The Bavarian Ice Fest (also known as Icefest) celebrates the best of winter with many invigorating outdoor events. The festival typically features frosty frivolity such as a Nordic ski race, dog sled rides, a snow sculpture competition, live ice sculpting, snowmobile sled rides, a Penguin Pub Crawl, and Rail Jam where skiers and snowboarders from a local team throw down on a rail feature. Kids' events include an ice cube scramble, snowball toss, and a Frisbee Sweep race, in which the goal is to use a broom to sweep a Frisbee from one end of Front Street to the other. Adult Icefest games include the Bavarian Mug Relay, tug of war, a relay snowshoe race, and Smooshing, a race unique to the festival where teams of four have their toes strapped to 10' long boards and try to maneuver and glide down the street tandem style. Icefest also includes a chili cook off and the Northwest Dog Sled Pulling Competition, a sanctioned event of the International Weight Pull Association. Top off the exciting weekend with a fireworks show, then head over to the Festhalle for movie night (no entry fee required).

Address: Front Street Park
Admission: Free admission. Activity registration fees are as follows: Adult 18 and up $5, Junior 12–17 $3, Youth 7–11 $3, Kid 4–6 no charge, Tot 1–3 no charge. Penny Day – One cent registration for an activity if you are active-duty military personnel. ID is required.
Parking: Street and parking lot
Accessible: Yes
Pets: No

Lodging: www.leavenworth.org/lodging
Website: www.leavenworth.org/event/2443
Attractions: Icicle Junction Activity Center, Nutcracker Museum, Cashmere Museum and Pioneer Village, Hidden Lake, Icicle River, Lake Minotaur, Waterfront Park.
Trivia: Originally headquartering the Great Northern Railroad in the early 1900s, Leavenworth's economy suffered greatly when the railroad relocated to Wenatchee. In 1962, the struggling community began to transform itself into the mock Bavarian village that now hosts one million tourists annually.
Directions: Leavenworth is easily accessible from the west coast via US-2, and the drive through the Cascades has been voted one of the most scenic drives in the States.

Washington has more than 750 wineries and 251 craft breweries.

Food & Agricultural Festivals

Washington State Apple Blossom Festival
Wenatchee, Chelan County
Last weekend in April, first weekend in May

It stands to reason that the oldest major festival in the state of Washington centers on apples. Established in 1919, this 11-day celebration occurs right around the time that the apple trees are in bloom. Enjoy art and craft vendors, and the Memorial Park Food Fair, which, in addition to traditional fair food, serves up several apple-related items such as apple fries, apple piroshkies, and of course, apples dipped in caramel. Festival events include a carnival (America's 7th largest); a golf tournament; singing and dancing entertainment; a youth day and youth parade; Art 4 Kidz contest (open to kids pre-k through 12th grade); 2.1K, 5K, and 10K runs; an apple pie and dessert bakeoff; a Blossoms and Brews beer tent; a pie-eating contest; an English style high tea; and the Washington State Apple Blossom Festival Grand Parade, which attracts 100,000 spectators. Also, you can take in the Classy Chassis Car Show and Parade just across the river in East Wenatchee.

Address: Riverfront Park, Memorial Park, and various locations
Admission: No admission fee, but individual events and performances may charge a fee
Parking: Street and parking lot
Accessible: Yes
Pets: No
Lodging: www.appleblossom.org/visitors/places-to-stay.html. Camping and RV is also available throughout the area.
Website: www.appleblossom.org
Facebook: www.facebook.com/AppleBlossomFestivalWenatchee
Attractions: Squilchuck State Park, Apple Capital Loop Trail, Pybus Public Market, Cascade Valley Wine Country
Trivia: Apples found their way to Washington State in 1826 as seeds on a Hudson's Bay Company sailing vessel. These seeds were planted at Fort Vancouver, WA in the spring of 1827. From this auspicious beginning, the Washington apple industry has grown to national significance, producing about 100 million boxes of apples each season.
Directions: Wenatchee is located 148 miles (2.5 hours) southeast of Seattle via I-90 E; 169 miles (2.5 hours) west of Spokane via I-90 W; and 115 miles (2 hours) north of Yakima via I-82 W and I-90 E.

Huckleberry Festival
Bingen, Klickitat County
Early September

The annual Huckleberry Festival promises "More fun with huckleberries than you would imagine possible," which staggers the mind with possibilities. One thing's for sure, the town of Bingen knows how to celebrate the much-sought-after berry, whose flavor, if you've never had the pleasure, is similar to a blueberry, only bolder and often tarter. The huckleberry is very difficult to cultivate commercially because they require elevations of 2,000–11,000 feet and thrive in acidic mountain soil. So, almost all huckleberries must be harvested by hand-picking in the mountains, which makes the delicious items available at the Huckleberry Festival a true labor of love. The event not only sells berries by the gallon, but also huckleberry ice cream, pie, jams, jellies, and candy bars. The festival features lots of live entertainment, a parade, art and craft vendors, and a talent show.

Address: Daubenspeck Park, Willow Street
Admission: Free
Parking: Free street and parking lot parking
Accessible: Yes
Lodging: http://mtadamschamber.com/stay
Website: http://huckleberry-fest.com
Facebook: www.facebook.com/pages/Huckleberry-Festival/255999637850094
Attractions: Gorge Heritage Museum, rafting on the White Salmon river, Beacon Rock State Park, local area wineries, Hood River County Fruit Loop scenic drive, Klickitat Trail, Guler Ice Cave and natural bridges
Trivia: The word "huckleberry" is the North American version of the English "hurtleberry" or "whortleberry." The word has had several different variances in American English slang. The term "huckleberry" has been used to mean something small or inconsequential, presumably because of the small size of the berry. The phrase "huckleberry over my persimmon" meant that something was beyond one's reach or abilities. There is some mystery as to how the phrase "I'm your huckleberry" grew to mean "I'm the right person for the job," but thanks to the 1993 movie *Tombstone*, Val Kilmer's Doc Holliday reintroduced the phrase as a fantastically wonderful movie line.
Directions: Bingen is located 65 miles east of Portland, OR and Vancouver, WA via I-84 E.

Wenatchee River Salmon Festival
Leavenworth, Chelan County
September

Northwest rivers are integral to the Pacific Northwest. Residents rely on the waters to provide electricity for homes, irrigation for crops, livelihoods for fishermen, and places to play, picnic, camp, and hike. Thousands of people of all ages and cultures come to the four-day Wenatchee River Salmon Festival each year to celebrate the return of wild salmon to the Wenatchee River. This natural-resource education event includes hands-on activities, and gives folks a unique opportunity to discover and appreciate the complexities of the natural world and the significance of salmon to people in the northwest.

Address: Leavenworth National Fish Hatchery, 12790 Fish Hatchery Road
Admission: Free
Parking: Free parking in hatchery parking lot. A free shuttle runs on Saturday from Leavenworth's Front Street to the Salmon Festival's main entrance
Accessible: Yes
Pets: No
Lodging: www.leavenworth.org/lodging.
Website: www.salmonfest.org
Facebook: www.facebook.com/pages/Wenatchee-River-Salmon-Festival/118986101559932
Attractions: Scenic Icicle Canyon, Bavarian-themed village of Leavenworth, Leavenworth Nutcracker Museum, Leavenworth National Fish Hatchery
Trivia: The Chinook, or King, is the largest salmon species, and can weigh more than 100 pounds.
Directions: Leavenworth is easily accessible from the west coast via US-2, and the drive through the Cascades has been voted one of the most scenic drives in the States.

Wenatchee Taste of the Harvest
Wenatchee, Chelan County
Last Saturday in September

Wenatchee Taste of the Harvest celebrates the Wenatchee valley's incredible harvest season and rich agricultural heritage. The event includes music; a farmers market; a 5K, 10K, and half-marathon run; food and art vendors; cooking demonstrations; and a film festival. In addition to a beer and wine garden, the event also includes a wine tasting area where you can sample as many as 20 tastes of award-winning wines from the best wineries in north central Washington. And after all of the delicious food you've sampled throughout the festival, you can burn off some calories by participating in jazzercise, yoga, or Zumba on the street.

Address: Downtown between 1st Street & Yakima Street
Admission: Free. The wine tasting area costs $20, and you can sample as many as 20 tastes.
Parking: Street and parking lot
Accessible: Yes
Pets: Yes
Lodging: http://wenatchee.org/listings/category/sleep
Website: www.wendowntown.org/events/taste-of-the-harvest
Facebook: www.facebook.com/WenatcheeTasteoftheHarvestFestival
Attractions: Squilchuck State Park, Apple Capital Loop Trail, Pybus Public Market, Cascade Valley Wine Country
Trivia: Chris DeGarm, one-time lead guitarist for the heavy metal band Queensryche, was born in Wenatchee in 1963.
Directions: Wenatchee is located 148 miles (2.5 hours) southeast of Seattle via I-90 E; 169 miles (2.5 hours) west of Spokane via I-90 W; and 115 miles (2 hours) north of Yakima via I-82 W and I-90 E.

Apple Pie Jamboree
Pateros, Okanogan County
Third weekend in July

Pateros is nestled up against the eastern edge of the Cascade Mountains at the confluence of the Columbia River and the Methow River, which means that the Apple Pie Jamboree not only celebrates the apple, but also the water activities that residents enjoy during the warm summer months. The Jamboree features a parade, art and craft vendors, food vendors, a jamboree jog, a hoop shoot fundraiser, a quilt show, bingo, a dunk tank, 3-on-3 basketball, kids' games, live music and entertainment including a comedy troupe from Seattle, a community dinner, and night-time fireworks. You can also break out your fishing pole and try your luck in the Ray Stanley Memorial Bass Tournament, or your golf clubs and swing your way through the golf tournament. One of the more exciting events is the Jet Ski racing and freestyle competitions. Riders compete for national points and a chance to earn a berth at the world finals. The racers take to the Columbia River on a closed, near-shore buoy course that features sharp turns and high-speed stretches. Freestylers demonstrate barrel rolls, the cowboy, and flips, as well as compete in a big air competition, which includes backflips and other stunts.

Address: Downtown
Admission: Free
Parking: Free street and parking lot parking
Accessible: Yes
Pets: Yes
Lodging: Camping is available at Alta Lake State Park, Lightning Pine RV, Whistlin' Pine Ranch, and many more beautiful areas surrounding Pateros.
Website: www.paterosapj.com
Facebook: www.facebook.com/pages/Apple-Pie-Jamboree/186604068049697
Attractions: Scenic Cascade Loop Hwy, Columbia River, Chelan River Gorge, Coulee Dam Casino, Molson Museum, balloon tours
Trivia: On July 17–18, 2014, much of Pateros was destroyed by the Carlton Complex wildfire—the largest wildfire in Washington state history. No injuries or fatalities were reported, but approximately 20% of the buildings in the city were reported destroyed. Remarkably, this only delayed the yearly Apple Pie Jamboree by a couple of weeks, and shortened the festivities a bit, which is a testament to the indomitable spirit and resiliency of Washingtonians in the face of disaster.
Directions: Pateros is located 200 miles (3.5 hours) east of Seattle via I-90 E and US-97 N; 142 miles (2.5 hours) northwest of Spokane via US-2 W/US Rte 2 W and WA-174 W; and 160 miles (3 hours) from Yakima via US-97 N.

Skewered Apple BBQ Competition
Selah, Yakima County
Early September (usually the first weekend after Labor Day weekend)

Tree Top hosts the annual Skewered Apple BBQ Competition at its headquarters in central Washington. Barbecue cooks compete for more than $25,000 in prize money. The event, which benefits local charities, includes cooking demos, live entertainment, food vendors, a Hog Callin' Hoedown, pie eating contests, and wine and beer—all amidst sunny fruit, wine, and hop country. The event is sanctioned and officiated by the Pacific NW BBQ Association. On Sunday, competitors turn in their meats to trained judges every hour beginning at 11 am until 4 pm. The best part is, samples may be available to the public after each meat is turned in.

Address: Tree Top campus, 220 E. 2nd Avenue
Admission: Day pass costs $10. A weekend pass costs $15.
Parking: Parking lot parking at Tree Top
Accessible: Yes
Pets: No
Lodging: The Yakima Valley offers many places to stay. A few locations are mentioned at the event website.
Website: www.skeweredapple.com
Facebook: www.facebook.com/skeweredapple
Attractions: More than 75 local wineries, Yakima River Canyon, Yakima Greenway, Oak Creek Wildlife Viewing Area, Selah Ridge Lavender Farm
Trivia: The first map of the Columbia River in central Washington was created by the Lewis and Clark Expedition in 1805. On that map, the Selah region was named "Selartar," which was probably a mistranslation of a tribal word because local tribes did not use the letter R in their dialect. In 1850, the missionary Father Charles Marie Pandosy is credited with referring to the area as Selah, which is not only close to the original tribal name for the area, but is a biblical word that generally means to pause and think.
Directions: Selah is located 90 miles northwest of the Tri-Cities via I-82 W; 140 miles (2 hours) southeast of Seattle via I-90 E and I-82 E; and 200 miles (3 hours) southwest of Spokane via I-90 W and I-82 W.

Wapato Tamale Festival
Wapato, Yakima County
Saturday, early in October

The small town of Wapato in the Yakima Valley has a population that is around 75% Hispanic Latino, making it one of the most Hispanic communities in the state of Washington. The yearly Wapato Tamale Festival is a chance to celebrate the Hispanic history, culture, and deliciousness. The event includes art and craft vendors, a car show, dancing, kids' activities, live music, and lots of food, including, of course, mouth-watering tamales. The tamale cooking contest is open to anyone. Just bring a dozen tamales to the judging table by noon. Top three winners get cash prizes.

Address: Downtown
Admission: Free admission. Entry fee for the tamale contest is $25.
Parking: Free street and parking lot parking
Accessible: Yes
Lodging: Yakima Valley Visitor's Bureau, www.visityakima.com/newSite/yakima-valley-accommodations.asp
Website: www.wapato-city.org/calendarofevents.html
Attractions: American Hop Museum, Toppenish murals, Toppenish National Wildlife Refuge, Fort Simcoe State Park, Northern Pacific Railway Museum, Yakama Native Cultural Heritage Museum, Yakima Valley Rail and Steam Museum, Yakama Nation's Legends Casino
Trivia: The name Wapato is of Yakama origin. "Wa pa too" is an aquatic plant that produces an edible tuber root that was of great value to native Yakamas and settlers. Other common names of this species of plant are arrowhead, duck potato, katniss, swan potato, and tule potato.
Directions: Wapato is located 15 miles south of Yakima on Hwy 97.

Washington produces more apples than any other state in the union.

Music

Basin Summer Sounds
Ephrata, Grant County
Third weekend in July

Billing itself as the largest free contemporary music and arts festival in the Northwest, Basin Summer Sounds features more than merely a progressive mix of live music. It takes place on the beautiful grounds of the Grant County Courthouse, which was constructed in 1919 and is on the National Register of Historic Places. The two-day event features food and commercial vendors, a huge wine and beer garden, a charity 3-on-3 basketball tournament, children's activities, visual arts, and a car and cycle show. The festival features performers from all over the northwest and beyond.

Address: Grant County Courthouse, 35 C Street NW
Admission: Free
Parking: Street and parking lot parking
Accessible: Yes
Pets: Service animals only allowed in the beer and wine garden
Lodging: www.tourgrantcounty.com/ephrata
Website: http://basinsummersounds.com
Facebook: www.facebook.com/pages/Basin-Summer-Sounds/638407436188972
Attractions: Surf and Slide Water Park, Grandfather Cuts Loose the Ponies wild horse monument, Dry Falls, local area wineries
Trivia: Six miles from Ephrata lies the town of Soap Lake, which, in 2002, began plans to construct the world's largest Lava Lamp. Once completed, the groovy structure will tower 60 feet from the ground to the cap. Conceived by artist/architect Brent Blake, the project, not surprisingly, has turned out to be a bit more complicated, and more expensive than originally thought. There was a reason that no one had ever before completed a 60-foot functioning Lava Lamp. In addition to design and architectural challenges, the lamp, which will cost around $1 million to complete, is funded solely by donations and grassroots fundraising efforts, which means the timeline for completion is vague. On the Soap Lake Lava Lamp website, in addition to describing the tourism and aesthetic benefits of such a structure, the architects note the fact that a 60-foot Lava Lamp is just simply "very cool." And who can argue with that?

Directions: Ephrata is located 95 miles northwest of Yakima via I-82 W and I-90 E. It is also 123 miles (2 hours) west of Spokane via I-90 W.

Rock the Gap
Yakima, Yakima County
Saturday in late May or early June

The annual one-day Rock the Gap is one of Yakima's largest open-air concerts of the year. The evening, only for adults 21 and older, is filled with classic rock music, as well as a fantastic VIP dinner, local wine and beer, and a silent auction and dessert auction. All proceeds from the event benefit local children's programs and charities.

Address: Sarg Hubbard Park, 111 S. 18th Street
Admission: Dinner and concert tickets are $55 in advance, $60 at the door. Concert-only tickets are $20. VIP tables for eight are available for $500, which includes dinner, a souvenir glass, scrip for one drink per person, and the event's popular custom engraved rock (Rock the Gap—get it?).
Accessible: Yes
Pets: No
Lodging: http://visityakima.com/newSite/yakima-valley-accommodations.asp
Website: www.rockthegap.com
Facebook: www.facebook.com/rockthegap
Attractions: Fort Simcoe State Park, Yakima Valley wineries, Yakama Nation Museum, Toppenish Murals, Meadowbrook Family Fun Center, Cowiche Canyon
Trivia: In 2009, *Popular Mechanics* published an article stating that, according to the Center for UFO Studies, from the years 1947 to 2005, Yakima County has one of the highest UFO reporting rates, per capita, in the United States. Amongst less-populated counties Yakima ranks fourth in UFO reports (Washington's King County [Seattle metro area] ranks second for major metro counties). Yakima does house a military training zone, so that could be part—let's be honest, probably most—of the explanation. However, while visiting Yakima, should you find yourself witnessing strange lights or having eerie premonitions or some sort of probing, the article in *Popular Mechanics* (available at www.popularmechanics.com/technology/aviation/ufo/4304768) includes a helpful

checklist to go over before you make an official UFO sighting report. **Point 1: Is it Venus?**
Directions: Yakima is located 142 miles (2.5 hours) southeast of Seattle via I-90 E and 85 miles (1.5 hours) northwest of the Tri-Cities via I-82 W.

Wenatchee River Bluegrass Festival
Cashmere, Chelan County
Third weekend in June

The goal of the Wenatchee River Bluegrass Festival is to preserve early style acoustic music, and nurture the future of acoustic roots music in America. Pickers of all ages are invited to a weekend filled with bluegrass music, both on and off the main stage. The event includes adult and kid instrument workshops, old time music, a slow jam, a band scramble, and a meet-and-greet luau and potluck.

Address: Chelan County Expo Center/Fairgrounds, 5700 Wescott Avenue
Admission: A day pass costs $25 per person Friday or Saturday, and $10 per person on Sunday. A full weekend pass costs $30 per person. Children ages 12 and under are free.
Parking: Parking available in expo center/fairground parking lots
Accessible: Yes
Pets: Dogs allowed in campground only.
Lodging: Camping is available on site for $20 per campsite per night. Other lodging information can be found at: http://cashmerechamber.org/about/stay
Website: www.cashmerecoffeehouse.com/wrbfest.htm
Facebook: www.facebook.com/pages/Wenatchee-River-Bluegrass-Festival/268380441257
Attractions: Whitewater rafting and river tubing down the Wenatchee River, Aplets and Cotlets Candy Kitchen, Cashmere Museum and Pioneer Village, Cascade Scenic Loop Hwy
Trivia: Cashmere is home to Liberty Orchards, makers of internationally famous Aplets and Cotlets fruit and nut confections.
Directions: Cashmere is located on Hwy 2 on the Cascade Loop, midway between Leavenworth and Wenatchee. Look for signs in Cashmere directing you to the Chelan County Expo Center - Fairgrounds (Westcott off Sunset).

Lake Chelan Bach Fest
Chelan/Manson, Chelan County
Starts the second weekend in July

The Lake Chelan Bach Fest gathers musicians from all over the United States and Canada to present nine days of music ranging from classical to jazz, show tunes, orchestras, chamber music, and chorus. A Friday Night Classics Concert features the full Bach Fest orchestra and chorus. The final festival concert is usually performed in the evening at the Riverwalk Park Pavilion, near the Old Bridge coming into downtown Chelan. Guests are encouraged to bring lawn chairs or blankets for this delightful evening in the park.

Address: Various venues
Admission: An all-concert pass costs $50. Individual concert prices range from $6 to $15.
Parking: Street, parking lot
Accessible: Yes
Pets: No
Lodging: www.bachfest.org/links-to-chamber-of-commerce-hotels-wineries_8.html
Website: www.bachfest.org
Facebook: www.facebook.com/pages/Lake-Chelan-Bach-Fest/190383867683305
Attractions: Lake Chelan Wine Valley (featuring more than 20 wineries)
Trivia: Johann Sebastian Bach was the father of 20 children—seven with his first wife (and second cousin) Maria, and 13 with his second wife Anna, who was 17 years younger than he.
Directions: Lake Chelan is 200 miles (4 hours) northeast of Seattle via I-90 E and US-97 N; 160 miles (3.5 hours) north of Yakima via US-97 N; and 182 miles (4 hours) east of Spokane via US-2 W.

Watershed Festival
George, Grant County
First weekend in August

The annual Watershed Festival presents the biggest names in country music on one of the most beautiful outdoor stages in America—the Gorge Amphitheatre, on a plateau overlooking the mighty Columbia River. The amphitheater is a nine-time winner of *Pollstar Magazine's* award for Best Outdoor Music Venue, and has won the Top Amphitheater prize at the 2013 Billboard Touring Awards. The festival features multiple stages of live music, showcasing a mix of country music from superstars, newcomers, and local country acts.

Address: 754 Silica Road
Admission: A three-day festival pass costs $125. Single day passes are not available.
Parking: Ample on-site parking is available at the venue. Day parking in the general parking lot is free. Parking on county roads or private property is prohibited. Premier parking options are available for a fee.
Accessible: Yes
Pets: No
Lodging: Camping is available on site. Camping fees are sold per vehicle, and start at $125 for the full weekend. Showers, comfort stations, a convenience store, and an ATM are on site for all campers. The premier camping package costs a hefty $900 for the weekend, but is worth every penny if only for the simple fact that it is fabulously referred to as "Glamping." Glamping includes a furnished preset cottage-style tent in an exclusive, secluded area with great views, separate showers and comfort stations, concierge service, personal picnic tables, a continental breakfast, and free shuttle service to the event. Other lodging information can be found at the Quincy Valley Tourism website: www.quincyvalleytourism.org/accommodations.html
Website: http://watershedfest.com
Facebook: www.facebook.com/WatershedMusicFestival?ref=br_tf
Attractions: Quincy Lakes, local area wineries, Crescent Bar Recreation Area, Columbia River Gorge National Scenic area
Trivia: The city of George, Washington is the only city in the country to bear the full name of a president. On the city's July 4th celebration every year, a group called the Georgettes makes the "world's largest cherry pie," which weighs in at nearly half a ton and serves 1,800 people. The 8 ft. by 8 ft. square crust contains 75 gallons of pie filling.
Directions: George is 70 miles northeast of Yakima via I-82 W and I-90 E. It is also 131 miles (2 hours) southwest of Spokane via I-90 W.

Jazz in the Valley
Ellensburg, Kittitas County
Last weekend in July

The Jazz in the Valley Festival is a celebration of jazz and blues, which takes place annually in historic downtown Ellensburg. Enjoy the many intimate performances, in a diversity of musical styles, all within a jazz framework. Performance venues are all within walking distance of each other. While enjoying the wide range of jazz and blues, attendees can sip a variety of microbrews and wine at the Main Stage Beer Garden. On Saturday afternoon, enjoy a Sip 'n' Sample where you can taste some of the Northwest's premium wines that are paired with specialty food items (such as chocolates, breads, and cheeses). The wine tasting events include a silent wine and art auction. The farmers market, on 4th Avenue between Ruby and Pearl streets runs concurrently with the festival. The entire family can enjoy this event—children are welcome at all performance venues.

Address: 4th Street & Pearl Street in Historic Downtown
Admission: Full festival pass for all three days costs $40. Day and evening passes are also available: Friday night and Saturday night passes from 8 pm to midnight cost $15 each; Saturday afternoon noon to 7 pm costs $15; Sunday 10:30 am to 4:30 pm costs $10. Wine tasting events cost $12 per person and include a souvenir wine glass.
Parking: Street and parking lot parking
Accessible: Yes
Pets: No
Lodging: www.jazzinthevalley.com/lodging.html
Website: www.jazzinthevalley.com
Facebook: www.facebook.com/pages/Jazz-in-the-Valley/334629474446?fref=ts
Attractions: Kittitas County Historical Museum, Children's Activity Museum
Trivia: Central Washington University in Ellensburg houses the Chimpanzee and Human Communication Institute (CHCI), which, until 2013, housed chimpanzees who learned to communicate with humans and each other using American Sign Language (ASL). Inhabitants of the facility included Washoe, the first non-human to learn to communicate using American Sign Language. Her vocabulary consisted of more than 350 words. Some of these words she, in turn, taught to her adopted son Loulis. Washoe is honored with a statue in a tiny park just west of the Liberty Theatre in downtown Ellensburg.
Directions: Ellensburg is located 108 miles (2 hours) east of Seattle on I-90 E; 120 miles (2 hours) northwest of the Tri-Cities; and 170 miles (2.5 hours) west of Spokane on I-90 W.

Central Washington County Fairs

Chelan
Cashmere
www.chelancountyfair.com

Douglas/North Central Washington District Fair
Waterville
www.douglascountywa.net/ncwfair

Grant
Moses Lake
www.gcfairgrounds.com

Kittitas
Ellensburg
www.kittitascountyfair.com

Klickitat
Goldendale
www.klickitatcountyfair.com

Okanogan
Okanogan
http://okanogancounty.org/fair/index.html

Yakima/Central Washington State Fair
Yakima
www.statefairpark.org/p/central-wa-state-fair

Eastern Region

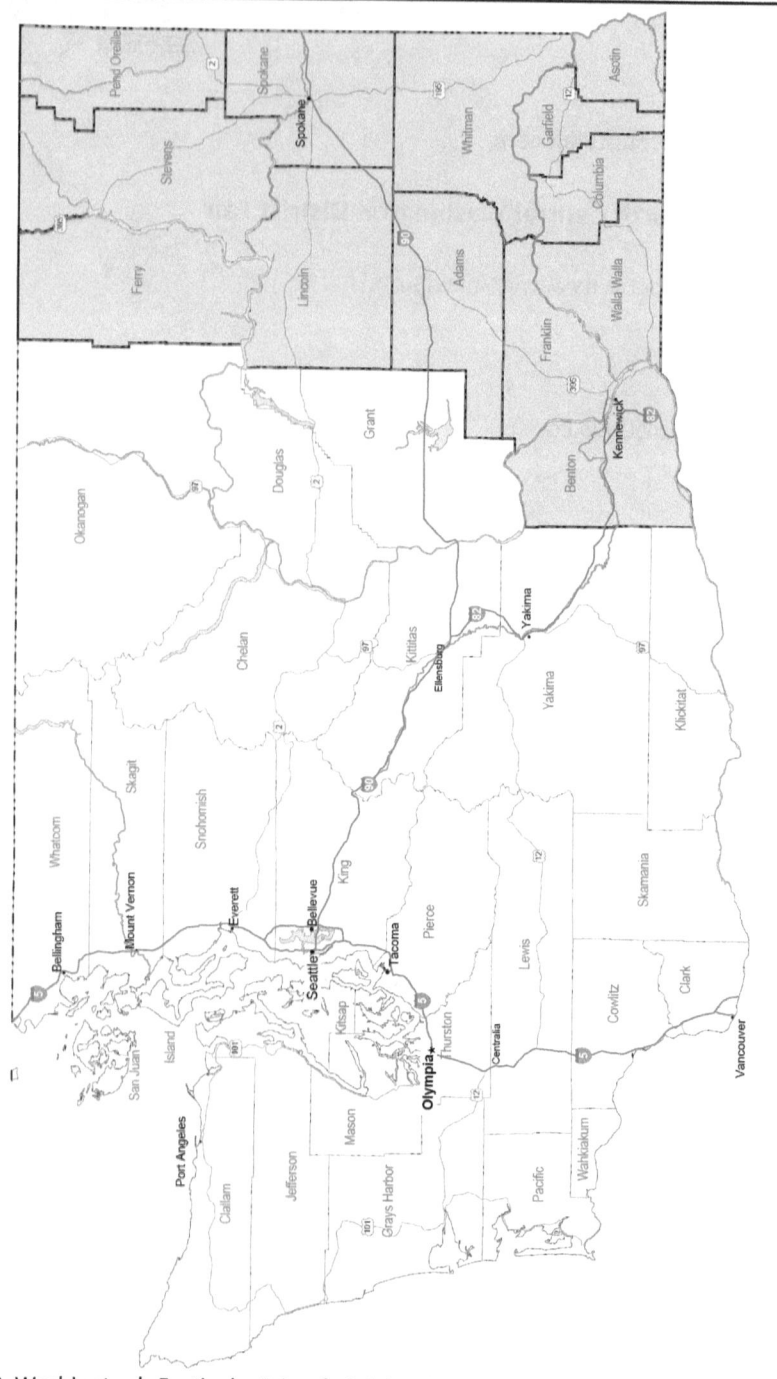

Eastern Washington

Eastern Washington is a dichotomy of geography and climate. The Okanogan Highlands in the far northeast corner of the state make up part of the Rocky Mountain foothills, and are populated with few people, but with plenty of steep mountains, green forests, and fantastic driving scenery, which makes it hard to imagine a better place to host the town of Republic's Motorcycle Rally.

Spokane, the population center of the eastern border, began as a trading post and transportation hub. Though it was the smallest city to host the World's Fair (1974), it has grown to become the second largest city in the state. You can experience the Spokane area's unique—and quirky—personality at events like the indie-rock music festival Elkfest, the Inland Craft Beer Festival, and the GetLit! Literary Festival.

Further south, the semi-arid lands of the Columbia Plateau and the Palouse region provide plenty of grazing land for cattle, and some of the most fertile soil in the nation. Events like Odessa's Deutschesfest, Pullman's National Lentil Festival, and Palouse's Cabin Fever Brew Fest celebrate the indomitable (and thirsty) spirit of the hard-working farmers who helped cultivate the land into what is now a vast legume- and wheat-growing area. It is this region that makes Washington the 4th largest wheat-producing state in the nation.

The Tri-Cities (which comprises Kennewick, Richland, and Pasco) lies at the confluence of the Yakima, Snake, and Columbia Rivers (you may have heard of them), which spent millennia carving out a beautiful landscape that is highlighted by events like the Great Prosser Balloon Rally. And in this region that sees only 5–7 inches of rain each year, the waterways provide hot summertime relief, as well as endless recreational delights, which are celebrated at the hugely popular Tri-Cities Water Follies.

In such a large agricultural and farming region, it stands to reason that food would be the focal point of many of the local celebrations. Pasco's Fiery Foods Festival and Spokane's Pig Out in the Park provide treats for every taste bud.

Other intriguing events in Eastern Washington include Richland's Ye Merrie Greenwood Renaissance Faire, Kennewick's Columbia River Cowboy Gathering and Music Festival, and Curlew's Barrel Derby Days festival, which recreates exciting moments in the city's bootlegging past.

Art Events

Get Lit! Literary Festival
Cheney, Spokane County
Second week in April

The Get Lit! Festival began in 1998 as a one-day marathon of literary readings sponsored by Eastern Washington University Press and EWU's Department of Creative Writing. By 2004, more than 10,000 people from Spokane and the surrounding region came to enjoy the event. The Get Lit! Festival is a weeklong celebration that connects the community with local, new, and nationally known writers. Every year, Get Lit! partners with other educational institutions to bring 40 authors to Spokane for a series of readings, workshops, panel discussions, poetry slams, and special events. Past festivals have featured authors such as Kurt Vonnegut, Jane Smiley, Richard Russo, Salman Rushdie, Rita Dov, and Sarah Vowell.

Address: Various locations throughout the Spokane area
Admission: Most events are free and open to the public. Headliner events (one each evening) cost $15 for the general public, but are free to all high-school and college students with a valid ID. You can buy a festival pass for $40 that gets you in to all three of the headliner events.
Parking: Various street and paid parking lot parking
Accessible: Yes
Pets: No
Lodging: The Red Lion River Inn (509.326.5577), at 700 N. Division Street, is within walking distance of many festival venues, and it offers a special festival rate for attendees. Find more information at: www.visitspokane.com/hotels
Website: http://outreach.ewu.edu/getlit/2528.xml
Facebook: www.facebook.com/EWUGetLitPrograms
Attractions: Riverside Park, Spokane Falls, Mt. Spokane, Turnbull National Wildlife Refuge, Cat Tales Zoological Park, Silverwood Theme Park, Northwest Museum of Arts and Culture, Couer d'Alene Casino
Trivia: Outside of the Spokane Opera House sits a bronze statue memorial of astronaut Michael Anderson, who was a native of Cheney. Anderson was the payload commander whowas killed on the ill-fated space shuttle Columbia that disintegrated during reentry into earth's atmosphere on February 1, 2003. The statue depicts Anderson kneeling with his helmet in one hand, and a dove in the other.
Directions: Cheney is 17 miles southwest of Spokane.

Beer, Wine & Spirits

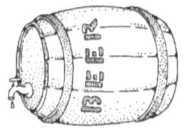

Horse Heaven Hills Trail Drive
Paterson/Prosser, Benton County
Third Saturday in July

Horse Heaven Hills Wine Growers Association is home to 25% of Washington State's vineyard acreage, and the source of four of the state's 100-point wines. For the Horse Heaven Hills Trail Drive, load up in your faithful steed (two-wheel or four-wheel drive, makes no difference), and, while enjoying the area's dramatic vistas, head off to various stops within the Horse Heaven Hills wine area to sample some of the regions delicious wines. Meet and chat with the area's growers and vintners. A Trail Ticket gets you a logo glass and wine tasting at all stops. The trip takes 4–5 hours, and designated drivers are strongly encouraged. At the end of the trail, wind down your day with a catered barbecue and live music.

Address: Choice of pickup at Crow Butte Park, located in the town of Paterson at 1 Crow Butte State Park Road, or in Prosser at the Best Western Inn at Horse Heaven, 259 Merlot Drive
Admission: Prices range from $25 for the barbecue only to $100 for the full VIP tour, including bus transportation. Kids 12 and younger eat free at the barbecue.
Parking: Free
Accessible: Yes
Pets: No
Lodging: Camping available at Crow Butte Park: www.crowbutte.com. Lodging also available at Best Western Inn at Horse Heaven (509.786.7977).
Website: www.horseheavenhillswinegrowers.org/annual-trail-drive-event.html
Facebook: www.facebook.com/horseheavenhills
Attractions: Prosser Farmers Market, 30+ local wineries, the historic Princess Theater, Benton County Museum
Trivia: About 10 miles outside of Prosser lies the mystery that is Gravity Hill. Drive to the spot, which is difficult to find amidst all of the roads that traverse the rolling hills in the area, line your car up on the conveniently spray-painted starting line, put your car in neutral, and your car, seemingly, rolls uphill. Optical illusion? Perhaps, but many who have

experienced the thrill of their car racing at speeds of up to 10 miles per hour in an unanticipated direction state that their GPS devices showed an increase in elevation. Spooky.

Directions: Paterson is located 40 minutes southwest of the Tri-Cities on WA-14.

Inland NW Craft Beer Festival
Spokane, Spokane County
Last weekend in September

This beer-tasting festival celebrates the craft beer of the Inland Northwest. The two-day event features great beer, food, and music in the outfield grass of Avista Stadium. It hosts 30 craft breweries pouring more than 70 types of beer, including all of your typical flavors (with a northwest flair), as well as interesting flavors such as pumpkin, lavender, blackberry, cranberry-pumpkin, lemon cream, peach pie, sour cherry, honey basil, huckleberry, jalapeno, mango, and toasted coconut and marshmallow. And if the unique flavors aren't enough of an incentive, the creative names of some of the brews will surely coax you into trying a sip: Hoodoojuju Pumpkin Spice Beer (Bale Breaker Brewing), Rye Not? (Diamond Knot Craft Brewing), Space Dust IPA (Elysian Brewing), Wiggly Butt IPA (English Setter Brewing), Fish Vicious Circle (Fish Brewing), Bonfire Ale (Fremont Brewing), Saint Dorothy (Laht Neppur Brewing), Blackfill (No-Li Brewhouse), Hoppy Bitch IPA (Northwest Brewing), Alpha Madness (Paradise Creek Brewery), Falling Backwards (Republic Brewing), Wicked Riff (Twelve Bar Brews), Roundabout Confusion (Twelve String Brewing), and Smokey the Beer Porter (Waddell's Brewing).

Address: Avista Stadium, 602 N. Havana Street
Admission: Tickets cost $15 in advance, $20 at the door (military discount tickets are $15 at the door). Admission includes a commemorative tasting cup and six 5-oz sample tastes. Additional tokens can be purchased for $1.50 each, or four for $5.
Parking: Parking is free outside the stadium.
Accessible: Yes
Pets: No
Lodging: The Courtyard-Marriott (509.456.7600) is the official hotel of the Inland NW Craft Beer Festival.
Website: http://washingtonbeer.com/inlandnwcraftbeerfestival

Facebook: None
Attractions: Manito Park and Botanical Gardens, John A. Finch Arboretum, Mt. Spokane State Park, Cat Tales Zoological Park, Cathedral of St. John the Evangelist
Trivia: The inland Northwest, including eastern Washington and northern Idaho, is home to plenty of amazing breweries. To showcase the variety, local craft brewers and other sponsors have created the Inland NW Ale Trail, which is a touring challenge of around 30 of the craft microbreweries throughout the region. Visitors and local craft beer enthusiasts can pick up a map highlighting participating INWCB breweries. Ale Trail participants receive a stamp as they visit each brewery. Once they've collected 12 stamps, participants are eligible to receive a prize of a 32-oz growler. Find a map and more information at http://inlandnwaletrail.com.
Directions: If traveling into Spokane in I-90 E, take the Thor/Freya St exit (I-90 #283 B). Now on 3rd. St, go through two lights, then take a left on Havana St (follow signs to Fairgrounds). Go through the three-way stop, then the light on Sprague Ave, and cross the railroad tracks .The stadium is on the right. If traveling into Spokane on I-90 W, take the Broadway exit (I-90 #286), then take a right off the exit onto Broadway Ave heading west. Proceed about two miles. The stadium is on the left.

Palouse Cabin Fever Brew Fest
Palouse, Whitman County
Early February

In an area where the average January temperature is 25°, and the average amount of daylight is only around 8.5 hours, the Palouse Cabin Fever Brew Fest, although certainly not one of the larger beer festivals in the state, is surely one of the most highly anticipated. Palouse Cabin Fever Brew Fest promises to bring a little fun to the doldrums of winter. Begun as a fundraiser in 2013 for the Palouse Community Center, organizers have been delighted with its resounding success—festival tickets have sold out each year. The event includes several local breweries offering their favorite brews to those looking to escape the mundane of winter. Because Palousians (Palousites?) are a hardy folk, this festival is both an indoor and an outdoor event. Fire pits and heaters help warm the outside area, and, of course, the beer helps warm you up also, but dress accordingly. Food and snacks are available for purchase.

Address: Palouse Community Center, 230 E Main

Admission: Tickets cost $15 in advance and $20 at the door (if any tickets are still available on the date of the event). Your ticket purchase ensures that you receive your commemorative pint glass, which you must have to get your six 4-oz beer tastes. Extra beer tastes can be purchased for $1 each, and full pints are only $3.

Parking: Free parking lot and street parking

Accessible: Yes

Pets: No

Lodging: The Palouse RV Park (www.visitpalouse.com/rvpark.html) is a great facility within walking distance of the Brew Fest. The nearby town of Pullman also has lodging accommodations www.pullmanchamber.com/visit-pullman/where-to-stay/. Moscow, ID is also quite close http://moscowchamber.chambermaster.com/list/mc/183-182-184.

Facebook: www.facebook.com/PalouseCabinFeverBrewFest

Attractions: Roy M. Chatters Newspaper and Printing Museum, Palouse River, Palouse Scenic Byway, Elberton Ghost Town, Codger Pole, Palouse Falls State Park, Palouse Discovery Science Center

Trivia: Seventeen miles outside of Palouse, in the nearby town of Colfax, lies the 65-foot tall Codger Pole, reportedly the tallest chainsaw carving in the world. The pole commemorates a 1988 reunion football game between Colfax and the town of St. John. The original game was played in 1938, and replayed 50 years later by those players still living. The pole depicts the faces of the players.

Directions: Palouse is 65 miles south of Spokane on WA-27 South.

Ethnic & Cultural Celebrations

Ye Merrie Greenwood Renaissance Faire
Richland, Benton County
Last weekend in June

Ye Merrie Greenwood Faire is an Elizabethan-era festival set in the year 1585. The event includes more than 100 professional acts, eight stages, jousting, food and drink, historical re-enactment, and children's entertainment. Enjoy English country dancing, madrigals, musicians, puppets, jugglers, story tellers, magicians, and stilt walkers. And, as always, the audience is encouraged to sing and dance along and pretend they are in Merrie Old England. Village merchants offer an array of period clothing, weaponry, accessories, and toys.

Address: Howard Amon Park, 900 Amon Park Road N, one block east from the corner of George Washington Way and Lee Blvd.
Admission: Adults/teens $9 for one day, $12 for two days. Seniors/children ages 5–12 $7 for one day, $9 for two days. Children under age 5 are free. A two-day family pass for two adults and two children ages 5–12 runs $38.
Accessible: Yes
Pets: No
Lodging: www.yemerriegreenwoodfaire.org/maps_and_lodging.htm
Website: www.yemerriegreenwoodfaire.org
Facebook: www.facebook.com/pages/Ye-Merrie-Greenwood-Renaissance-Faire/288486720923
Attractions: Hanford Nuclear Reservation, local area wineries, Columbia and Yakima Rivers, Sacagawea Heritage Trail, Badger Mountain Centennial Preserve
Trivia: In the actual year 1585, a group of 107 colonists, set forth by Sir Walter Raleigh, landed in America on Roanoke Island hoping to establish the first permanent English settlement in what is now the state of North Carolina. When a relief ship returned the following year, it found the colony abandoned. To this day, no one is sure of what happened to the colonists at what has now been nicknamed the "Lost Colony."
Directions: Richland is located 145 miles (2 hours) southwest of Spokane via I-90 W and US-395 S; 220 miles (3.5 hours) east of Portland, OR via I-84 E; and 80 miles (1.5 hours) east of Yakima via I-82 E.

Pioneer Days
Davenport, Lincoln County
Third weekend in July

With a population of around 1,700 people, the town of Davenport is the largest town in Lincoln County, which is reportedly the second-largest producer of wheat in the United States (following Whitman County, also in Washington). Lincoln County produces as many as 25 million bushels of wheat a year. Pioneer Days is a chance to take a break from the summer work and celebrate the history of this agricultural area with neighbors, friends, and visitors. This event features activities such as the Pioneer Plod Fun Run, Road Knights Classic Car Show, Pioneer Days Parade, Lions Club Barbeque in the Park, live music in the park, teen dance, farmers market, food and craft vendors, and a beer garden. The annual sidewalk chalk art contest takes place throughout the downtown area. The belly flop contest winner takes home the "Golden Flipper" award.

Address: Downtown Davenport
Admission: Free
Parking: Street and parking lot parking
Accessible: Yes
Pets: Yes
Lodging: www.visitlincolncountywashington.com/Accommodations.html
Website: www.pioneerdays.org
Facebook: www.facebook.com/DavenportPioneerDays
Attractions: Lake Roosevelt National Recreation Area, Fort Spokane, Lincoln County Historical Museum, Odessa Historisches Museum, Rocky Ford/Goose Butte Recreation Area
Trivia: The National UFO Reporting Center (NUFORC) is located in Davenport in a decommissioned U. S. Air Force ICBM missile base.
Directions: Davenport is 35 miles west of Spokane on US-2 W.

Deutschesfest
Odessa, Lincoln County
Third full weekend in September

Deutschesfest is a celebration of rich and colorful German traditions of the German Russians who settled in the Odessa area at the beginning of the 20th century. Through hard work, they turned the once-desolate

Lincoln County into one of the world's richest grain growing areas. But hard work wasn't the only thing that filled their days. They always made time to get together with friends and family to enjoy good food and drink, music, and dancing. Deutschesfest, which attracts as many as 20,000 visitors every year, is a celebration of this German heritage. The streets are alive with revelers and authentic German music. Other bands provide old time rock and roll of the '50s and '60s, country rock, and big-band era music. The food circus (aka the Festplatz) serves everything from krautranza to strudel. The Biergarten serves all sorts of refreshments, including domestic and German beers, locally crafted beers, and locally made German sausage. Events include a fun run, a parade, a tricycle race, an art show, a bake sale, a horseshoe tournament, a vintage quilt show, and a genealogy room.

Address: Downtown
Admission: Free. Bier Garten charges a $5 entry fee ($3 on Thursday).
Parking: Plenty of free parking on residential streets adjacent to downtown
Accessible: Yes
Lodging: Lodging is tough if you don't plan ahead. The town has one motel, La Collage Inn (509.982.2412) that offers a fun theme-roomed stay. But the inn has only 12 rooms, and festival dates are often booked up to a year in advance. As many as 600 RVs flood the town in the days before the festival. Odessa's Reiman Park and the Finney Field sports complex offer RV and camping spots on a first-come, first-served basis. You can also reserve a spot at Odessa Golf Club and RV Park (509.982.0093), but that is also often booked up a year in advance. To get the best spots, plan ahead and come early.
Website: www.deutschesfest.com
Facebook: www.facebook.com/odessafest
Attractions: Odessa Historisches Museum, Odessa Golf Club, Channeled Scablands, Fishtrap Lake hike, Fort Spokane, Odessa Craters
Trivia: The Channeled Scablands is an area that contains geologic features unique to Eastern Washington. Around 14,000 years ago, the Missoula Floods carved channels through the flat land, creating canyons of carved basalt columns. On this scenic drive, you see unique draining patterns, immense potholes and ripple marks, and large boulders that were deposited by the flood.
Directions: Odessa is centrally located in east-central Washington, at the crosswords of State Hwys 28 and 21, and is just 18 miles north of

I-90, at the Hwy 21 exit #206. It is 200 miles from Seattle, 75 miles from Spokane, 140 miles from Yakima, 100 miles from Wenatchee, 100 miles from the Tri-Cities, 110 miles from Walla Walla, and 110 miles from Pullman.

Spokane Japanese Obon Festival
Spokane, Spokane County
Late July, early August

Obon, or Bon, is a Buddhist custom to honor past ancestors. The Japanese Obon Festival at the Spokane Buddhist temple celebrates this by hosting a bazaar type event that includes Japanese food, art, crafts, music, martial arts, and games for kids. The event hosts a parade on Saturday. Exhibits throughout the weekend include Ikebana (flower arranging), Sumi-E (ink painting), bonsai, an anime/manga group dressed in Cosplay, and Nuido (embroidery). Demonstrations include karate, aikido, kendo, and taiko drumming. Some of the delicious food at the event includes chicken teriyaki rice bowls, curry rice bowls, fresh salads, mochi, senbei, teriyaki dogs, and green tea smoothies. Each day's festivities are topped off with the highlight of the festival—a taiko drum performance, and Bon Odori (or Bon), dancing. Don't forget to take a tour of the temple while you're there.

Address: Spokane Buddhist Temple, 927 S Perry
Admission: Free entry, charge for food and games
Parking: Free parking at the temple and street parking
Accessible: Yes
Pets: No
Lodging: www.visitspokane.com/hotels
Website: www.spokanebuddhisttemple.org/#sthash.5FwSj0qL.dpuf
Facebook: www.spokanebuddhisttemple.org
Attractions: Manito Park and Botanical Gardens, Bing Crosby Theater, Mt. Spokane State Park, Riverfront Park, Spokane Falls, Northwest Museum of Arts and Culture
Trivia: The original Buddhist church was destroyed by arson fire on April 23, 1992. However, the original shrine of Amida Buddha was saved by firefighters and is used in the rebuilt church at the same location.
Directions: From I-90 W, take exit 283A. Take S Altamont St and E 9th Ave to S Perry St and turn left. The temple is on the left.

Scottish Fest and Highland Games
Prosser, Benton County
Third Saturday in June

This event packs a lot of activities into one day. The Parade of Tartans ushers in the welcoming ceremony, then festivities begin with the boom of black powder and the billowing grey smoke of the infamous anvil launch. Next comes the heavy athletic competitions, which include hammer throw for distance, light and heavy weights for distance, stone throw for distance, sheaf toss for height, weight for height over bar, and caber toss for flipping accuracy. The sanctioned Highland Dance competition features Scottish Highland dances (jigs, reels, flings, and sword dances) that were performed by men in pre-battle preparations and victory celebrations, plus national dances that were developed after the Highland Dances were banned by the English. The Bonny Knees contest puts brave kilted men in front of a panel of blindfolded women who feel for excellent bone structure, strength of calf, and skin texture, and decide who has the bonniest knees. Other activities include Celtic music, pipe bands, youth athletics (for ages 7–13), Celtic crafts, children's fun, food, the Flying Anvil Pub, MacPherson's Farm, trebuchets, and the Firemen's Challenge. Trace your Scottish roots or delve into the history of Scotland by talking with clan and society members throughout the day.

Address: Port of Benton Wine and Food Park Festival Grounds, 2840 Lee Road
Admission: General Admission is $8; for kids ages 5–12 years and adults 65 and older the cost is $5. Children under the age of 4 get in free.
Parking: Free, across Lee Rd to the south of the festival site
Accessible: Yes
Pets: No
Lodging: www.tourprosser.com/index.php/stay-directory
Website: www.prosserscottishfest.org
Facebook: www.facebook.com/ProsserScottishFest
Attractions: Prosser Farmers Market, 30+ local wineries, the historic Princess Theater, Benton County Museum, Bill's Berry Farm, Sage Bluff Alpaca farm, Natural Maximum Alpaca Farm
Trivia: Scottish law allows that a criminal trial may end in one of three verdicts: guilty, not guilty, or not proven. The "not proven" verdict is often referred to as the Scottish Verdict.
Directions: Prosser and the festival grounds are easy to get to coming

from either the east or the west along I-82. Take Exit 82 to Wine Country Rd. Go right (east) along Wine Country Rd to Benitz Rd and turn left (north) on Benitz Rd. Cross the railroad tracks and turn right on to Lee Rd, and arrive at the event grounds.

Spokane Highland Games
Spokane Valley, Spokane County
Early August

Spokane Highland Games provide a charming Scottish day-adventure full of fun, entertainment, and athletic games. Traditional activities include massed bands, pipe band exhibitions, individual piping, heavy athletics, highland dancing, and children's games. Enjoy Celtic music and Scottish country dancing throughout the day. Watch sheepdog and blacksmith demonstrations, tug-of-war competitions, and reenactments. Stop at a clan tent to discover whether you have Scottish ancestry, and shop at the Scottish and Celtic merchant booths. Up for an adventure? Join in the haggis tasting, learn about its history, and discover how it is made today. Display your talents by entering the shortbread contest or the Photos of Scotland contest.

Address: Spokane County Fair and Expo Center, 404 N. Havana Street
Admission: Adults $10, seniors (60+) $8, youth (11–17) $8, children (6–10) $5, children under 5 get in free.
Parking: Free parking at the event
Accessible: Yes
Pets: No
Lodging: www.visitspokane.com/hotels. Overnight camping facilities are available on site. Contact the Spokane County Fair and Expo Center at 509.477.2770 for further information.
Website: http://spokanehighlandgames.org/SpokaneHighlandGames/Welcome.html
Facebook: www.facebook.com/pages/Spokane-Scottish-Highland-Games/70659246405
Attractions: Mt. Saint Michael, Mt. Spokane State Park, Riverfront Park Carousel, Spokane Falls
Trivia: The unicorn is Scotland's official animal.
Directions: Located five minutes from downtown Spokane, the Spokane County Fair and Expo Center is easily accessible via I-90.

Ritzville Western Art Show and Historic Ritzville Days
Ritzville, Adams County
May/Memorial Day weekend

The annual Western Art Show helps celebrate public art and attract attention to the city's efforts to revitalize its downtown through the use of art. The event, which is held entirely within the boundaries of Ritzville's National Historic District, features more than 60 artists and their artwork that captures the spirit of the West, rural living, Native American life, wildlife, and agriculture. The show features free entertainment (including gunfight reenactments), a street dance on Saturday night, youth art activities, artists' quick draws, artist demonstrations, rope-making demonstrations, and of course, food vendors. The event also includes a Dutch oven, three-pot cook-off on Saturday (consisting of bread, a main dish, and a dessert), and Dutch oven demonstrations on Sunday. The winning team earns the right to compete at the world championships.

Address: Main Avenue and Washington Street
Admission: Free
Parking: Street and parking lot parking
Accessible: Yes
Lodging: http://ritzvillechamber.chambermaster.com/list/QuickLink-Members/lodging-travel-15.htm
Website: www.ritzvillewesternart.com/home.html
Facebook: www.facebook.com/pages/Ritzville-Western-Art-Show-Historic-Ritzville-Days/374229772480
Attractions: The Burroughs Home, National Pacific Railroad Depot, Ritzville metal sculptures, Ritzville Water Park, Palouse Falls
Trivia: The eruption of Mt. St. Helens on May 18, 1980 brought the town of Ritzville to a standstill. The enormous ash cloud emitted from the volcano traveled directly over the small town, dropping four to six inches of ash. Visibility was terrible, breathing was difficult, and travel was impossible—more than 2,500 motorists were stranded, and the town was cut off from the outside world for five days. Ritzville residents were still shoveling ash months after the eruption.
Directions: Ritzville is 60 miles southwest of Spokane on I-90 and 80 miles northeast of the Tri-Cities.

Columbia River Cowboy Gathering and Music Festival

Kennewick, Benton County
Second weekend in April

This festival's goal is to preserve the western way of life and honor cowboy heritage through music, poetry, and western arts and goods. Festival organizers are dedicated to creating an event that is wholesome, family oriented, and affordable. In addition to plenty of live entertainment, the event includes a Cowboy Idol Contest and open mic performances. A kiddie corral provides activities for the kids. Sunday morning opens with a breakfast buffet, which is followed by cowboy church and gospel concert.

Address: Benton County Fairgrounds, 1500 S Oak Street
Admission: Advance ticket prices: general admission is $15 each day (includes the evening concert); tickets with reserved concert seats are $20 each day for all day and the evening concert. Gate prices: general admission is $25, tickets with reserved concert seats are $30 (if available). Daytime-only passes, available at the gate, cost $5.
Parking: Parking is available at the fairgrounds
Accessible: Yes
Pets: No info
Lodging: Clover Island Inn in Kennewick provides a discounted rate for event attendees. Call 866.586.0542. Camping is also available from Thursday night to Saturday night for $15 a night.
Website: http://columbiarivercowboygathering.com
Facebook: www.facebook.com/pages/Columbia-River-Cowboy-Gathering-and-Music-Festival/150932944952298
Attractions: Hanford Reach National Monument, Sacagawea Heritage Trail, Badger Mountain Centennial Preserve, Cable Bridge (Ed Hendler Bridge), vineyards and farms, Ice Age Floods National Geologic Trail, McNary National Wildlife Refuge
Trivia: At the Southridge Sports Complex in southern Kennewick stands a 9/11 World Trade Center memorial monument. The central part of the monument is a 35' twisted column of steel, weighing nearly 6,000 pounds, that was salvaged from the destroyed World Trade Center towers in New York in 2011. The monument was dedicated on the 10th anniversary of the 9/11 attack.
Directions: From I-82 take exit 395 and turn left on 10th St if you're coming from the Yakima area, or right on 10th St if you're coming from Oregon. Stay on 10th. The fairgrounds is on your right.

Family Fun

The Great Prosser Balloon Rally
Prosser, Benton County
Fourth weekend in September

Balloon pilots from all over the Northwestern United States converge on Prosser to participate in the annual Great Prosser Balloon Rally. Weekend festivities include sunrise hot air balloon launches, night glow (where hot air balloons are anchored and illuminated from within against the dark night sky), a harvest festival, a farmers market, and a street-painting festival. Start off the festival at the sunrise launch on Friday morning. Arrive early (about 6:15 am) at the Prosser Airport to watch the pilots prepare the giant balloons. You may even be one of the lucky spectators who is asked to assist the balloon pilots inflate, chase, and recover the hot air balloons.

Address: Prosser Airport, 1433 Paterson Road
Admission: Admission is free. Gates at the Art Fiker Stadium open at 5:30 pm. Admission for the stands is free. However, there is a charge for the limited seating inside the fenced area near the track and inside the playing field.
Parking: Free
Accessible: Yes
Pets: No
Lodging: Camping is available at Crow Butte Park www.crowbutte.com. Other lodging information www.tourprosser.com/index.php/stay
Website: www.prosserballoonrally.org
Facebook: www.facebook.com/GreatProsserBalloonRally
Attractions: Prosser Farmers Market, 30+ local wineries, the historic Princess Theater, Benton County Museum, Bill's Berry Farm, Sage Bluff Alpaca farm, Natural Maximum Alpaca Farm
Trivia: One of Prosser's most notable residents was Harold R. McCluskey, the "Atomic Man." McCluskey was a chemical operations technician at the Hanford Plutonium Finishing Plant, just outside of Washington's Tri-Cities. On August 30, 1976, an exploding glove box exposed McCluskey to americium-241 (a plutonium byproduct) at a level that was 500 times the level that doctors deem safe over a lifetime. This exposure was, and is, the highest dose of radiation from americium ever recorded. He was placed in isolation for five months, and was released to return home to

Prosser in 1977 when his body's radiation count had fallen by 80%. Eight years after the exposure, his body still contained enough radiation to set off a Geiger Counter. He died of heart failure in 1987 (he had experienced significant heart issues well before the accident), and autopsy results showed no signs of cancer. He is buried in the Prosser Cemetery.
Directions: Prosser is located 35 miles west of the Tri-Cities on I-82 W.

Othello Sandhill Crane Festival
Othello, Adams County
Late March, early April

The Othello Sandhill Crane Festival highlights the spring return of Sandhill cranes to the greater Othello area and Columbia National Wildlife Refuge. The three-day festival includes a variety of entertaining and educational activities for the whole family to enjoy. The festival provides many tours for crane viewing, or you can go on a specialty tour, which, in the past, has included a Columbia National Wildlife Refuge/Potholes area wildlife tour, Missoula Floods and Channeled Scablands geology tour, Lower Grand Coulee birding tour, and a Wahluke Slope/Shrub Steppe birding tour. Your admission on Saturday gives you access to various informative and educational lectures that are repeated throughout the day on topics such as falconry, Missoula Flood and Channeled Scablands, Othello area history, shrub-steppe flora and fauna, owls of eastern Washington, and spring migration in the Columbia basin. Children's programs and an art contest for all ages are part of the weekend's activities. Saturday evening hosts a banquet and silent auction.

Address: Othello High School, 340 S 7th Avenue
Admission: Adult admission is $10, seniors $7, and children 12 and older $7. Children under age 12 get in for free. Tours cost extra.
Parking: Free
Pets: No
Lodging: http://othellosandhillcranefestival.org/index.php?option=com_content&view=article&id=51&Itemid=80
Website: http://othellosandhillcranefestival.org
Facebook: www.facebook.com/pages/Othello-Sandhill-Crane-Festival/204363422909694
Attractions: Othello Community Museum, Coulee Corridor Scenic Byway, Potholes State Park, Columbia National Wildlife Refuge

Trivia: Sandhill cranes can travel 350 miles per day while migrating, at speeds that range from 15–50 miles per hour, and at heights up to 12,000 feet. The crane has a trumpet-like call so loud it can be heard for over a mile. Sandhill cranes mate for life, and can live as long as 25 years in the wild, much longer in captivity.
Directions: From Spokane: (100 miles), take US-395 south to US-26 west. Follow US-26 to Othello. Turn right onto 1st Ave. Follow 1st Ave to Main St to 7th Ave. Turn right on 7th Ave. Othello High School is located on the right in the second block. From Tri-Cities: (54 miles), take US-395 north to the Hwy 17/Othello exit. Follow Hwy 17 north to Cunningham Rd and turn left. Cunningham Rd becomes Main St when you get to Othello. Turn left at the light on 7th Ave. Othello High School is located on the right in the second block.

Tri-Cities Water Follies
Kennewick, Benton County
Last weekend in July

Bring your family and friends to the shores of the Columbia River for an action-packed, energy filled weekend that includes the world's fastest race boats, vintage hydroplanes, Grand Prix hydroplanes, one-liter hydroplanes, and the exciting Over-the-River Air Show, plus vendors, amenities, and a beer garden along the shoreline. This event is home of the Columbia Cup for Unlimited Hydroplanes, which is one of the premier hydroplane racing events in the country. Tens of thousands of spectators from throughout the northwest and across the country line the river for this high-speed weekend, while countless others watch on television and the Internet. Meet the hydroplane drivers, as well as air show pilots and performers at an autograph session on Saturday.

Address: Columbia Park, 5111 Columbia Park Trail
Admission: Children age 5 and younger are free all weekend. Weekend two-day admission: adults $25, children 6–12 $10. Saturday general admission ticket (available at the gate): adults $15, children 6–12 $5. Sunday general admission ticket (available at the gate): adults $25, children 6–12 $5. A one-day Pit Access Pass (does not include park admission) costs $10 each day. A three-day Pit Access Pass, which does include park admission, costs $45.
Parking: Two major parking areas are available on the weekend of the

festival. Columbia Park in Kennewick, entrance off Hwy 240, charges $5 for Friday and Saturday, $10 for Sunday. No in and out privileges. Your car is charged a parking fee each time it enters the lot. Parking is also available in Pasco, just off Sylvester Street, which is free on Friday, $5 on Saturday, and $10 on Sunday.
Accessible: Yes
Pets: No
Lodging: www.waterfollies.com/plan-your-visit/travel-lodging
Website: www.waterfollies.com
Facebook: www.facebook.com/pages/Tri-City-Water-Follies/170534656327243
Attractions: Hanford Reach National Monument, Sacagawea Heritage Trail, Badger Mountain Centennial Preserve, Cable Bridge (Ed Hendler Bridge), vineyards and farms, Ice Age Floods National Geologic Trail, McNary National Wildlife Refuge
Trivia: During boat races in 1996, Kennewick Man was discovered along the shores of the Columbia River when two festival attendees took a break from the races to drink some beer in a clump of woods just upstream from the race course. When the college buddies waded into the water, one of them stubbed his toe on what turned out to be the skull of a man who lived 9,200 years ago. It is one of the most complete ancient skeletons ever found.
Directions: The HAPO Columbia Cup is held just west of the Hwy 395 Bridge, aka "The Blue Bridge."

Barrel Derby Days
Curlew, Ferry County
First Sunday in June

Barrel Derby Days is a town celebration that is based on dubious beginnings. According to tradition, during Prohibition, bootleggers from Midway, British Columbia would float barrels of illegal whiskey down the Kettle River, across the Canadian border, past customs officials, and down to the town of Curlew, where the barrels were pulled out of the water. In celebration of those bootlegging days, the town of Curlew drops a barrel off the Midway Bridge (just south of British Columbia), and townsfolk and visitors buy tickets for a chance to give their best guess as to what time the barrel will arrive at the Curlew bridge. These days, the barrel is filled with just plain water, but that doesn't dampen the festivities. Other events at Barrel Derby Days include a pancake breakfast, 5K and 10K fun runs, a parade, hoop jam tournaments, 4-H activities, an ice cream social, and face painting.

Address: River Street
Admission: Ticket fee to guess how long it will take the barrel to reach the bridge
Parking: Free
Accessible: Yes
Pets: Yes
Lodging: www.ferrycounty.com/category/business/lodging-business
Website: www.ferrycounty.com/activities/attractions/barrel-derby-days
Attractions: Antique Auto and Truck Museum, Ansorge Hotel Museum, the Old Swimming Hole, Curlew Bridge, Ferry County Fair Carousel, Historic Malo Store, Stonerose Interpretive Center and Fossil Site
Trivia: Ten and-a-half miles from Curlew, in a small graveyard overlooking the Kettle River, lies the remains of Ranald MacDonald, who died in 1894, and is recognized by many as the first native English-speaker to teach the English language in Japan. Japan's isolationist policy in the mid-1800s prohibited foreigners from setting foot on Japanese soil. Determined to visit the country that fascinated him, in 1848, MacDonald convinced a whaling ship captain to set him afloat in a small boat off the coast of Japan. When he reached shore, he pretended he was shipwrecked. He was arrested, but officials soon realized that he could be an asset. Although Japan was closed to foreigners, many American and British ships were regularly approaching the shores, and no one in Japan spoke English well enough to communicate. Fourteen samurai were sent to study English under his tutelage. His pupils included Einosuke Moriyama, eventually one of the chief interpreters to handle the trade-agreement negotiations between Commodore Perry and the Tokugawa Shogunate, which helped open Japan to the west. MacDonald died at his daughter's home in Curlew, and was buried in a small Indian cemetery (his father was a Hudson's Bay fur trader and his mother was a Chinook named Raven). MacDonald's grave site is the smallest state park in Washington State.
Directions: Curlew is located in the northeast corner of Washington in Ferry County, 22 miles from the town of Republic, and 10 miles from the Canadian border (close to Grand Forks, British Columbia).

Valleyfest
Spokane Valley, Spokane County
September

Valleyfest presents a free showcase of visual and performing arts, education, science, and recreation to those families who might otherwise not have the means to experience them. The three-day event provides entertainment for the entire family, an opportunity to meet and have fun with neighbors, and recognition of area youth for their talents. The festival has three entertainment stages; Hot Air Balloons over Valleyfest; a pancake breakfast; beer, wine, and food; more than 200 vendors; a car show; robotics and astronomy demonstrations; Bloomfest Baby and Mother Expo; bed races; a triathlon (boat, bike, run); StepUp for Down Syndrome Walk; and Responsible Dog Ownership Day, which includes disc dog competitions, and agility and flyball demonstrations.

Address: Mirabeau Point Park/CenterPlace Regional Event Center, 2426 N. Discovery Place
Admission: Free
Parking: Parking is free at the Spokane Valley Mall. A shuttle runs from the parking lot near the Red Robin at the mall to Valleyfest. Cost is 75 cents for all-day riding. Limited parking is also available at Pinecroft Business Center and at CenterPlace.
Accessible: Yes
Pets: Yes
Lodging: Camping is available at Mirabeau Meadows, 13500 Mirabeau Pkwy. Hotel information at: www.valleyfest.org/hotels.html
Website: www.valleyfest.org
Facebook: www.facebook.com/pages/Valleyfest/192485200527
Attractions: Spokane River, Centennial Trail, Mullan road monuments, Valley Heritage Museum, CenterPlace Gallery
Trivia: The winter of 1968–69 was a whopper in Spokane Valley. Registering 77.5" of snow that winter ranked 9th for total snowfall. But what made it unusual was that a majority of the snow fell in the month of January (it snowed 20 of the 31 days). Coupled with freezing temperatures down to −19°, the snow accumulated to a total of 42" before the winter weather started to let up.
Directions: Spokane Valley is located between Spokane, and Post Falls, Idaho. From I-90 E, take exit 289. Turn left on to N Pines Rd, then take the first right on E Indiana Ave. Travel 0.7 miles, then turn left on Mi-

rabeau Pkwy. Take the first left on to Mansfield Ave, then take the first right on to N Discovery Place. The event center is on the right. From I-90 W, take exit 291A, turn right on to N Evergreen Rd, then take the first left on E Indiana Ave. Travel 0.5 miles, and then take the first right on to Mirabeau Pkwy. Take the first left on to E Mansfield Ave, the take the first right on to N Discovery Place. The event center is on the right.

Down River Days
Ione, Pend Oreille County
Last weekend of July

It's hard to be a snowmobile in northern Washington in the summer time. Waiting for those cold, snowy winter days—where you can cavort and roam free—is agonizing. If only there were a way to keep your skis busy during those warm, sunny months. . . At the summer Down River Days in Ione, snowmobiles get just that chance. The annual snowmobile water cross takes place at Lone City Park. This event, which, at first blush seems ill-conceived, is actually tremendously exciting to watch. For each heat, two snowmobiles line up on the sandy banks of the Pend Oreille River, and when given the "go" sign, race as fast as they can across the river to the other side. Remarkably deft on the water, snowmobiles do have the unpleasant habit of sinking if speed is not maintained. So, the key to these races seems to be: just don't stop. The festivities also include a cowboy breakfast, a parade, a tug-of-war competition, a wakeboard competition, a mower obstacle course, live music, a Barbie Jeep ride (where racers zoom down a course in toy vehicles that are entirely too small), a softball tournament, a street dance, train rides, a beer garden, and art, craft, and food vendors.

Address: Ione City Park, Downtown
Admission: Free. A Lions scenic train ride costs $15 for adults (13 and older), $10 for children (ages 2–12), and $10 for seniors 64 and older. Children under 2 ride free.
Parking: Free street and parking lot parking.
Accessible: Yes, but wheelchairs may have trouble on the riverbank terrain.
Lodging: www.porta-us.com/lodging.html
Website: http://downriverdays.com
Facebook: www.facebook.com/IoneDownRiverDays

Attractions: Box Canyon Dam, North Pend Oreille Lions Club Excursion Train Ride, Serendipity Golf Course, Crawford State Park, International Selkirk Loop, Cutter Theater and Museum, Mill Pone Flume Historic Site
Trivia: Fifteen miles outside of Ione, on a Forest Service Road, stands what remains of the Shoe Tree. For decades, visitors have been hanging or attaching shoes to the old-growth cedar tree leaving it covered with hundreds of flip flops, sneakers, baby shoes, cowboy boots, and heels. Unfortunately, this regional landmark caught fire in 2010, and all of the shoes, as well as a good portion of the tree, were burned. The Forest Service discouraged the community from starting a new shoe tree.
Directions: Ione is approximately 85 miles north of Spokane. From Spokane, take Hwy 2 north to the town of Newport. Take Hwy 20 for 46 miles to Hwy 31, which runs right through downtown Ione. Take a right on Main St and the City Park is one block up on the left.

Republic Motorcycle Rally
Republic, Ferry County
Mid-July

Nestled deep in the Okanogan mountain range, the town of Republic was founded by gold prospectors in the late 19th century. These days, the tiny town draws more motorcycles than miners to the annual Republic Motorcycle Rally. The three-day event includes exciting arena racing, lawnmower racing, live music, a poker run, bike games for all ages, and Sunday chapel.

Address: Ferry County Fairgrounds, 14 Lawson Way on Hwy 20
Admission: $20 per person for the weekend, $10 for a Saturday-only pass, $5 camping per night for a tent, $15 per night for electric and water hookups.
Parking: Free
Accessible: Yes
Pets: Yes
Lodging: www.ferrycounty.com/category/business/lodging-business
Website: www.republicrally.com
Facebook: www.facebook.com/pages/Republic-Motorcycle-Rally-Association/175178417406
Attractions: Stonerose Interpretive Center and Fossil Site, Ferry County Carousel, car racing at Eagle Track Raceway, Ferry County Historical Cen-

ter, Lake Roosevelt National Scenic Area, Pacific Northwest Scenic Trail
Trivia: The town of Republic lies on the remains of an ancient lake that, in the Eocene Epoch, teemed with plants, insects, and fish. This makes the area a great place to find fossils. At the Stonerose Interpretive Center and Fossil Site, you can either rent or bring your own tools, and go treasure hunting in the fossil beds themselves. You can take home your find (up to three fossils per day). On a school field trip in 2000, Azure Belgarde unearthed a previously unknown species of big-headed fly. The species was subsequently named in her honor: Metanephrocerus belgardeae.

Directions: Republic is located between Wauconda and Sherman Passes at the intersection of SR-20 and SR-21 in the north central part of the state. Ferry County Fairground is located 3.5 miles northeast of Republic on Hwy 20.

There are over 40,000 miles of rivers and streams and more than 8,000 lakes in Washington.

Food & Agricultural Celebrations

Pend Oreille Valley Lavender Festival
Newport, Pend Oreille County
Early July

The Lavender Festival takes place when the lavender is in full bloom along the Pend Oreille River. Spend the weekend browsing through the open-air market of more than 75 booths featuring unique local artists, artisans, and lavender growers. Talk with lavender specialists about how to grow and process lavender. Relax and eat lunch while listening to music in the wine garden. Enjoy the micro-brew garden, many delicious food options, and children's art activities. Learn how to make a lavender wand, and watch demonstrations such as model airplanes, fly-tying, spinning, and basket weaving.

Address: City Park at First and Calispel
Admission: Adults $6 for one day, $10 for4 a two-day pass. Kids under 12 get in free
Parking: Free
Accessible: Yes
Pets: No
Lodging: http://business.newportareachamber.com/list/category/lodging-travel-17
Website: www.povlavenderfestival.com
Facebook: www.facebook.com/pages/Pend-Oreille-Valley-Lavender-Festival/321372011227541
Attractions: Pend Oreille Historical Museum, Albeni Falls Dam, Camden Creek Lavender Farm, International Selkirk Loop
Trivia: Lavender is a flowering plant in the mint family. In history, it has been referred to as spikenard, nardus, or nard.
Directions: From Spokane, take US-2 W and travel north for 40 miles to the town of Newport. Turn left onto S Calispel Ave, then a left on 2nd St. City Park is on your right.

Spokane Lilac Festival

Spokane, Spokane County
Third weekend in May

Since 1938, Spokane has been honoring the military, recognizing local youth, and showcasing the community at the Lilac Festival. According to local legend, the first lilac bush traveled to Spokane all the way from Minnesota in a trunk in the year 1882 and was planted at a nearby homestead. Thirteen years later in 1896, the Spokane Floral Association held its first meeting and soon after the Spokane Parks Department began to officially promote Spokane as "The Lilac City,"' which is still the city's official nickname. The festival includes a Royal Tea Party, a Queen's Luncheon, a golf tournament, a military luncheon, a car show, and the main event, the Armed Forces Torchlight Parade.

Address: Various locations downtown
Admission: Free
Parking: Street parking
Accessible: Yes
Pets: Welcome at some events
Lodging: The Davenport Hotel (800.899.1482), has been the host hotel for the festival, and it provides special room rates for festival attendees. More information at: www.visitspokane.com/hotels
Website: http://spokanelilacfestival.org
Facebook: www.facebook.com/pages/Spokane-Lilac-Festival/140022989381638
Attractions: Riverside Park, Spokane Falls, Mt. Spokane, Turnbull National Wildlife Refuge, Cat Tales Zoological Park, Silverwood Theme Park, Northwest Museum of Arts and Culture, Couer d'Alene Casino
Trivia: When WWII ended, President Harry S. Truman led an effort to establish a single holiday for citizens to come together and thank our military members for their patriotic service. This led to the creation of Armed Forces Day in 1949. Because the Spokane Lilac Festival enthusiastically supports the military, they modified the annual celebration to include an Armed Forces Day Parade. For a few years, the festival included two parades. Eventually, the military parade and flower parade merged into one creating the Spokane Lilac Festival Armed Forces Torchlight Parade, which is reportedly the largest Armed Forces Torchlight Parade in the nation.
Directions: Find downtown Spokane and look for the various events.

Fiery Foods Festival
Pasco, Franklin County
Mid-September

Are your taste buds up for some excitement? If you appreciate the hotter things in life, then the Fiery Foods Festival is for you. This multicultural event is a place where you can bring the entire family, listen to great music, shop local vendors, and taste exciting food. The Restaurant Show and Competition features more than 25 restaurants serving up their spiciest foods, and fans judge the winning dish. Think your salsa can stand the heat of competition? Enter your favorite recipe in the Red Hot Salsa contest. The festival also features live cultural dancing, kids' activities, and a display of new and classic cars. For those who don't like their food to cause them to break out in a sweat, the festival features plenty of milder fare as well.

Address: West Lewis Street and S 4th Avenue
Admission: Free
Parking: Street and parking lot parking
Accessible: Yes
Lodging: www.visittri-cities.com/visitors/hotels
Website: http://fieryfoodsfestival.com
Facebook: www.facebook.com/DowntownPasco
Attractions: More than 150 local wineries, Franklin County Historical Museum, Yakama Nation Museum, Yakama Nation Legends Casino, Sacagawea Heritage Trail, Hanford Nuclear Reservation
Trivia: The heat intensity of a pepper is measured in Scoville Heat Units. Mild peppers, such as bell peppers, banana peppers, and paprika rate from 0–1,000 on the Scoville scale. Spicier types such as the jalapeño rate from 3,500–10,000 on the scale. The hottest peppers on record are the Trinidad Moruga Scorpion (originating in Trinidad and Tobago) and the Carolina Reaper (originating in South Carolina). These peppers clock in at around 2,000,000–2,200,000 heat units, making them roughly 400 times more potent than a jalapeño.
Directions: From Spokane, take I-90 to US-395 S to N. Oregon St. Drive two miles south on North Oregon St and turn right on Lewis St. Continue to 4th Ave. From Portland, take I-84 E for 171 miles, and take the I-82 W exit (exit 179). Take exit 113 for US-395 N, take the Lewis St exit on the left, and take Lewis St to 4th Ave.

Pig Out in the Park

Spokane, Spokane County
Last week in August

Pig Out in the Park is Spokane's annual six-day food and entertainment festival. Located at Spokane's beautiful Riverfront Park, the event features 45 great food booths, three adult beverage gardens, and 70 free concerts on three stages. Browse through the art and craft booths. During special hours only, vendors offer a $3 bite of an item from their booth menu, so you can diversify your pig out.

Address: Riverfront Park
Admission: Free
Parking: Street parking and various paid parking. Park and Ride alternatives are also available where you can park your car and ride a bus to the event.
Accessible: Yes
Pets: No
Lodging: www.visitspokane.com/hotels
Website: www.spokanepigout.com
Facebook: www.facebook.com/PigOutSpokane
Attractions: Riverside Park, Spokane Falls, Mt. Spokane, Turnbull National Wildlife Refuge, Cat Tales Zoological Park, Silverwood Theme Park, Northwest Museum of Arts and Culture, Couer d'Alene Casino
Trivia: The Benewah Milk Bottles are two distinctive architectural landmarks in Spokane. The milk-bottle shaped buildings were built in the 1930s as advertisements for the Benewah Creamery Company, which operated them as concession stands. The bottles are located on W. Garland Street and S. Cedar Street, the latter of which is visible from I-90 and is registered on the National Register of Historic Places. The Garland Street building is currently a small burger and milkshake restaurant.
Directions: From I-90, take the US-2 N/US-395 N exit 281 toward Newport/Colville/Spokane Arena. Turn slight right to S Division St/US-2 E/US-395. Turn left onto W Spokane Falls Blvd. Riverfront Park is four blocks up on the right.

Marcus CiderFest
Marcus, Stevens County
First Saturday in October

Every year, the town of Marcus celebrates autumn, apples, and community with the Marcus CiderFest. Termed the "Biggest Little Festival in Northern Washington," the town of nearly 200 people hosts this event, which features lots of freshly made cider, pressed on site, which you can purchase by the cup, half-gallon, or gallon. The event also includes a pancake breakfast, a kids' carnival, a parade, a food court, more than 100 art and craft vendors, live music, a car show, and a beer garden. CiderFest also offers a variety of homemade pies, cookies, cakes, and other delicious treats to satisfy your sweet tooth.

Address: Downtown, just off Hwy 25
Admission: Free
Parking: Free
Accessible: Yes
Pets: Yes
Lodging: www.marcusciderfest.com/come-stay-or-play.html
Website: www.marcusciderfest.com
Attractions: Pacific Northwest National Scenic Trail, Colville National Forest, Kaniksu National Forest, Lake Roosevelt National Recreation Area, Little Pend Oreille National Wildlife Refuge
Trivia: When the Grand Coulee Dam was built, the town was forced to relocate to higher ground. The original site of the town is submerged under the waters of what is now Lake Roosevelt.
Directions: The town of Marcus lies along Hwy 25, five miles north of Kettle Falls. If you are traveling from Spokane on Hwy 395, Marcus is located approximately 85 miles north, 15 miles northwest of Colville, on the banks of Lake Roosevelt.

National Lentil Festival
Pullman, Whitman County
Late August (weekend before classes resume at nearby Washington State University)

Washington's Palouse region produces approximately 25% of lentils in the United States, so it provides a perfect place to gather and celebrate the tasty legume. The event kicks off on Friday with free chili from what organizers call "the world's largest bowl of lentil chili"—a 350-gallon stainless steel vat. The event includes a fun run, a pancake breakfast on Saturday, a parade, live music, a local microbrew beer and wine garden, games and activities for the whole family, food, and art and craft booths. Learn about the history of the lentil in Washington and how lentils are grown, and meet Tase T. Lentil, the festival's mascot. The cooking demonstration stage features experts divulging their lentil cooking secrets, and showing you dishes that you can make at home. The Lentil Cook-Off pits five finalists against each other as they prepare their favorite recipes for a panel of judges. One hundred lucky festival-goers are allowed to sample the top five dishes and vote for a people's choice award.

Address: East Spring Street, across from the Brelsford WSU Visitor Center located at 150 E. Spring St.
Admission: Free
Parking: Pullman has several free parking lots that are within walking distance from the festival. You can also park free on both Main Street and Paradise Street
Accessible: Yes
Lodging: www.pullmanchamber.com/visit-pullman/where-to-stay.
Website: www.lentilfest.com
Facebook: www.facebook.com/LentilFest
Attractions: Hell's Canyon, Palouse Discovery Science Center, Palouse Scenic Byway, Palouse Falls State Park, and many museums at Washington State University
Trivia: The Giant Palouse Earthworm (Driloleirus americanus) was first unearthed by Frank Smith near Pullman, Washington in 1897. These giant white earthworms can grow to three feet in length, and live in the deep, rich soils of the Palouse bunchgrass prairies. The scientific name Driloleirus means "lily-like worm," reflecting the peculiar flowery aroma the worm emits when handled. Thought to be extinct in the 1980s, a few specimens have been unearthed in the early 2000s.
Directions: The festival takes place near the Brelsford WSU Visitor Center in Pullman. From WA-27, take WA-270 (Paradise St) east, which becomes Main St. Turn left on Spring St, and the event is on the left.

Music

Rockin' on the River
Clarkston, Asotin County
Mid to late July

Rockin' on the River is a music event held on the banks of the Snake River each summer. In the past, the event, which supports local community organizations, featured headline acts such as Joan Jett and the Blackhearts, Scott Weiland, Everclear, and Presidents of the U.S.A. So bring your lawn chairs, blankets, and sunscreen (average temperature is 90 degrees in July) and enjoy rockin' out to live music in a fantastic outdoor venue.

Address: Port of Clarkston, Gateway Golf Center Grounds, 725 Port Way
Admission: $32 in advance, $40 at the gate. Children 5 and under are free.
Parking: $2 per vehicle
Accessible: Yes
Pets: No
Lodging: www.rockinontheriver.org
Website: www.rockinontheriver.org
Facebook: www.facebook.com/pages/Rockin-on-the-River/92148378669
Attractions: Snake River, Hells Canyon, Nez Perce National Historic Park, Lewis and Clark Discovery Center, Jack O'Connor Hunting Heritage and Education Center, local area wineries, Chief Timothy State Park
Trivia: The Snake River begins in Yellowstone National Park and travels 1,078 miles through six U.S. states until it joins up with the Columbia River near Pasco, Washington. It is the largest tributary of the Columbia River.
Directions: The Rockin' on the River music event is held on the banks of the Snake River inside Gateway Golf Center, 725 Port Way Clarkston, WA. Take US-12 (Bridge St) to 5th St and turn north. The Gateway Golf Center is straight ahead.

Creation Festival

Kennewick, Benton County
Late July, early August

Each year Creation Fest provides a chance for Christians to put aside their theological differences and worship as one body. The four-day event is one of the nation's largest Christian music festivals, hosting more than 60 Christian rock, contemporary, and worship bands. Creation Fest also features Christian speakers and authors, a fringe stage (hosting mostly up-and-coming and/or harder Christian rock bands), a children's stage (entertainment geared toward smaller children), a Late Nite Cafe, camping, a petting zoo, baptisms, communion, fireworks, extreme sports, volleyball, giveaways, a candlelight service, a prayer tent, a youth pastor VIP tent, and other experience-based activities.

Address: 1500 S Oak Street
Admission: Full event tickets cost $70 for adults (12 years and older) and $29 for kids ages 6–12. Children under 5 get in free. One-day tickets cost $39 and two-day tickets cost $73.
Parking: $5 per vehicle fee per entry for day parking
Accessible: Yes. Also, if you have a diagnosed medical condition that prohibits you from walking moderate distances, you can camp in the handicapped area.
Pets: No
Lodging: Camping is available on a first come, first served basis for individuals or groups. Only pre-registered groups (15+ or more adults), who purchase full event AND camping tickets at the same time on the same form, are pre-assigned a location. Camping rates run from $15–$35. Tri-Cities lodging information: www.visittri-cities.com/visitors/hotels/kennewick-hotels
Website: http://creationfest.com/nw
Facebook: www.facebook.com/creationfest
Attractions: World Trade Center Monument, Clover Island Lighthouse, more than 160 local wineries, Hanford Reach Interpretive Center, Carousel of Dreams, Natural History Museum, Sacajawea State Park
Trivia: In 2010, the newest lighthouse in Washington State was constructed in Kennewick on Clover Island (on the Columbia River). According to the *Seattle Times*, it is the first lighthouse to be built in the U.S. since 1962.

Directions: From US-395 N, take exit 113. Travel 3 miles east. Turn right onto W 10th Ave, then turn right on S Oak St. The venue location is on the right. From US-395 S, 395 becomes N Oregon Ave/WA-397. From 397, turn right on E 10th Ave, then left on S Oak St. The venue location is on the right.

Newport Music Festival
Newport, Pend Oreille County
September/First weekend after Labor Day

The Newport Music Festival not only provides a weekend packed with great music, but also gives you the opportunity to interact with the performers. Each year, the festival gathers the best in Americana music which encompasses a wide range of sub-genres including alternative country, folk, bluegrass, Cajun, Celtic, old time, and cowboy. Although the focus is on regional talent, the event features professional acoustic artists and bands from across the country. Workshops taught by main-stage performers provide a way for you to meet and talk, ask questions, get advice, and learn new licks and songs. The event also features an open mic stage, as well as a band scramble, which sorts musicians according to the instrument they play, then randomly mixes them to form a group. Band scramble groups have one hour to come up with a creative name and rehearse two songs to present to the audience. The event also includes folk art and craft vendors, and plenty of food.

Address: 1033 1st Street
Admission: Weekend pass $40. Day passes are $15 for Friday, $20 for Saturday, and $10 for Sunday. Kids 12 and under are free.
Parking: Free street parking and parking on the grounds.
Accessible: Yes
Pets: No info
Lodging: http://business.newportareachamber.com/list/category/lodging-travel-17
Website: www.pvbluegrass.com
Facebook: www.facebook.com/NewportWAMusicFestival?ref=hl
Attractions: Pend Oreille Historical Museum, Albeni Falls Dam, Camden Creek Lavender Farm, International Selkirk Loop
Trivia: The term Pend Oreille derives from a French-Canadian fur trade moniker for local Indians who may have worn large ear pendants. Pend

d'Oreille is a French term that means "hangs from ear."
Directions: From Spokane, take US-2 north to Newport about 1 hour, to S Calispel Ave (Golden Spur Motel) and turn left. Travel five blocks to the park. For camping, turn left on 1st St, go about two blocks (second gate) and turn left into camping grounds. From Sandpoint, Idaho drive south on US-2 for 30 minutes through Newport to 1st St and turn right. Travel six blocks to the park.

Elkfest
Spokane, Spokane County
Early June

Elkfest is an outdoor indie music festival that is free to the public and draws more than 10,000 fans every year. Conceived by the owners of the Elk Public House pub and restaurant, Elkfest was originally created to piggy back with Spokane's yearly Art Fest celebration. However, the music festival quickly became large enough to be self-supporting, so the two events split, now occurring on different weekends. Event organizers strive to create the best neighborhood party in Spokane, and go about it with a grassroots approach, utilizing very little outside sponsorship. The festival, suitable for all ages, takes place on the streets of Spokane's historic Browne's Addition neighborhood. In addition to lots of fantastic indie music, the event includes a beer garden and food vendors.

Address: 1931 West Pacific Avenue
Admission: Free
Parking: Street and parking lot parking
Accessible: Yes
Lodging: www.visitspokane.com/hotels
Website: http://wedonthaveone.com/the-elk/elkfest
Facebook: www.facebook.com/pages/Elkfest/112591915421244
Attractions: Riverside Park, Spokane Falls, Mt. Spokane, Turnbull National Wildlife Refuge, Cat Tales Zoological Park, Silverwood Theme Park, Northwest Museum of Arts and Culture, Couer d'Alene Casino
Trivia: Although born in Tacoma, Washington Bing Crosby was raised in Spokane. He graduated from Gonzaga High School (now called Gonzaga Prep) in 1920, and enrolled at Gonzaga University. During his early college years, he joined his first musical group, the Musicaladers, who mainly performed at dances. The house that Crosby's father built still

sits on the campus of Gonzaga University. It houses academic offices upstairs, but the lower level is open to tourists.
Directions: From I-90 E, take exit 280. Turn left on S Walnut St, then turn left on W 2nd Ave. Turn right on S Cannon St. From I-90 W, take exit 280A, turn right on S Walnut St, then turn left on W 2nd Ave. Turn right on S Cannon St.

Walla Walla Chamber Music Festival
Walla Walla, Walla Walla County
Summer Series begins First Thursday in June (Winter Series held one weekend in January)

For three weeks, the Walla Walla Chamber Music Festival presents 20 artists performing at 24 venues throughout the Walla Walla area. From chamber music covering Beethoven and Tchaikovsky to Guns n' Roses and Pink Floyd, the festival emphasizes smaller, more intimate venues to promote close connection between audience and artist. The series includes four types of events. The Portrait of an Artist provides a window into the life and experiences of one of the talented artists who visits Walla Walla for the festival. It consists of a special recital, and a chance to meet the artist. The Tasting Music event takes place in a local winery. The audience gets to taste wine while listening to the performances. The Special Event highlights a special performance. The Festival Series is the main set of performances. The festival also includes at least one original work that premieres at the first main concert.

Address: Various locations throughout the Walla Walla area
Admission: A Festival Series ticket starts at $20. Student tickets are $8 and a family ticket costs $45, which admits two adults and up to four children. Both Portrait of an Artist and Tasting Music tickets cost $17.50 each. Special Event tickets cost $20. An all-access Silver pass costs $70. The festival also includes several free community outreach performances and rehearsals.
Parking: Varies
Accessible: Yes
Pets: No
Lodging: www.wallawalla.org/lodging/lodging.html
Website: www.wwcmf.org

Facebook: www.facebook.com/pages/Walla-Walla-Chamber-Music-Festival/306509828842?ref=br_tf

Attractions: Art Walla Public Art Walking Tour, 27 wine tasting rooms, Fort Walla Walla Museum, Whitman Mission National Historic Site, Tamastslikt Cultural Institute, McNary National Wildlife Refuge, Walla Walla Farmers Market

Trivia: William West Anderson, better known as actor Adam West, was born in Walla Walla in 1928. He attended Walla Walla High School during his freshman and sophomore years, then moved to Seattle to finish high school. He returned to Walla Walla to attend Whitman College where he graduated with a Bachelor of Arts degree in Literature, and a minor in Psychology. Although acting in television roles since 1954, West is still best known for his portrayal of Batman in the campy TV series of the same name that ran from 1966 to 1968.

Directions: Walla Walla is located approximately 50 miles east of the Tri-Cities via US-12 E; 180 miles (3 hours) south of Spokane via I-90 W, US-395 S, US-12 E; and 242 miles (4 hours) east of Portland via I-84 E.

The Seattle Seahawks' fans have twice set the Guinness World Record for the loudest crowd noise at a sporting event.

Eastern Washington County Fairs

Adams
Othello
www.adamscountyfair.org

Asotin
Asotin
www.asotincountyfairandrodeo.org

Benton/Franklin
Kennewick
www.bentonfranklinfair.com

Columbia
Dayton
www.facebook.com/pages/Columbia-County-Fair/207207172768205

Ferry
Republic
http://ferrycountyfair.com

Garfield
Pomeroy
www.co.garfield.wa.us/GarfieldCountyFairandRodeo

Lincoln
Davenport
www.co.lincoln.wa.us/Fairboard/Fairboard.htm

Pend Oreille
Cusick
www.povn.com/pocofair

Southeast Spokane
Rockford
www.sespokanecountyfair.org

Spokane County Interstate Fair
Spokane Valley
www.spokanecounty.org/fair/sif

Stevens/Northeast Washington
Colville
www.co.stevens.wa.us/NE_WA_Fair/new_fair_home_page.htm

Walla Walla
Walla Walla
www.wallawallafairgrounds.com

Whitman/Palouse Empire
Colfax
http://palouseempirefair.org

Index

Art Events
Anacortes Arts Festival, **139**
Art and Wine Fusion, **180**
Bellevue Festival of the Arts, **87**
Eatonville Arts Festival, **92**
Ellensburg Film Festival, **182**
Friday Harbor Film Festival, **138**
Get Lit! Literary Festival, **220**
International Art Festival, **141**
Island Shakespeare Festival, **136**
Juan de Fuca Festival of the Arts, **7**
Kirkland Summerfest Art and Music Festival, **88**
Kitsap Arts and Crafts Festival, **11**
National Western Art Show and Auction, **181**
Olympia Film Festival, **50**
Port Townsend Film Festival, **10**
RainFest and River and Ocean Days, **6**
Recycled Arts Festival, **49**
San Juan Island Summer Arts Fair, **137**
Seattle International Film Festival, **89**
Seattle Outdoor Theater Festival, **90**
Sorticulture, Everett's Garden Art Festival, **140**
Trout Lake Festival of the Arts, **183**
Westport Art Festival, **8**

Beer, Wine & Spirits
Anacortes Spring Wine Festival, **143**
Bremerton Summer Brewfest, **13**
Everett Craft Beer Festival, **145**
Far West Beer Fest, **13**
Fresh Hop Ale Festival, **188**
Gig Harbor Beer Festival, **100**
Great Grandview Grape Stomp, **187**
Horse Heaven Hills Trail Drive, **221**
Inland NW Craft Beer Festival, **222**
Kirkland Uncorked, **93**
Lake Chelan Crush Festival, **185**
Olympia Brew Fest, **53**
Olympic Club Brewfest, **52**
On the Road to Paradise, Mount Rainier Fall Wine and Brew Festival, **99**
Palouse Cabin Fever Brew Fest, **223**
Seattle International Beerfest, **95**
Seattle Wine and Food Experience, **98**
Skagit Wine and Beer Festival, **144**
Snake in the Glass Passport Party, **189**
Snohomish on the Rocks Distillery Festival, **146**
Tumwater Artesian Brewfest, **54**
Vancouver Brewfest, **51**
Washington Brewer's Festival, **94**
Wine Rocks, **97**
WinterHop BrewFest, **186**

Ethnic & Cultural Celebrations
Aki Matsuri Fall Festival, **102**
Bellingham Scottish Highland Games, **151**
Bridge of Aloha Festival, **150**
Cinco de Mayo Festival, **193**
Columbia River Cowboy Gathering and Music Festival, **232**
CroatiaFest, **107**
Deutschesfest, **226**
Eagle Festival, **19**
Flute Quest, Native American Flute Festival, **102**
Gold Dust Days, **148**
Highlander Festival, **60**
Hood Canal Highland Celtic Festival, **19**
June Faire, **15**
Lacey Ethnic Celebration, **57**
Lummi Stommish Water Festival, **149**
Maifest, **191**
Midsommarfest, **103**
Northwest Folklife Festival, **105**
Oktoberfest (Friday Harbor), **152**
Oktoberfest (Leavenworth), **195**
Oktoberfest Northwest, **110**
Oshogatsu in Olympia, **59**
Pacific Northwest Scottish Highland Games and Clan Gathering, **108**
Pioneer Days, **226**
Polish Festival Seattle, **106**
Quileute Days, **16**
Ritzville Western Art Show and Historic Ritzville Days, **231**

Rusty Scupper's Pirate Daze, **21**
Scottish Fest and Highland Games, **229**
Spirit of the West Cowboy Gathering, **192**
Spokane Highland Games, **230**
Spokane Japanese Obon Festival, **228**
Spring Barrel Tasting, **196**
Summer White Party, **197**
Swede Day Midsommer Festival, **58**
Three Days of Aloha in the Pacific Northwest/Ho'Ike and Hawaiian Festival, **56**
Viking Fest, **17**
Yakima Folklife Festival, **194**
Ye Merrie Greenwood Renaissance Faire, **225**

Family Fun
Allyn Days/Geoduck Festival, **26**
Amboy Territorial Days, **64**
Aquafest, **157**
Bald Eagle Days, **64**
Barrel Derby Days, **236**
Bavarian Ice Fest, **202**
Bigfoot Bash and Bounty, **69**
Capital Lakefair, **67**
Down River Days, **239**
Gigantic Bike Festival, **113**
Logger's Playday, **24**
Loggerodeo, **158**
Longview Squirrel Fest, **65**
Mahogany and Merlot Vintage Boat Show, **200**
Maryhill Festival of Speed, **198**
Mason County Forest Festival, **27**
McCleary Bear Festival, **25**
Moisture Festival, **112**
Omak Stampede, **201**
Othello Sandhill Crane Festival, **234**
Puget Sound Bird Fest, **156**
Quincy Hot Air Balloon and Wine Festival, **199**
Renton River Days, **118**
Republic Motorcycle Rally, **240**
Ring of Fire and Hope, **160**
Sandsations, **62**
Seafair, **119**
Seattle Hempfest, **114**
Snohomish Pumpkin Hurl and Medieval Faire, **155**
Snoqualmie Railroad Days, **120**
Steampunk Festival and the Fantastical Mr. Flip's Carnival of Wonders and Curiosities, **154**
Tacoma Maritime Fest, **116**
The Great Prosser Balloon Rally, **233**
Tri-Cities Water Follies, **235**
Valleyfest, **238**
Washington State International Kite Festival, **63**
Whaling Days, **23**
Winlock Egg Day Festival, **66**

Food and Agricultural Festivals
Apple Pie Jamboree, **207**
Ballard Seafood Fest, **125**
Blackberry Festival, **29**
Chehalis Garlic Fest and Craft Show, **72**
Chocolate on the Beach Festival, **34**
Cranberrian Fair, **73**
Daffodil Festival, **122**
Dirty Dan Day Seafood Festival, **167**
Dungeness Crab and Seafood Festival (Crabfest), **32**
Fiery Foods Festival, **244**
Huckleberry Festival, **205**
Issaquah Salmon Days Festival, **124**
Marcus CiderFest, **246**
Marysville Strawberry Festival, **161**
Mossyrock Blueberry Festival, **70**
National Lentil Festival, **246**
Northwest Raspberry Festival, **161**
OysterFest, **35**
Pacific Northwest Mushroom Festival, **75**
Pend Oreille Valley Lavender Festival, **242**
Penn Cove Musselfest, **164**
Pig Out in the Park, **245**
Rhododendron Festival, **31**
Rhubarb Days, **122**
Sequim Lavender Festival, **30**
ShrimpFest, **36**
Skagit River Salmon Festival, **165**

Skagit Valley Tulip Festival, **162**
Skewered Apple BBQ Competition, **208**
South Sound BBQ Festival, **74**
Spokane Lilac Festival, **243**
Taste of Hood Canal, **38**
Taste Washington, **126**
Wapato Tamale Festival, **209**
Washington State Apple Blossom Festival, **204**
Wenatchee River Salmon Festival, **206**
Wenatchee Taste of the Harvest, **206**
Woodland Tulip Festival, **71**

Music
America's Classic Jazz Festival, **81**
Basin Summer Sounds, **211**
Bellingham Festival of Music, **171**
Birch Bay Music Festival, **172**
Bluegrass from the Forest Festival, **43**
Bumbershoot, **129**
Columbia Gorge Bluegrass Festival, **78**
Creation Festival, **249**
Darrington Bluegrass Festival, **173**
Decibel Festival, **130**
DjangoFest Northwest, **174**
Doe Bay Festival, **170**
Earshot Jazz Festival, **132**
Elkfest, **251**
Galway Bay's Irish Music Festival, **40**
Jazz in the Valley, **215**
Laid Back Attack, **128**
Lake Chelan Bach Fest, **214**
Newport Music Festival, **250**
Oak Harbor Music Festival, **169**
Olympic Music Festival, **41**
Rock the Gap, **212**
Rockin' on the River, **248**
Seattle Chamber Music Festival, **131**
Vancouver Wine and Jazz Festival, **80**
Walla Walla Chamber Music Festival, **252**
Watershed Festival, **214**
Wenatchee River Bluegrass Festival, **213**
XFest NW, **77**

Washington County Fairs
Adams (Othello), **254**
Asotin (Asotin), **254**
Benton/Franklin (Kennewick), **254**
Chelan (Cashmere), **217**
Clallam (Port Angeles), **45**
Clark (Ridgefield), **83**
Columbia (Dayton), **254**
Cowlitz (Longview), **83**
Douglas/North Central Washington District Fair (Waterville), **217**
Ferry (Republic), **254**
Garfield (Pomeroy), **254**
Grant (Moses Lake), **217**
Grays Harbor (Elma), **45**
Jefferson (Port Townsend), **45**
King (Enumclaw), **133**
Kitsap (Bremerton), **45**
Kittitas (Ellensburg), **217**
Klickitat (Goldendale), **217**
Lewis/Southwest Washington (Chehalis), **83**
Lincoln (Davenport), **254**
Mason (Shelton), **45**
Okanogan (Okanogan), **217**
Pacific (Menlo), **83**
Pend Oreille (Cusick), **254**
Pierce (Graham), **133**
San Juan (Harbor), **176**
Skagit (Mt. Vernon), **176**
Skamania (Stevenson), **83**
Snohomish/Evergreen (Monroe), **176**
Southeast Spokane (Rockford), **254**
Spokane County Interstate Fair (Spokane Valley), **254**
Stevens/Northeast Washington (Colville), **254**
Thurston (Olympia), **83**
Wahkiakum (Skamokawa), **83**
Walla Walla (Walla Walla), **254**
Washington State Fair (Puyallup), **133**
Whatcom/Northwest Washington (Lynden), **176**
Whidbey Island (Langley), **176**
Whitman/Palouse Empire (Colfax), **254**
Yakima/Central Washington State Fair (Yakima), **217**

Explore Oregon!
Oregon's Festivals, Faires & Celebrations!
Visit www.gladeyepress.com

From truffles and brews to mosquito fests and didgeridoo, in Oregon there's always something to do!

Whether you're a newcomer, just passing through, or a native, Oregon offers a rich variety of experiences for the intrepid, fun-seeking traveler—from craft brew and wine fests to food and flowers, music, film and the arts, and family events.

Pick up a copy and begin your Oregon adventure now!

GladEye Press
Springfield, OR 97478
(541) 747-4514
www.gladeyepress.com